D0777305

REVISED EDITION

The Complete Guide to
Forecasting Real World Company
Performance

STRATEGIC BUSINESS FORECASTING

REVISED EDITION

The Complete Guide to
Forecasting Real World Company
Performance

STRATEGIC BUSINESS FORECASTING

JAE K. SHIM, PH.D.

Professor of Business Administration
California State University at Long Beach

S^t_L

St. Lucie Press
Boca Raton   London
New York   Washington, D.C.

Library of Congress Cataloging-in-Publication Data

Shim, Jae K.
    Strategic business forecasting : the complete guide to forecasting real world company
performance / Jae K. Shim.—Rev. ed.
    p. cm.
    Includes bibliographical references and index.
    ISBN 1-57444-251-1 (alk. paper)
    1. Business forecasting. I. Title.
    HD30.27 .S48 2000
    658.4′0355—dc21   99-056213
                                                                    CIP

© 2000 by CRC Press LLC
St. Lucie Press is an imprint of CRC Press LLC

No claim to original U.S. Government works
International Standard Book Number 1-57444-251-1
Library of Congress Card Number 99-056213
Printed in the United States of America   1 2 3 4 5 6 7 8 9 0
Printed on acid-free paper

PREFACE

Business forecasting is of extreme importance not only to business economists working for corporations, but also to managers at practically all levels. Top managers must make long-term strategic decisions. Middle managers use sales forecasts to develop their departmental budgets. Every plan for production, purchasing, manpower, and finance follows from sales forecasting.

This book is designed for business professionals such as directors of forecasting and planning, forecast managers, directors of strategic planning, marketing, or information systems, advertising managers, CFOs, financial officers, controllers, treasurers, financial analysts, purchasing agents, and managers of sales, production, brand/product, new products, supply chains, logistics, material management, and scheduling.

The goal of *Strategic Business Forecasting* is to provide readers with a working knowledge of the fundamentals of business forecasting that can be applied in the real world regardless of firm size. It walks you through not only basic forecasting methodology, but also its practical applications. All aspects of business forecasting are discussed, making this book a comprehensive, valuable reference.

There are three unique aspects to this book:

1. It is practical, avoiding theoretical, rigorous, and mathematical discussions as much as possible. It gets directly into how to use forecasting, when to use it, what it is used for, and what resources are required. The book includes many practical examples, applications, illustrations, guidelines, measures, checklists, rules of thumb, tips, graphs, diagrams, and tables to aid your comprehension.

2. It incorporates the use of computer technology—especially the PC. Actual computer printouts obtained from spreadsheet programs such as *Microsoft Excel, Lotus 1-2-3, Quatrro Pro*, spreadsheet-based add-ins (such as *Fore CaZc*), and popular software packages such as *SPSS, Minitab, SAS, Forecast Pro, Sibyl/Runner*, and *Micro TSP* are displayed and explained.

3. The book goes far beyond simple sales forecasting. It encompasses a wide range of topics of major importance to practical business managers, including cash flow forecasting, cost prediction, earnings forecasts, bankruptcy prediction, foreign exchange forecasting, and interest rate forecasting.

Throughout, you will find the book quick reading, practical, up-to-date, intriguing, and useful. Keep this book handy for regular, easy reference throughout your professional business career.

After reviewing popular books on the subject from the viewpoint of many years' teaching and consulting experience in this subject, I am thoroughly convinced that none of them has the unique practicality of this book. That's the very reason that I decided to embark on this project.

Special thanks to Professor Joel G. Siegel for his outstanding editorial assistance and Allison Shim for her word processing and spreadsheet work.

Jae K. Shim
Los Alamitos, California

ABOUT THE AUTHOR

JAE K. SHIM, Ph.D., is Professor of Business at California State University, Long Beach. He received his M.B.A and Ph.D. degrees from the University of California at Berkeley (Haas School of Business). For over twenty years Dr. Shim has been an industrial consultant and government advisor in the areas of financial and sales forecasting, corporate planning modeling, and information systems development.

Dr. Shim has published numerous articles in accounting, finance, economics, and operations research journals, including *Journal of Business Forecasting, Decision Sciences, Financial Management, Long Range Planning, Business Economics, Econometrica, Journal of Operational Research Society, OMEGA, Journal of Systems Management, Journal of Urban Economics,* and *Annals of Regional Science.*

Dr. Shim has over 50 books to his credit. He is a co-author of *Handbook of Financial Analysis, Forecasting, and Modeling, Managerial Economics, Operations Management,* and the best-selling *Vest-Pocket MBA,* and received the 1982 Credit Research Foundation Outstanding Paper Award for one of his articles on financial forecasting.

TABLE OF CONTENTS

PART I
INTRODUCTION

CHAPTER 1
FORECASTING AND
MANAGERIAL
PLANNING

Business, more than any other occupation, is a continual dealing with the future; it is continual calculation, an instinctive exercise in foresight.

Henry R. Luce

Probably the most important function of business is forecasting. A forecast is a starting point for planning. Yet managers in both private and public organizations typically operate under conditions of uncertainty or risk.

The objective of forecasting is to reduce risk in decision making. In business, forecasts are the basis for capacity planning, production and inventory planning, manpower planning, planning for sales and market share, financial planning and budgeting, planning for research and development, and top management's strategic planning. Sales forecasts are especially crucial to many financial management activities, including budgets, profit planning, capital expenditure analysis, and acquisition and merger analysis. Figure 1.1 on page 4 illustrates how sales forecasts relate to various managerial functions.

WHO USES FORECASTS?

Every manager uses forecasts. Marketing managers use sales forecasts to determine optimal sales force allocations, set sales goals, and plan promotions and advertising, not to mention market share, prices, and trends in new product development. Production planners need forecasts in order to schedule production activities, order materials, establish inventory levels, and plan shipments. Forecasts are also necessary to plan for material requirements (purchasing and procurement), labor scheduling, equipment purchases, maintenance, and changes in plant capacity.

Figure 1.1-—SALES FORECASTS AND MANAGERIAL FUNCTIONS

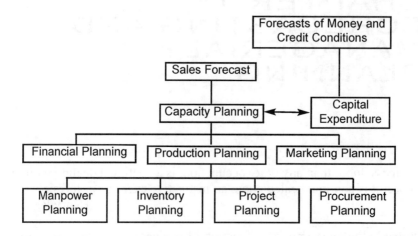

As Figure 1.1 demonstrates, as soon as a company makes sure that it has enough capacity, the production plan is developed. If the company does not have enough capacity, it must make planning and budgeting decisions for capital spending for capacity expansion.

On this basis, the financial manager must estimate future cash inflow and outflow, plan cash and borrowing needs, and forecast cash flows and the rates of expenses and revenues needed to maintain corporate liquidity and operating efficiency. In planning for capital investments, future economic activity must be predicted so that returns or cash inflows accruing from the investment may be estimated.

Forecasts must also be made of money and credit conditions, including interest rates, so that the cash needs of the firm may be met at the lowest possible cost to help balance the flow of funds in the organization. The finance and accounting functions must also forecast interest rates to support the acquisition of new capital, the collection of accounts receivable, and for planning working capital needs and capital equipment expenditure. Sound predictions of foreign exchange rates are increasingly important to financial managers of multinational companies (MNCs).

Long-term forecasts are needed to plan for changes in the company's capital structure. Decisions about whether to issue stock or debt in order to maintain the desired financial structure of the firm require forecasts of money and credit conditions.

The personnel department requires a number of forecasts. Workers must be hired and trained, and, for these personnel, benefits must be provided competitive with those available in the local labor market. Trends that affect such variables as labor turnover, retirement age, absenteeism, and tardiness must be forecast.

Managers of nonprofit institutions and public administrators must also make forecasts. Hospital administrators face the problem of forecasting the health care needs of the community. In order to do this efficiently, projections must be made about growth in absolute number in the size of population, changes in the number of people in various age groupings, and the varying medical needs of these different age groups.

Universities forecast student enrollments, cost of operations, and often what level of funds will be provided by tuition and by government appropriations or grants.

The service sector, which today accounts for two-thirds of US gross domestic product (GDP), includes companies as varied as banks, insurance companies, restaurants, and cruise ships. They need various projections for their operational and long-term strategic planning. A bank, for example, has to forecast demands of various loans and deposits as well as money and credit conditions so that it can determine the cost of the money it lends.

TYPES OF FORECASTS

The types of forecasts used by businesses and other organizations may be classified in several categories, depending on the objective and the situation for which a forecast is to be used. Four types are discussed below.

1. *Sales Forecasts:* As already noted, sales forecasts give the expected level of sales for the company's goods or services throughout some future period; they are instrumental in the company's planning and budgeting functions, and are key to other forecasts and plans.

2. *Financial Forecasts:* Although the sales forecast is the primary input to many financial decisions, other financial forecasts need to be made independent of sales forecasts. These include forecasts of such financial variables as earnings, the amount of external financing needed, cash flows, and the likelihood corporate bankruptcy.

3. *Economic Forecasts:* These statements of expected future business conditions are published by government agencies and private economic forecasting firms. A business can use these forecasts to

develop its own forecasts about how the external business environment will affect demand for its product. Economic forecasts cover a variety of topics including GDP, levels of employment, interest rates, and foreign exchange rates.

4. ***Technological Forecasts:*** A technological forecast is an estimate of rates of technological progress. Certainly, software makers are interested in the rates of technological advancement in computer hardware and its peripheral equipment. Technological changes will provide many businesses with new products and materials to offer for sale while giving other companies competition from other businesses. Technological forecasting is probably best performed by experts in the particular technology.

FORECASTING METHODS

A company may choose from a wide range of forecasting techniques, though there are only four basic approaches to forecasting (see Figure 1.2):

Figure 1.2—FORECASTING METHODS

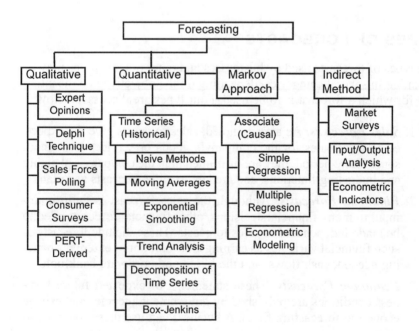

1. ***Qualitative approach*** (forecasts based on judgment and opinion).
   - Executive opinions
   - Delphi technique
   - Sales force polling
   - Consumer surveys
   - PERT-derived techniques for eliciting opinions from experts

2. ***Quantitative approach***
   a. Forecasts based on historical data
   - Naive methods
   - Moving averages
   - Exponential smoothing
   - Trend analysis
   - Decomposition of time series
   - Box-Jenkins

   b. Associative (causal) forecasts
   - Simple regression
   - Multiple regression
   - Econometric modeling

   c. Forecasts based on consumer behavior (Markov approach)

   d. Indirect methods
   - Market surveys
   - Input-output analysis
   - Economic indicators

Quantitative models work superbly as long as there is little or no systemic change in the environment. When patterns or relationships do change, the objective models by themselves are of little use. It is here that the qualitative approach based on human judgment is indispensable. Because judgmental forecasting is also based on observation of existing trends, it too is subject to a number of shortcomings, but it has the advantage of being able to identify systemic change more quickly and better interpret its effects on the future.

We will discuss the qualitative method in this Chapter; quantitative methods will be taken up later.

SELECTING A FORECASTING METHOD

The choice of a forecasting technique is significantly influenced by the stage of the product life cycle and sometimes by the type of firm or the industry for which a decision is being made.

In the beginning of the product life cycle, relatively small expenditures are made for research and market investigation. During the product introduction phase, these expenditures start to increase. In the rapid growth stage, because decisions involve considerable amounts of money, a high level of accuracy is desirable. After the product has entered the maturity stage, decisions are more routine, involving marketing and manufacturing. These are important considerations in choosing a sales forecast technique.

After evaluating the particular stages of the product along with firm and industry life cycles, a further probe is necessary. Instead of selecting a forecasting technique by using whatever seems applicable, decision-makers should determine what is appropriate. Some techniques are quite simple and inexpensive; others are extremely complex, require significant amounts of time to develop, and may be quite expensive. Some are best suited for short-term projections; others are better prepared for intermediate or long-term forecasts.

The choice of technique or techniques depends on the following criteria:

1. How much will it cost to develop the forecasting model compared with the potential gains resulting from its use? The choice is one of benefit-cost trade-off.

2. How complicated are the relationships that must be forecast?

3. Is the forecast for short-run or long-run purposes?

4. How much accuracy is desired?

5. Is there a minimum tolerance level of error?

6. What data are available? Techniques vary in the amount of data they require.

THE QUALITATIVE APPROACH

The qualitative or judgmental approach can be useful in formulating short-term forecasts and can also supplement projections based on the use of any of the qualitative methods. Four of the better known qualitative forecasting methods are executive opinions, the Delphi method, sales-force polling, and consumer surveys.

EXECUTIVE OPINIONS

In this approach, the subjective estimates of executives or experts from sales, production, finance, purchasing, and administration are averaged to generate a forecast about future sales. Usually this method is used in conjunction with a quantitative method such as trend extrapolation. Members of the management team modify the resulting forecast based on their own expectations.

The advantage of this approach is that the forecasting is done quickly and easily, without the need for elaborate statistics. Also, in the absence of adequate data the jury of executive opinions may be the only feasible means of forecasting.

The disadvantage is "group think," a set of problems inherent to those who meet as a group. Foremost among these problems are high cohesiveness, strong leadership, and insulation of the group. With high cohesiveness, the group becomes increasingly conforming through group pressure that stifles dissension and critical thought. Strong leadership fosters group pressure for unanimous opinion. Insulation of the group tends to separate the group from any outside opinions.

THE DELPHI METHOD

Delphi is a group technique in which a panel of experts is individually questioned about their perceptions of future events. Figure 1.3 on page 10 offers an example of how it works. Because the experts do not meet as a group, the possibility that consensus is reached only because of dominant personality factors is reduced. Instead, the forecasts and accompanying arguments are summarized by an outside party and returned along with further questions to the experts. This continues until the group reaches consensus, often after only a few rounds. This method is quite effective for long-range forecasting.

The questionnaire format eliminates the disadvantages of group think. There is no committee or debate. The experts are not influenced by peer pressure to forecast a certain way. The main disadvantage is thought to be low reliability, as well as lack of consensus.

Figure 1.3—AN EXAMPLE OF THE USE OF THE DELPHI METHOD

1 Population (in Millions)	2 Midpoint	3 Number of Panelists	4 Probability Distribution of Panelists	5 Weighted Average (2 X 4)
30 and above		0	.00	0
20-30	25	1	.05	1.25
15-19	17	2	.10	1.70
10-14	12	2	.10	1.20
5-9	7	7	.35	2.45
2-4	3	8	.40	1.20
Less than 2	1	0	.00	0
Total		**20**	**1.00**	**7.80**

Case example: In 1982, 20 college-educated representatives from different parts of the United States were asked to estimate the population of Bombay, India. None of the panelists had been to India since World War 1. The population was estimated to be 7.8 million, very close to the actual population.

Source: Singhvi, Surendra. "Financial Forecast: Why and How?" *Managerial Planning.* March/April 1984.

SALES-FORCE POLLING

Some companies use as a forecast source sales people who have continual contacts with customers. They believe that sales people, who are closest to the ultimate customers, have significant insights into the future market. Forecasts based on sales-force polling may be averaged to develop a future forecast, or they may be used to modify other forecasts that have been generated internally in the company.

The advantages to sales-force polling are that (1) it is simple to use and understand, (2) it uses the specialized knowledge of those closest to the action, (3) it can place responsibility for attaining the forecast in the hands of those who most affect the actual results, and (4) the information can be easily broken down by territory, product, customer, or salesperson.

The disadvantages include the possibility of salespeople being overly optimistic or pessimistic, and of inaccuracies due to broader economic events that are largely beyond their control.

CONSUMER SURVEYS

Some companies conduct their own market surveys of consumer purchasing plans. These may consist of telephone contacts, personal interviews, or questionnaires. Extensive statistical analysis is usually applied to survey results in order to test hypotheses generated regarding consumer behavior.

PERT-DERIVED FORECASTS

A technique known as PERT (Program Evaluation and Review Technique) has been useful in producing estimates based on subjective opinions such as executive opinions or sales-force polling. The PERT methodology requires that the expert provide three estimates: (1) pessimistic (a), (2) the most likely (m), and (3) optimistic (b). The theory suggests that these estimates combine to form an expected value, or forecast, as follows:

$$EV = (a + 4m + b)/6$$
with a standard deviation (σ) of
$$\sigma = (b - a)/6$$
where EV = expected value (mean) of the forecast,
σ = standard deviation of the forecast

For example, suppose that management of a company believes that next year's sales will be $300,000 if the economy is in recession and $330,000 if the economy is in prosperity. Their most likely estimate is $310,000. The PERT method generates an expected value of sales as follows:

$$EV = (\$300,000 + 4(\$310,000) + \$330,000)/6 = \$311,667$$
with a standard deviation of
$$\sigma = (\$330,000 - \$300,000)/6 = \$5,000$$

There are two distinct advantages to this method:

1. It is often easier and more realistic to ask the expert to give a range of estimates than a specific forecast value.
2. The PERT method includes a measure of dispersion (the standard deviation) that makes it possible to develop probabilistic statements. In the above example, for instance, the forecaster is 95 per-

cent confident that the true value of likely sales lies between plus or minus two standard deviations from the mean ($311,667). That is, the true value can be expected between $301,667 and $321,667.

A WORD OF CAUTION

It is important to realize that forecasting is not an exact science like mathematics; it is an art. The quality of forecasts tends to improve over time as the forecaster gains more experience. Evidence shows, however, that forecasts using qualitative techniques are not as accurate as those using quantitative techniques.

Humans possess unique knowledge and inside information not available to quantitative methods. Surprisingly, however, empirical studies and laboratory experiments have shown that their forecasts are not more accurate than those of quantitative methods. Humans tend to be optimistic and underestimate the future uncertainty. In addition, the cost of forecasting with judgmental methods is often considerably higher than when quantitative methods are used.[1]

To create a reasonable forecast, a forecaster must use both qualitative and quantitative techniques.

COMMON FEATURES AND ASSUMPTIONS OF FORECASTING

Though forecasting techniques are clearly quite different from each other, there are certain features and assumptions that underlie them all:

1. Forecasting techniques generally assume that the underlying causal relationship that existed in the past will continue in the future. In other words, most of our techniques are based on historical data.

2. Forecasts are very rarely perfect. Therefore, for planning purposes, allowances should be made for inaccuracies. (For example, the company should always maintain a safety stock in anticipation of stockouts.)

3. Forecast accuracy decreases as the time period (the time "horizon") covered by the forecast increases. Generally speaking,

---

[1]Makridakis, S., "The Art and Science of Forecasting" *International Journal of Forecasting*, Vol. 2, 1986, p. 17.

because of the greater uncertainty a long-term forecast tends to be less accurate than a short-term forecast.

4. Forecasts for groups of items tend to be more accurate than forecasts for individual items, since forecasting errors among items in a group tend to cancel each other out. For example, industry forecasting is more accurate than individual firm forecasting.

STEPS IN THE FORECASTING PROCESS

There are six basic steps in the forecasting process (see Figure 1.4, page 14). They are:

1. Determine the what and why of the forecast and what will be needed, including the level of detail required (e.g., by region, by product, etc.), the amount of resources (e.g., computer hardware and software, manpower, etc.) that can be justified, and the level of accuracy desired.

2. Establish a time horizon, short or long-term, one year or five, etc.

3. Select a forecasting technique.

4. Gather the data and develop a forecast.

5. Identify any assumptions made in preparing and using the forecast.

6. Monitor the forecast to see if it is performing in a manner desired. Develop an evaluation system for this purpose. If not, go to step 1.

Figure 1.4—THE FORECASTING PROCESS

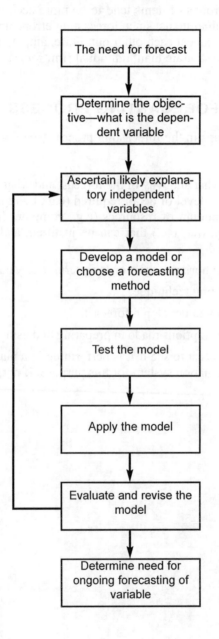

CHAPTER 2
FORECASTING,
BUDGETING, AND
BUSINESS VALUATION

The sales forecast is the first step in the preparation of a budget and a master plan for the company. A master budget is a formal statement of management's expectation regarding the organization's sales, expenses, volume, and other financial transactions for a specified period. Simply put, a budget is a set of projected or planned financial statements. It consists basically of a pro forma income statement, pro forma balance sheet, and cash budget.

A budget is a tool for both planning and control. At the beginning of the period, the budget sets a standard; at the end, it serves as a control device to help management measure how well it performed against the standard so that future performance may be improved.

There are two broad categories of budget:

1. *Operating*, reflecting the results of operating decisions.

2. *Financial*, reflecting the financial decisions of the firm.

The operating budget consists of a pro forma income statement and budgets for sales, production, direct materials, direct labor, factory overhead, and selling and administrative expense.

The financial budget consists of the cash budget and a pro forma balance sheet.

To prepare a budget you must:

1. Prepare a sales forecast.

2. Determine expected production volume.

3. Estimate manufacturing costs and operating expenses.

4. Determine cash flow and other financial effects.

5. Formulate projected financial statements.

Figure 2.1 summarizes the relationships among the various components of the comprehensive (master) budget, the master plan of the company.

Figure 2.1—MASTER BUDGET

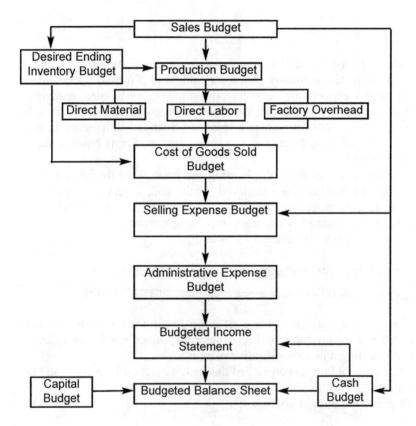

AN ILLUSTRATION

To demonstrate how all these budgets are put together, we will use a manufacturing company, the Morton Company, that produces and markets a single product. We will assume that the company develops the master budget on a quarterly basis.

THE SALES BUDGET

The outcome of the sales forecast is a sales budget. Preparing the master budget starts with the sales budget, since estimated sales volume influences nearly all the other items in the master budget. The sales budget ordinarily indicates the quantity of each product expected to be sold. After sales volume has been estimated, the sales budget is constructed by multiplying the expected sales in units by the expected unit selling price. Table 2.1 is an example of a relatively uncomplicated sales budget; it will become more complicated as the number of products, sales regions, and other subdivisions increases. Generally, the sales budget includes a projection of expected cash collections from credit sales, which will be used later for cash budgeting.

Table 2.1—THE MORTON COMPANY'S BUDGET FOR THE YEAR ENDING DECEMBER 31, 20B

	Quarter				
	1	2	3	4	Total
Expected sales in units	800	700	900	800	3,200
Unit sales price	x $80	x $80	x $80	x $80	x $80
Total sales	$64,000	$56,000	$72,000	$64,000	$256,000

Schedule of Expected Cash Collections

	1	2	3	4	Total
Accounts receivable 12/31/20A	9,500[1]				$9,500
1st quarter sales ($64,000)	44,800[2]	$17,920[3]			62,720
2nd quarter sales ($56,000)		39,200	$15,680		54,880
3rd quarter sales ($72,000)			50,400	$20,160	70,560
4th quarter sales ($64,000)				44,800	44,800
Total cash collections	$54,300	$57,120	$66,080	$64,960	$242,460

[1] The entire $9,500 accounts receivable balance is assumed to be collectible in the first quarter.
[2] 70 percent of a quarter's sales are collected in the quarter of sale.
[3] 28 percent of a quarter's sales are collected in the quarter following, and the remaining 2 percent are uncollectible.

THE PRODUCTION BUDGET

After sales are budgeted, the production budget is determined (see Table 2.2); the number of units expected to be manufactured to meet forecast sales needs and inventory requirements is set forth. The expected volume of production is determined by subtracting the estimated inventory at the beginning of the period from the sum of the units expected to be sold and the desired inventory at the end of the period.

Table 2.2—THE MORTON COMPANY'S PRODUCTION BUDGET FOR THE YEAR ENDING DECEMBER 31, 20B

	Quarter				
	1	2	3	4	Total
Planned unit sales (from Table 2.1)	800	700	900	800	3,200
Desired ending inventory[1]	70	90	80	100[2]	100
Total needs	870	790	980	900	3,300
Less: Beginning inventory[3]	80	70	90	80	80
Units to be produced	790	720	890	820	3,220

[1]10 percent of the next quarter's sales.
[2]Estimated.
[3]The same as the previous quarter's ending inventory.

THE DIRECT MATERIAL BUDGET

When the level of production has been computed, a direct material budget should be constructed to show how much material will be required and how much must be bought to meet this production requirement. The amount to be bought will depend on both expected usage of materials and inventory levels. The formula for the computation is:

Purchase in units = Usage + Desired ending material inventory units – Beginning inventory units

The direct material budget is usually accompanied by a computation of expected cash payments for materials. A sample direct material budget is shown in Table 2.3.

Table 2.3—THE MORTON COMPANY'S DIRECT MATERIAL BUDGET FOR THE YEAR ENDING DECEMBER 31, 20B

	Quarter				
	1	2	3	4	Total
Units to be produced					
(from Table 2.2)	790	720	890	820	3,220
Material needs per unit (lbs.)	X 3	X 3	X 3	X 3	X 3
Material needs for production	2,370	2,160	2,670	2,460	9,660
Desired ending inventory of					
materials[1]	216	267	246	250[2]	250
Total needs	2,586	2,427	2,916	2,710	9,910
Less: Beginning inventory of					
materials[3]	237	216	267	246	237
Materials to be purchased	2,349	2,211	2,649	2,464	9,673
Unit price per lb.	X 2	X 2	X 2	X 2	X 2
Cost	$4,698	$4,422	$5,298	$4,928	$19,346

Schedule of Expected Cash Disbursements

	1	2	3	4	Total
Accounts payable, 12/31/20A	$2,200				$2,200
1st quarter purchases ($4,698)	2,349	2,349[4]			4,698
2nd quarter purchases ($4,422)		2,211	2,211		4,422
3rd quarter purchases ($5,298)			2,649	2,649	5,298
4th quarter purchases ($4,928)				2,464	2,464
Total disbursements	**$4,549**	**$4,560**	**$4,860**	**$5,113**	**$19,082**

[1]10 percent of the next quarter's units needed for production.
[2]Estimated.
[3]The same as the prior quarter's ending inventory.
[4]50 percent of a quarter's purchases is paid for in the quarter of purchase; the remainder is paid for in the following quarter.

THE DIRECT LABOR BUDGET

The production budget also provides the starting point for the preparation of the direct labor budget. To compute direct labor requirements, expected production volume for each period is multiplied by the number of direct labor hours required to produce a single unit. The result is then multiplied by the direct labor cost per hour to obtain budgeted total direct labor costs (see Table 2.4).

Table 2.4—THE MORTON COMPANY'S DIRECT LABOR BUDGET FOR
THE YEAR ENDING DEDEMBER 31, 20B

	Quarter				
	1	2	3	4	Total
Units to be produced					
(from Table 2.2)	790	720	890	820	3,220
Direct labor hours per unit	X 5	X 5	X 5	X 5	X 5
Total hours	3,950	3,600	4,450	4,100	16,100
Direct labor cost per hour	X 5	X 5	X 5	X 5	X 5
Total direct labor cost	$19,750	$18,000	$22,250	$20,500	$80,500

THE FACTORY OVERHEAD BUDGET

The factory overhead budget is a schedule of all manufacturing costs
other than direct materials and direct labor, among them depreciation,
property taxes, and factory rent. In developing the cash budget, we must
remember that because depreciation does not entail a cash outlay, it must
be deducted from total factory overhead in computing the cash disburse-
ment for factory overhead, as shown in Table 2.5.

Table 2.5—THE MORTON COMPANY'S FACTORY OVERHEAD BUDGET
FOR THE YEAR ENDING DECEMBER 31, 20B

Assume:
- Total factory overhead budgeted = $6,000 fixed (per quarter), plus $2 per hour of
  direct labor.
- Depreciation expenses are $3,250 each quarter.
- All overhead costs involving cash outlays are paid for in the quarter incurred.

	Quarter				
	1	2	3	4	Total
Budgeted direct labor hours					
(from Table 2.4)	3,950	3,600	4,450	4,100	16,100
Variable overhead rate	X 2	X 2	X 2	X 2	X 2
Variable budgeted overhead	7,900	7,200	8,900	8,200	32,200
Fixed budgeted overhead	6,000	6,000	6,000	6,000	24,000
Total budgeted overhead	13,900	13,200	14,900	14,200	56,200
Less: Depreciation	3,250	3,250	3,250	3,250	13,000
Cash disbursement for overhead	10,650	9,950	11,650	10,950	43,200

THE SELLING AND ADMINISTRATIVE EXPENSE BUDGET

The selling and administrative expense budget (see Table 2.6) lists the operating expenses that will be incurred in selling the products and in managing the business.

Table 2.6—THE MORTON COMPANY'S SELLING AND ADMINISTRATIVE EXPENSE BUDGET FOR THE YEAR ENDING DECEMBER 31, 20B

	Quarter				
	1	2	3	4	Total
Expected sales in units	800	700	900	800	3,200
Variable selling and administrative expense per unit[1]	X 4	X 4	X 4	X 4	X 4
Budgeted variable expense	$3,200	$2,800	$3,600	$3,200	$12,800
Fixed selling and administrative expenses:					
Advertising	1,100	1,100	1,100	1,100	4,400
Insurance	2,800				2,800
Office supplies	8,500	8,500	8,500	8,500	34,000
Rent	350	350	350	350	1,400
Taxes			1,200		1,200
Total budgeted selling and administrative expenses[2]	$15,950	$12,750	$14,750	$13,150	$56,600

[1]Assumed. It includes sales agents' commissions, shipping, and supplies.
[2]Paid for in the quarter incurred.

THE CASH BUDGET

The cash budget is prepared for the purpose of cash planning and control. It presents the expected cash inflows and outflows for a designated period. This budget helps management keep cash balances that reasonably relate to its needs. It helps avoid keeping too much cash idle as well as possible cash shortages. A typical cash budget (see Table 2.7) has four major sections:

1. The *receipts* section, which takes into account the beginning cash balance, cash collections from customers, and other receipts.

2. The *disbursements* section, which comprises all cash payments planned during the budget period.

3. The *cash surplus* or *deficit* section, which simply shows the difference between the cash receipts section and the cash disbursements section.

4. The *financing* section, which provides a detailed account of any borrowings and repayments expected during the budgeting period.

Table 2.7—THE MORTON COMPANY'S CASH BUDGET FOR THE YEAR ENDING DECEMBER 31, 20A

Assume:
- The company desires to have a $5,000 minimum cash balance at the end of each quarter.
- All borrowing and repayment must be in multiples of $500 at an interest rate of 10 percent per annum. Interest is computed and paid as the principal is repaid. Borrowing takes place at the beginning of each quarter and repayment is at the end of each quarter.

	From Table	Quarter 1	2	3	4	Total
Cash balance, beginning		10,000[1]	9,401	5,461	9,106	10,000
Add: Receipts						
Collections from customers	2.1	54,300	57,120	66,080	64,960	242,460
Total cash available		64,300	66,521	71,541	74,066	252,460
Less: Disbursements						
Direct materials	2.3	4,549	4,560	4,860	5,113	19,082
Direct labor	2.4	19,750	18,000	22,250	10,500	80,500
Factory overhead	2.5	10,650	9,950	11,650	10,950	43,200
Selling and administrative	2.6	15,950	12,750	14,750	13,150	56,600
Machinery purchase	Given		24,300			24,300
Income tax	Given	4,000				4,000
Total disbursements		54,899	69,560	53,510	49,713	227,682
Cash surplus (deficit)		9,401	<3,039>	18,031	24,353	24,778
Financing:						
Borrowing			8,500			8,500
Repayment				<8,500>		<8,500>
Interest				<425>		<425>
Total financing			8,500	<8,925>		<425>
Cash balance, ending		$9,401	$5,461	$9,106	$24,353	$24,353

[1]From balance sheet for preceding year.

THE BUDGETED INCOME STATEMENT

The budgeted income statement summarizes the various projections of revenue and expenses for the budgeting period; for control purposes the budget can be divided into quarters or even months depending on the need. A sample budgeted income statement is provided in Table 2.8.

Table 2.8—THE MORTON COMPANY'S BUDGETED INCOME STATEMENT FOR THE YEAR ENDING DECEMBER 31, 20B

Sales (3,200 units at $80)	$256,000	
Less: Cost of goods sold (3,200 units at $48.5)	155,200	
Gross margin		100,800
Less: Operating expenses		
Selling and administrative	55,600	
Less: Interest expense	425	56,025
Income before taxes		43,775
Less: Income taxes (20%)[1]		8,755
Net income		$35,020

[1]Assumed.

THE BUDGETED BALANCE SHEET

The budgeted balance sheet is developed by adjusting the balance sheet for the year just ended using all the activities that are expected to take place during the budgeting period. Some reasons why the budgeted balance sheet must be prepared:

(a) It could disclose unfavorable financial conditions that management might want to avoid.

(b) It helps management perform a variety of ratio calculations.

(c) It highlights future resources and obligations.

"WHAT-IF" SCENARIOS

With the aid of computer technology, budgeting can be an effective device for evaluation of "what-if" scenarios, allowing management to move toward finding the best course of action among various alternatives. If managers do not like what they see on the budgeted financial statements in terms of various financial ratios such as liquidity, activity (turnover), leverage, profit margin, and market value ratios, they can always alter their contemplated decision and planning set and test alternatives through simulation.

USING AN ELECTRONIC SPREADSHEET

Tables 2.1 through 2.8 showed the detail required to formulate a master budget. However, in practice a short-cut approach to budgeting using computer technology is quite common. Figure 2.2 shows how to develop a projected income statement using a spreadsheet such as Excel. A spreadsheet program allows financial managers to evaluate various "what-if" scenarios.

FORECASTING AND BUSINESS VALUATION

Forecasting has never been an exact science. It never will be. The reason is that crystal-balling the future is always a challenge in anybody's life. It is something every human being strives to achieve, because you and I will always try to minimize uncertainty or risk. It's true that if you can make the right forecast about something in your life, you can easily make a fortune overnight. It can be a stock price, interest rate, foreign exchange rate, or even a lottery. You pick the winning six numbers. You become an instant millionaire. You picking the right stock—same result, though probably not instantly. How about predicting where an interest rate or a foreign exchange rate is heading and when? Ask George Soros. You can similarly make a fortune in options or forward contracts, and so forth.

Business valuation relates to determining the value you put on an asset, such as stock, bond, real estate, a business, or a targeted business to be acquired, to name a few. A question that comes up all the time is: How much are you willing to pay for a piece of real estate, a business, etc? From a business standpoint, prediction and business valuation have a lot to do with each other. For buying or selling a business, a valuation might be important for establishing an asking or offering price.

To determine the value of a business, you must find the present value of its expected future cash flows using the investor's required rate of return. The basic valuation model can be defined mathematically:

$$V = \sum_{t=1}^{n} \frac{C_t}{(1+r)^t}$$

Figure 2.2—PROJECTED INCOME STATEMENT

	1	2	3	4	5	6	7	8	9	10	11	12	Total	%
Sales	$60,000	$63,000	$66,150	$69,458	$72,930	$76,577	$80,406	$84,426	$88,647	$93,080	$97,734	$102,620	$955,028	100%
Less: Variable costs														
Cost of sales	$25,200	$26,460	$27,783	$29,172	$30,631	$32,162	$33,770	$35,459	$37,232	$39,093	$41,048	$43,101	$401,112	42%
Operating expenses	$3,000	$3,150	$3,308	$3,473	$3,647	$3,829	$4,020	$4,221	$4,432	$4,654	$4,887	$5,131	$47,751	5%
CM	$31,800	$33,390	$35,060	$36,812	$38,653	$40,586	$42,615	$44,746	$46,983	$49,332	$51,799	$54,389	$506,165	53%
Less: FC Operating expenses	$10,000	$10,000	$10,000	$10,000	$10,000	$10,000	$10,000	$10,000	$10,000	$10,000	$10,000	$10,000	$120,000	13%
Net income (NI)	$21,800	$23,390	$25,060	$26,812	$28,653	$30,586	$32,615	$34,746	$36,983	$39,332	$41,799	$44,389	$386,165	40%
Less: Tax	$6,540	$7,017	$7,518	$8,044	$8,596	$9,176	$9,785	$10,424	$11,095	$11,800	$12,540	$13,317	$115,849	12%
NI after tax	$15,260	$16,373	$17,542	$18,769	$20,057	$21,410	$22,831	$24,322	$25,888	$27,533	$29,259	$31,072	$270,315	28%

where   V   =   intrinsic value or present value of an asset
          C_t =   expected future cash flows or earnings in period
                        $t = 1, ..., n$
          r   =   investor's required rate of return

For example, the value of a common stock is the present value of all expected future cash inflows to the investor in the form of dividends and future selling price. At least in theory, the price you are willing to pay to buy a stock is the present worth of the expected future earning power of the stock. The classic *discounted cash flow (DCF)* model is used for this purpose.

Sound forecast of future cash flows or earning power is vital for business valuations.

CONCLUSION

Forecasting is essential to planning and budgeting. It is needed wherever the future financing needs are being estimated. Basically, forecasts of future sales and their related expenses provide a company with the information it needs to plan other activities of the business.

This chapter has emphasized budgets. The process involves developing a sales forecast and using it to generate those budgets needed by the company. Once developed, the budget provides management with a means of controlling the activities of the business as well as monitoring actual performance and comparing it to budget goals.

Budgeting can be done easily with electronic spreadsheet software, as was illustrated in this chapter, but there are many specialized software products available for budgeting.

Budgeting also helps clarify the relationship between forecasting and business valuations. How much you are willing to pay for a business, stock, or real estate is essentially the present worth of its expected future (forecast) earnings.

PART II
FORECASTING
METHODS

CHAPTER 3
MOVING AVERAGES
AND SMOOTHING
METHODS

This Chapter discusses several forecasting methods based on historical data that fall into the quantitative approach category, including naive models, moving averages, and exponential smoothing methods. Time series analysis and regressions are covered in future chapters.

NAIVE MODELS

Naive forecasting models are based exclusively on historical observation of sales or other variables such as earnings and cash flows. They do not attempt to explain the underlying causal relationships that produce the variable being forecast.

Naive models may be classified into two groups. One consists of simple projection models. These models require inputs of data from recent observations, but no statistical analysis. The second group is made up of models that, while naive, are complex enough to require a computer. Classical decomposition, moving average, and exponential smoothing models are some examples.

The advantage of a naïve model is that it is inexpensive to develop, store data, and operate.

The disadvantage is that it does not consider any causal relationships that may underlie the forecasted variable.

Here are three typical naïve models:

1. The simplest naive model is to use the actual sales of the current period to forecast the next period. Let us use the symbol Y'_{t+1} as the forecast value and the symbol Y_t as the actual value. Then,

$$Y'_{t+1} = Y_t$$

2. If you consider trends, then

$$Y'_{t+1} = Y_t + (Y_t - Y_{t-1})$$

This model adds the latest observed absolute period-to-period change to the most recent observed level of the variable.

3. If you want to incorporate the rate of change rather than the absolute amount, then

$$Y'_{t+1} = \frac{Y_t}{Y_{t-1}}$$

Example 3.1

Consider the following sales data:

Month	20x1 Monthly Sales of Product
1	$3,050
2	$2,980
3	$3,670
4	$2,910
5	$3,340
6	$4,060
7	$4,750
8	$5,510
9	$5,280
10	$5,504
11	$5,810
12	$6,100

If we develop forecasts for January 20X2 based on the three models set out above:

1. $Y'_{t+1} = Y_t = \$6,100$

2. $Y'_{t+1} = Y_t + (Y_t - Y_{t-1}) = \$6,100 + (\$6,100 - \$5,810)$
$$= \$6,100 + \$290 = \$6,390$$

3. $Y'_{t+1} = Y_t \dfrac{Y_t}{Y_{t-1}}$

$$= \$6,100 \text{ x} \frac{\$6,100}{\$5,810} = \$6,100 \ (1.05) = \$6,405$$

Naive models can be applied, with very little need of a computer, to develop forecasts for sales, earnings, and cash flows. For forecasting efficiency, however, they must be compared with more sophisticated models such as the regression (Chapter 5) and Box-Jenkins (Chapter 8) methods.

SMOOTHING TECHNIQUES

Smoothing techniques are a higher form of naive model. There are two typical forms: moving average and exponential smoothing. Moving average is the simpler.

MOVING AVERAGE

Moving averages are averages that are updated as new information is received. With the moving average, a manager simply uses the most recent observations to calculate an average that is used as the forecast for the next period.

Example 3.2

Assume that the marketing manager has the following sales data:

	Date	Actual Sales (Y_t)
Jan.	1	46
	2	54
	3	53
	4	46
	5	58
	6	49
	7	54

In order to predict the sales for the seventh and eighth days of January, the manager has to pick a number of observations to be used for averaging purposes. Let us consider two cases, one a six-day moving average and the other a three-day average (see Figure 3.1).

Case 1

$$Y'_7 = \frac{46 + 54 + 53 + 46 + 58 + 49}{6} = 51$$

$$Y'_8 = \frac{54 + 53 + 46 + 58 + 49 + 54}{6} = 52.3$$

Case 2

$$Y'_7 = \frac{46 + 58 + 49}{3} = 51$$

$$Y'_8 = \frac{58 + 49 + 54}{3} = 53.6$$

Figure 3.1—MOVING AVERAGE CALCULATIONS

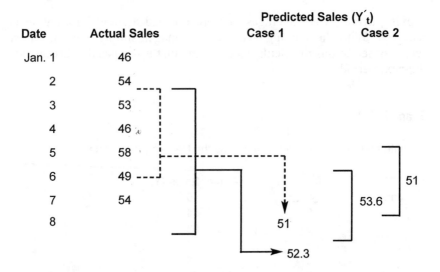

		Predicted Sales (Y'_t)	
Date	**Actual Sales**	**Case 1**	**Case 2**
Jan. 1	46		
2	54		
3	53		
4	46		
5	58		
6	49		51
7	54		53.6
8		51	
		52.3	

In terms of the weights given to observations, in case 1 the old data received a weight of 5/6 and the current observation got a weight of 1/6. In case 2 the old data received a weight of only 2/3 while the current observation received a weight of 1/3. The marketing manager's choice of the number of periods to use in a moving average is thus a measure of the relative importance attached to old versus current data.

The moving average is simple to use and easy to understand. However, it has two shortcomings:

- It requires you to retain a great deal of data and carry it from forecast period to forecast period.
- All data in the sample are weighted equally. If more recent data are more valid than older data, why not give them greater weight?

The forecasting method known as exponential smoothing gets around these disadvantages.

EXPONENTIAL SMOOTHING

Exponential smoothing is a popular technique among financial managers for short-run forecasting. It uses a weighted average of past data as the basis for a forecast. The procedure gives greatest weight to more recent information and less weight to observations in the more distant past. The reason for this is that the future is more dependent upon the recent than on the distant past. The method is known to be effective when there is randomness and no seasonal fluctuations. One of its disadvantages, however, is that it does not take into account industrial or economic factors such as market conditions, prices, or the effects of competitors' actions.

THE MODEL

The formula for exponential smoothing is:

$$Y'_{t+1} = \alpha\ Y_t + (1 - \alpha)\ Y'_t$$

or alternatively,

$$Y'_{new} = \alpha\ Y_{old} + (1 - \alpha)\ Y'_{old}$$

where

$\quad Y'_{new}$ = Exponentially smoothed average to be used as the forecast.
$\quad Y_{old}$ = Most recent actual data.
$\quad Y'_{old}$ = Most recent smoothed forecast.
$\quad \alpha$ = Smoothing constant.

The higher the α, the greater the weight given to the more recent information.

Example 3.3

The data on sales are as follows:

Time Period (t)	Actual Sales*(Y_t)
1	$60.0
2	64.0
3	58.0
4	66.0
5	70.0
6	60.0
7	70.0
8	74.0
9	62.0
10	74.0
11	68.0
12	66.0
13	60.0
14	66.0
15	62.0

*In thousands of dollars.

To begin the exponential smoothing process, we must have the initial forecast. The first smoothed forecast to be used can be either first actual observations, or an average of the actual data for a few periods.

For illustrative purposes, let us use a six-period average as the initial forecast Y'_7 with a smoothing constant of α = 0.40.

Then Y'_7 = $(Y_1 + Y_2 + Y_3 + Y_4 + Y_5 + Y_6) / 6$

= $(60 + 64 + 58 + 66 + 70 + 60) / 6 = 63$

Note that actual sales in Y'_7 = 70. Then Y'_8 is computed as follows:

$$Y'_8 \quad = \quad \alpha\, Y_7 + (1 - \alpha)\, Y'_7$$
$$= \quad (0.40)(70) + (0.60)(63)$$
$$= \quad 28.0 + 37.80 = 65.80$$

Similarly,

$$Y'_9 \quad = \quad \alpha\, Y_8 + (1 - \alpha)\, Y'_8$$
$$= \quad (0.40)(74) + (0.60)(65.80)$$
$$= \quad 29.60 + 39.48 = 69.08$$

and

$$Y'_{10} \quad = \quad \alpha\, Y_9 + (1 - \alpha)\, Y'_9$$
$$= \quad (0.40)(62) + (0.60)(69.08)$$
$$= \quad 24.80 + 41.45 = 66.25$$

Using the same procedure, the values of Y'_{11}, Y'_{12}, Y'_{13}, Y'_{14}, and Y'_{15} can be calculated. Table 3.1 shows a comparison between actual sales and sales predicted by the exponential smoothing method.

Table 3.1—Comparison of Actual Sales and Predicted Sales

Time period (t)	Actual sales (Y_t)	Predicted sales (Y'_t)	Difference ($Y_t - Y'_t$)	Difference^2 ($Y_t - Y'_t)^2$
1	$60.0			
2	64.0			
3	58.0			
4	66.0			
5	70.0			
6	60.0			
7	70.0	63.00	7.00	49.00
8	74.0	65.80	8.20	67.24
9	62.0	69.08	-7.08	50.13
10	74.0	66.25	7.75	60.06
11	68.0	69.35	-1.35	1.82
12	66.0	68.81	-2.81	7.90
13	60.0	67.69	-7.69	59.14
14	66.0	64.61	1.39	1.93
15	62.0	65.17	-3.17	10.05
				$307.27

Given the negative and positive differences between actual sales and predicted sales, the forecaster can use a higher or lower smoothing constant (a) in order to adjust the prediction as quickly as possible to large fluctuations in the data series. For example, if the forecast is slow in reacting to increased sales (i.e., if the difference is negative), the forecaster might want to try a higher value. For practical purposes, the optimal may be picked by minimizing what is known as the *mean squared error* (MSE), which will be discussed in more detail in Chapter 9:

$$\text{MSE} = \sum_{t=1}^{n} (Y_t - Y'_t)^2 / (n - i)$$

Where

i = the number of observations used to determine the initial forecast (in our example, i = 6).

In our example,

MSE = 307.27 / (15 − 6) = 307.27/9 = 34.14

The idea is to select the α that minimizes MSE, which is the average sum of the variations between historical sales data and the values forecast for the corresponding periods.

COMPUTER SMOOTHING

As a manager, you will be confronted with complex problems requiring large amounts of sample data. You will also need to try different values of α for exponential smoothing. Virtually all forecasting software has an exponential smoothing routine. Figure 3.2 is a sample output from a computer program for exponential smoothing.

Notice that the best α for this particular example is .9, because it gives the lowest MSE.

Figure 3.2—EXPONENTIAL SMOOTHING PROGRAM—SINGLE SMOOTHING

Period	Actual Value	Estimated Value	Error
1	117.00	.00	
2	120.00	117.00	

The value of the exponential smoother is .1:

Period	Actual Value	Estimated Value	Error
3	132.00	117.30	14.70
4	141.00	118.77	22.23
5	140.00	120.99	19.01
6	156.00	122.89	33.11
7	169.00	126.20	42.80
8	171.00	130.48	40.52
9	174.00	134.54	39.46
10	182.00	138.48	43.52

The total absolute error in estimates is 255.34.
The mean squared error is 1,136.48.

The value of the exponential smoother is .2:

Period	Actual Value	Estimated Value	Error
3	132.00	117.60	14.40
4	141.00	120.48	20.52
5	140.00	124.58	15.42
6	156.00	127.67	28.33
7	169.00	133.33	35.67
8	171.00	140.47	30.53
9	174.00	146.57	27.43
10	182.00	152.06	29.94

The total absolute error in estimate is 202.24.
The mean squared error is 690.23.

The value of the exponential smoother is .3:

Period	Actual Value	Estimated Value	Error
3	132.00	117.90	14.40
4	141.00	122.13	18.87
5	140.00	127.79	12.21
6	156.00	131.45	24.55
7	169.00	138.82	30.18
8	171.00	147.87	23.13
9	174.00	154.81	19.19
10	182.00	160.57	21.43

The total absolute error in estimate is 163.66.
The mean squared error is 447.49.

The value of the exponential smoother is .4:

Period	Actual Value	Estimated Value	Error
3	132.00	118.20	13.80
4	141.00	123.72	17.28
5	140.00	130.63	9.37
6	156.00	134.38	21.62

Figure 3.2—EXPONENTIAL SMOOTHING PROGRAM—SINGLE SMOOTHING, con't.

Period	Actual Value	Estimated Value	Error
7	169.00	143.03	25.97
8	171.00	153.42	17.58
9	174.00	160.45	13.55
10	182.00	165.87	16.13

The total absolute error in estimate is 135.3.
The mean squared error is 308.97

The value of the exponential smoother is .5:

3	132.00	118.50	13.50
4	141.00	125.25	15.75
5	140.00	133.12	6.88
6	156.00	136.56	19.44
7	169.00	146.28	22.72
8	171.00	157.64	13.36
9	174.00	164.32	9.68
10	182.00	169.16	12.84

The total absolute error in estimate is 141.16.
The mean squared error is 226.07.

The value of the exponential smoother is .6:

3	132.00	118.80	13.20
4	141.00	126.72	14.28
5	140.00	135.29	4.71
6	156.00	138.12	17.88
7	169.00	148.85	20.15
8	171.00	160.94	10.06
9	174.00	166.98	7.02
10	182.00	171.19	10.81

The total absolute error in estimate is 98.13.
The mean squared error is 174.23.

The value of the exponential smoother is .7:

3	132.00	119.10	12.90
4	141.00	128.13	12.87
5	140.00	137.14	2.86
6	156.00	139.14	16.86
7	169.00	150.94	18.06
8	171.00	163.58	7.42
9	174.00	168.77	5.23
10	182.00	172.43	9.57

The total absolute error in estimate is 85.76.
The mean squared error is 140.55.

Figure 3.2—EXPONENTIAL SMOOTHING PROGRAM—SINGLE SMOOTHING, *con't.*

Period	Actual Value	Estimated Value	Error
The value of the exponential smoother is .8:			
3	132.00	119.40	12.60
4	141.00	129.48	11.52
5	140.00	138.70	1.30
6	156.00	139.74	16.26
7	169.00	152.75	16.25
8	171.00	165.75	5.25
9	174.00	169.95	4.05
10	182.00	173.19	8.81

The total absolute error in estimate is 76.05.
The mean squared error is 117.91.

Period	Actual Value	Estimated Value	Error
The value of the exponential smoother is .9:			
3	132.00	119.70	12.30
4	141.00	130.77	10.23
5	140.00	139.88	.02
6	156.00	140.00	16.00
7	169.00	154.40	14.60
8	171.00	167.54	3.46
9	174.00	170.65	3.35
10	182.00	173.67	8.33

The total absolute error in estimate is 68.30.
The mean squared error is 102.23.

Summary Results
The exponential smoother .1 with a mean squared error of 1,136.48
The exponential smoother .2 with a mean squared error of 690.23
The exponential smoother .3 with a mean squared error of 447.49
The exponential smoother .4 with a mean squared error of 308.97
The exponential smoother .5 with a mean squared error of 226.07
The exponential smoother .6 with a mean squared error of 174.23
The exponential smoother .7 with a mean squared error of 140.55
The exponential smoother .8 with a mean squared error of 117.91
The exponential smoother .9 with a mean squared error of 102.23

ADJUSTING FOR TREND

When the data show a sign of trend, we can add a trend factor to account for it. This situation can be handled by using another weighting (smoothing) constant. Thus, it involves two smoothings. First, the original data are smoothed, then the resulting values are smoothed as if they were original values.

These double-smoothed values have two useful properties:

1. They are smoother than the single-smoothed values, which means they will provide a clearer indication of the trend.

2. The double-smoothed values lag the single-smoothed values by about as much as the single-smoothed values lag the original data. Consequently, by adding the difference between single- and double-smoothed values to the single-smoothed values, the resulting series will approximate the original series.

Finally, by including an allowance for trend in the forecast, the forecasts will give a fairly good indication of future values. Both smoothing and double lagging can be seen in Figure 3.3.

Figure 3.3—DATA, FORECASTS, AND SMOOTHED VALUES
The exponentially smoothed forecast adjusted for trend is:

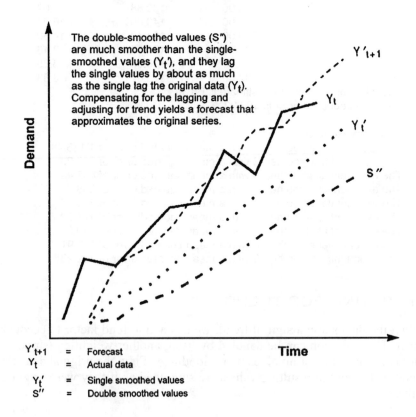

The double-smoothed values (S″) are much smoother than the single-smoothed values (Y_t'), and they lag the single values by about as much as the single lag the original data (Y_t). Compensating for the lagging and adjusting for trend yields a forecast that approximates the original series.

Y'_{t+1}	=	Forecast
Y_t	=	Actual data
Y_t'	=	Single smoothed values
S''	=	Double smoothed values

$$Y'_{t+1} = \text{Single} + (\text{Single} - \text{Double}) + \text{Trend}$$
$$\text{smoothed} \quad (\text{smoothed} \quad \text{smoothed}) \quad \text{adjustment}$$
$$= Y'_t + (Y'_t - S''_t) + b_t$$

where $Y'_t = \alpha Y_{t-1} + (1 - \alpha) Y'_{t-1}$ and the trend adjustment, bt, can be approximated by the amount of change each period in S'', that is:

$$b_t = S''_t - S''_{t-1}$$

Example 3.4

This example shows PC computer sales for a store in New York over the past 10 years. Using trend-adjusted exponential smoothing with a single smoothing constant of $\alpha = .4$ and a double smoothing constant of $\alpha = .3$, prepare a forecast for period 11.

Period	Unit sales
1	700
2	724
3	720
4	728
5	740
6	742
7	758
8	750
9	770
10	775

Step by step, these are the calculations (the results are shown in Table 3.2):

Step 1: Smooth the data using the equation $Y'_t = (.4) Y_{t-1} + (1 - .4) Y'_{t-1}$. Using the first data point, 700, as the beginning forecast, the results are shown in Table 3.2 in the Y'_t column.

Step 2: Smooth the Y'_t values using the equation $S''_t = Y'_{t-1} + .3(Y_t - S''_{t-1})$, with 700 as the first value. The results are shown in the S''_t column.

Step 3: Compute the trend adjustment, bt, using the equation $b_t = S''_t - S''_{t-1}$. The results are shown in column bt.

Step 4: Determine the forecast for each period using the equation $Y'_t + (Y'_t - S''_t) + bt$. The forecasts are shown in the last column.

Table 3.2—Calculations for Trend-Adjusted Forecast

t	Y_t (data)	Y'_t (single)	S''_t (double)	$S''_t - S''_{t-1}$ (b_t)	Forecast
1.	700.00	700.00	700.00		
2.	724.00	709.60	702.88	2.88	700.00
3.	720.00	713.76	706.14	3.26	719.20
4.	728.00	719.46	710.14	3.99	724.64
5.	740.00	727.67	715.40	5.26	732.77
6.	742.00	733.40	720.80	5.40	745.21
7.	758.00	743.24	727.53	6.73	751.41
8.	750.00	745.95	733.06	5.52	765.68
9.	770.00	755.57	739.81	6.75	764.36
10.	775.00	763.34	746.87	7.06	778.08
11.					786.87

Figure 3.4—FORECASTS, AND SMOOTHED VALUES (Table 3.2 values)

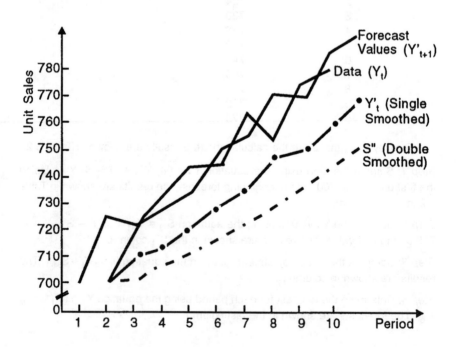

Data, forecasts, and smoothed values are plotted in Figure 3.4 on page 42. (Again, virtually all forecasting software will calculate forecasts based on exponential smoothing with trends.)

CONCLUSION

Among the quantitative forecasting methods, naive techniques are based solely on previous experience. Smoothing approaches include moving average and exponential smoothing. Moving averages and exponential smoothing employ a weighted average of past data in deriving the forecast.

CONCLUSION

CHAPTER 4
REGRESSION
ANALYSIS

Regression analysis is a statistical procedure for estimating mathematically the average relationship between a dependent variable and any independent variables. *Simple regression* involves one independent variable, such as price or advertising, in a demand function; *multiple regression* takes into account two or more variables, such as price and advertising, together. Here are some typical applications of simple regression:

1. Total manufacturing cost is explained by only one activity variable (such as either production volume or machine hours), i.e., $TC = a + b\,Q$.

2. The return on a security is a function of the return on a market portfolio (such as Standard & Poor's 500), i.e., $r_j = a + \beta r_m$ where β = beta, a measure of uncontrollable risk.

3. Consumption is a function of disposable income, i.e., $C = a + b\,Y_d$, where b = marginal propensity to consume.

4. Demand is a function of price, i.e., $Q_d = a - bP$.

5. Average time to be taken is a function of cumulative production, i.e., $Y = a\,X^{-b}$ where b represents a learning rate in the learning curve phenomenon.

6. Trend analysis attempts to detect a growing or declining trend of time series data, i.e., $Y = a + bt$, where t = time.

In this chapter, we will discuss simple (linear) regression to illustrate the *least-squares method*, which means that we will assume the relationship $Y = a + bX$.

THE LEAST-SQUARES METHOD

The regression method includes all the observed data and attempts to find a line of best fit. To find this line, a technique called the least-squares method is used widely for estimating parameter values.

To explain the least-squares method, we define error as the difference between the observed value and the estimated one and denote it with u. Symbolically,

$$u = Y - Y'$$

where   Y = observed value of the dependent variable
             Y' = estimated value based on $Y' = a + bX$

The least-squares criterion requires that the line of best fit be such that the sum of the squares of the errors (or the vertical distance in Figure 4.1 from the observed data points to the line) is a minimum:

$$\Sigma u^2 = \Sigma(Y - a - bX)^2$$

Figure 4.1—Y AND Y'

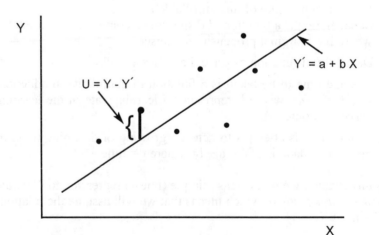

Using differential calculus we obtain the following equations, called normal equations:

$$\Sigma Y = na + b \Sigma X$$
$$\Sigma XY = a\Sigma X + b\Sigma X^2$$

Solving the equations for b and a yields

$$b = \frac{n\Sigma XY - (\Sigma X)(\Sigma Y)}{n\Sigma X^2 - (\Sigma X)^2}$$

$$a = \overline{Y} - b\overline{X}$$

where $\overline{Y} = \Sigma Y / n$ and $\overline{X} = \Sigma X / n$.

Example 4.1

To illustrate the computations of b and a, we will refer to the data in Table 4.1. All the sums required are computed and shown below.

Table 4.1—COMPUTED SUMS

Advertising X*	Sales Y*	XY	X²	Y²
9	15	135	81	225
19	20	380	361	400
11	14	154	121	196
14	16	224	196	256
23	25	575	529	625
12	20	240	144	400
12	20	240	144	400
22	23	506	484	529
7	14	98	49	196
13	22	286	169	484
15	18	270	225	324
17	18	306	289	324
174	225	3,414	2,792	4,359

*In thousands of dollars.

Using the data in Table 4.1, then:

$$\Sigma X = 174; \; \Sigma Y = 225; \; \Sigma XY = 3,3414; \; \Sigma X^2 = 2,792.$$

$$\overline{X} = \Sigma X / n = 174 / 12 = 14.5; \; \overline{Y} = \Sigma Y / n = 225 / 12 = 18.75.$$

Substituting these values into the formula for b first:

$$b = \frac{n\Sigma XY - (\Sigma X)(\Sigma Y)}{n\Sigma Y^2 - (\Sigma X)^2} = \frac{(12)(3,414) - (174)(225)}{(12)(2,792) - (174)^2} = \frac{1,818}{3,228} = 0.5632$$

$$a = \overline{Y} - b\overline{X} = 18.75 - (0.5632)(14.5) = 18.75 - 8.1664 = 10.5836$$

Thus, $Y' = 10.5836 + 0.5632\, X$

Example 4.2

Assume that the advertising allocation for next year is $10; projected sales for the next year would be computed as follows:

$$\begin{aligned} Y' &= 10.5836 + 0.5632\, X \\ &= 10.5836 + 0.5632\,(10) \\ &= \$16.2156 \end{aligned}$$

Note that ΣY^2 is not used here but rather is computed for r-squared (R^2).

USE OF LOTUS 1-2-3

In reality you do not compute the parameter values a and b manually. Spreadsheet programs such as *Lotus 1-2-3* have a regression routine that you can use without any difficulty. Figure 4.2 presents a Lotus regression output. At this juncture, we note from the output only that:

$$a = 10.58364$$
$$b = 0.563197$$

That is, $Y' = 10.58364 + 0.563197\, X$

Other statistics shown on the printout are discussed later in this chapter.

Figure 4.2—REGRESSION OUTPUT

Constant	10.58364	(a = 10.58364)
Standard error of Y estimate	2.343622	
R-squared	0.608373	
No. of observations	12	
Degrees of freedom	10	
X coefficient(s)	0.563197	(b = 0.563197)
Standard error of coefficient	0.142893	

The result shows:
Y′ = 10.58364 + 0.563197

A WORD OF CAUTION

Before attempting a least-squares regression approach, it is extremely important to plot the observed data on a diagram, called the scattergraph (Figure 4.3), so that you can make sure that a linear (straight-line) relationship existed between Y and X in the past sample.

Figure 4.3—SCATTER DIAGRAM

Sales (Y)

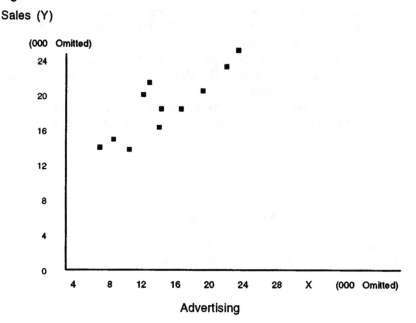

Advertising

If for any reason a nonlinear relationship is detected in the sample, the linear relationship we assumed—Y = a + bX—would not give us a good fit.

In order to obtain a good fit and achieve a high degree of accuracy, you should be familiar with statistics relating to regression such as r-squared (R^2) and t-value, which are also discussed later.

REGRESSION STATISTICS

Regression analysis is a statistical method. Hence, it uses a variety of statistical conventions to test the accuracy and reliability of the regression results. They include:

1. Correlation coefficient (R) and coefficient of determination (R^2)

2. Standard error of the estimate (S_e) and prediction confidence interval

3. Standard error of the regression coefficient (S_b) and t-statistic

CORRELATION COEFFICIENT (R) AND COEFFICIENT OF DETERMINATION (R^2)

The correlation coefficient R measures the degree of correlation between Y and X in a range of values from -1 to +1. More widely used, however, is the coefficient of determination, designated R^2 (read as r-squared). R^2 tells us how good the estimated regression equation is. In other words, it is a measure of "goodness of fit." The higher the R^2, the more confidence we may have in our estimate.

More specifically, R^2 represents the proportion of the total variation in Y that is explained by the regression equation. It has the range of values between 0 and 1.

Example 4.3

The statement "Sales is a function of advertising expenditure with R^2 = 70 percent" can be interpreted as "70 percent of the total variation in sales is explained by the regression equation or the change in advertising and the remaining 30 percent is accounted for by something other than advertising, such as price or income."

The coefficient of determination is computed as

$$R^2 = 1 - \frac{\Sigma(Y - Y')^2}{\Sigma(Y - \overline{Y})^2}$$

In a simple regression situation, however, there is a short cut available:

$$R^2 = \frac{(n\Sigma XY - (\Sigma X)(\Sigma Y))^2}{[n\Sigma X^2 - (\Sigma X)^2][n\Sigma Y^2 - (\Sigma Y)^2]}$$

Comparing this formula with the one for b, we see that the only additional information we need to compute R^2 is ΣY^2.

Example 4.4

We will use the data in Table 4.1 to illustrate the computation of various regression statistics: using the shortcut method for R^2,

$$R^2 = \frac{(1,818)^2}{[(3,228)(12)][(4,359) - (225)^2]} = \frac{3,305,124}{(3,228)(52,308 - 50,625)}$$

$$= \frac{3,305,124}{(3,228)(1,683)} = \frac{3,305,124}{5,432,724} = 0.6084 = 60.84\%$$

This means that about 60.84 percent of the total variation in sales is explained by advertising and the remaining 39.16 percent is still unexplained. A relatively low R^2 indicates that there is considerable room for improvement in our estimated forecasting formula (Y´ = \$10.5836 + \$0.5632X). Price or a combination of advertising and price might improve R^2.

STANDARD ERROR OF THE ESTIMATE (S_e) AND PREDICTION CONFIDENCE INTERVAL

The *standard error of the estimate*, S_e, is defined as the standard deviation of the regression. It is computed as:

$$S_e = \sqrt{\frac{\Sigma(Y - Y')^2}{n - 2}} = \sqrt{\frac{\Sigma Y^2 - a\Sigma Y - b\Sigma XY}{n - 2}}$$

This statistic can be used to gain some idea of the accuracy of predictions.

Example 4.5

Going back to our example data, S_e is calculated as:

$$S_e = \sqrt{\frac{4{,}359 - (10.5836)(225) - (0.5632)(3{,}414)}{12 - 2}}$$

$$= \sqrt{\frac{54.9252}{10}} = 2.3436$$

Suppose you wish to make a prediction regarding an individual Y value, perhaps a prediction about sales when advertising expense = \$10. Usually, we would like to have an objective measure of the confidence we can place in our prediction; one such measure is a *confidence (or prediction) interval* constructed for Y.

A confidence interval for a predicted Y, given a value for X, can be constructed in the following way:

$$Y' \pm tS_e \sqrt{1 + \frac{1}{n} + \frac{(X_p - \bar{X})^2}{\Sigma X^2 - \frac{(\Sigma X)^2}{n}}}$$

where Y' = the predicted value of Y given a value for X, and
         X_p = the value of independent variable used as the basis for prediction.

Note: t is the critical value for the level of significance employed. For example, for a significance level of 0.025 (equivalent to a 95 percent confidence level in a two-tailed test), the critical value of t for 10 degrees of freedom is 2.228 (see Table A.2 in the Appendix). As can be seen, the confidence interval is the linear distance bounded by limits on either side of the prediction.

Example 4.6

If you want a 95 percent confidence interval for your prediction, the range for the prediction, given an advertising expense of $10, would be between $10,595.10 and $21,836.10, determined as follows (note that from Example 4.2, Y' - 16.2156):

$$\$16.2156 \pm (2.228)(2.3436)\sqrt{1 + \frac{1}{12} \quad \frac{(10 - 14.5)^2}{2,792 - (174)^2 / 12}}$$

= $16.2156 ± (2.228)(2.3436) (1.0764)
= $16.2156 ± 5.6205

which means the range for the prediction, given an advertising expense of $10, would be between $10.5951 and $21.8361. Note that $10.5951 = $16.2156 – 5.6205 and $21.8361 = $16.2156 + 5.6205.

STANDARD ERROR OF THE REGRESSION COEFFICIENT (S_b) AND T-VALUE

The standard error of the regression coefficient, designated S_b, and the t-statistic are closely related. S_b is calculated as:

$$S_b = \frac{S_e}{\sqrt{\Sigma(X - \bar{X})^2}}$$

or in a short cut:

$$S_b = \frac{S_e}{\sqrt{\Sigma X^2 - X\Sigma\bar{X}}}$$

S_b gives an estimate of the range where the true coefficient will "actually" fall.

The t-value or t-statistic is a measure of the statistical significance of an independent variable X in explaining the dependent variable Y. It is determined by dividing the estimated regression coefficient b by its standard error S_b. It is then compared with the table t-value (Table A.2 in the Appendix). Thus, the t-statistic measures how many standard errors the coefficient is from zero.

Rule of thumb: Any t-value greater than +2 or less than –2 is acceptable. The higher the t-value, the greater the confidence we can have in the coefficient as a predictor. Low t-values indicate low reliability of the predictive power of that coefficient.

Example 4.7

The S_b for our example is:

$$S_b = \frac{2.3436}{\sqrt{2,792 - (14.5)(174)}}$$

$$= \frac{2.3436}{\sqrt{2,792 - 2,523}}$$

$$= \frac{2.3436}{\sqrt{269}} = .143$$

$$\text{Thus, t-statistic} = \frac{b}{S_b} = \frac{.5632}{.143} = 3.94$$

Since, t = 3.94 > 2.228, we conclude that the b coefficient is statistically significant. The table's critical value (cut-off value) for 10 degrees of freedom is 2.228 (from Table A.2).

To review:

1. The t-statistic is more relevant to multiple regressions that have more than one b.

2. R^2 tells you how good the forest (overall fit) is; the t-statistic tells you how good an individual tree (an independent variable) is.

The table t-value, based on a degree of freedom and a level of significance, is used:

1. To set the range—upper and lower limits—for the predicted value of the dependent variable.
2. To set the confidence range for regression coefficients.
3. As a cutoff value for the t-test.

Figure 4.4 shows an *Excel* regression output that contains the statistics we have discussed so far.

CONCLUSION

Regression analysis, the examination of the effect of a change in independent variables on the dependent variable, is a popular method for forecasting sales. This chapter discussed the well-known estimation technique, called the *least-squares method*.

To illustrate the method, we assume a simple regression that involves one independent variable in the form of $Y = a + bX$. In an attempt to obtain a good fit, we discussed various regression statistics. These statistics demonstrate how good and reliable an estimated equation is and help set the confidence interval for a prediction.

Most importantly, we discussed how to use spreadsheet programs such as *Lotus 1-2-3* to perform regressions, step by step. These programs calculate not only the regression equation but also all the regression statistics discussed in this chapter.

Figure 4.4—EXCEL REGRESSION OUTPUT

SUMMARY OUTPUT

Regression Statistics

Multiple R	0.779982858
R Square	0.608373258 (R^2)
Adjusted R square	0.569210584
Standard error	2.343622208 (S_e)
Observations	12

ANOVA

	df	SS	MS	F	Significance F
Regression	1	85.32434944	85.32434944	15.53451777	0.002768653
Residual	10	54.92565056	5.492565056		
Total	11	140.25			

	Coefficients	Standard Error (Sb)	t Stat	P-value*	Lower 95%	Upper 95%	Lower 95%	Upper 95%
Intercept	10.58364312	2.17960878	4.855753573	0.000665624	5.727171277	15.4401497	5.727171277	15.44011497
Advertising	0.563197026	0.142893168	3.94138526	0.002768653	0.244811152	0.815829	0.244811152	0.815829

*The P-value for X variable (advertising in this example) = .00277, indicating a .277% chance that the true value of the X variable coefficient is equal to 0, implying a high level of accuracy about the estimated value of 0.563197.

The result shows:

Y' = 10.58364 + 0.563197 X

with:
(1) R-squared (R^2) = .608373 = 60.84%
(2) Standard error of the estimate (S_e) = 2.343622
(3) Standard error of the coefficient (S_b) = 0.142893
(4) t-value = 3.94

All of these results are the same as the ones manually obtained.

CHAPTER 5
MULTIPLE
REGRESSION

Multiple regression analysis is a powerful statistical technique that is perhaps the one most widely used by forecasters. Multiple regression attempts to estimate statistically the average relationship between a dependent variable (e.g., sales) and two or more independent variables (e.g., price, advertising, and income).

In reality, forecasters face more multiple regression situations than simple regression. In order to obtain a good fit and achieve a high degree of accuracy, they should be familiar with statistics relating to regression such as R-squared (R^2) and t-value. Furthermore, forecasters will have to perform additional tests unique to multiple regression.

APPLICATIONS

Applications of multiple regression are numerous. Multiple regression analysis is used:

1. To find the overall association between the dependent variable and a host of explanatory variables. Overhead costs, for example, are explained by volume, productivity, and technology.
2. To attempt to identify the factors that influence the dependent variable. For example,
   a. Factors critical in affecting sales include price levels, advertising expenditures, consumer take-home income, taste, and competition.
   b. Financial analysts might seek causes of a change in stock prices or price-earnings (P-E) ratios by analyzing growth in earnings,

variability of earnings, stock splits, inflation rates, beta, and dividend yields.

    c. Advertising directors study the impact on consumer buying of advertising budgets, advertising frequency, media selection, and the like.

    d. Personnel managers attempt to determine the relationship between employee salary levels and a host of factors such as industry type, union leadership, competitive salaries, unemployment, skill levels, and geographical location.

3. As a basis for providing sound forecasts of the dependent variable. For example, cash collections from customers are sometimes forecast from credit sales of prior months because cash collections lag behind sales.

THE MODEL

The multiple regression model takes the following form:

$$Y = b_o + b_1 X_1 + b_2 X_2 ... + b_k X_k + u$$

where
    Y = dependent variable,
    $X's$ = independent (explanatory) variables,
    $b's$ = regression coefficients, and
    u = error term.

Example 5.1

When a simple regression is not good enough to provide a satisfactory fit (as indicated typically by a low R-squared), the manager should use multiple regression. This is an example of both simple and multiple regressions and their spreadsheet printouts. The sales manager is trying to develop a model for forecasting annual sales for toothpaste using advertising budgets for the current year and two previous years. Assuming the data in Table 5.1, Figure 5.1 presents two regression results:

Table 5.1—ANNUAL DATA FOR TOOTHPASTE SALES WITH CURRENT AND PREVIOUS ADVERTISING BUDGETS (in millions of dollars)

Year	Sales(Y_t)	Advertising Budget(X_t)	X_{t-1}	X_{t-2}
1990	113.750	15.000		
1991	124.150	14.000	15.000	
1992	133.000	15.400	14.000	15.000
1993	126.000	18.250	15.400	14.000
1994	162.000	17.300	18.250	15.400
1995	191.625	23.000	17.300	18.250
1996	189.000	19.250	23.000	17.300
1997	210.000	23.056	19.250	23.000
1998	224.250	26.000	23.056	19.250
1999	245.000	28.000	26.000	23.056

Figure 5.1—TWO REGRESSION RESULTS

Regression Output:

Constant	-9.59129
Standard error of Y estimate	16.06997
R-squared	0.894576
No. of observations	10
Degrees of freedom	8

X coefficient(s)	9.107319
Standard error of coefficient	1.105363
t-statistic	8.239210

Regression Output:

Constant	-37.8770
Standard error of Y estimate	12.16478
R-squared	0.940992
No. of observations	8
Degrees of freedom	5

X coefficient(s)	4.970408	6.934206
Standard error of coefficient	1.522161	1.821730
t-statistic	3.265362	3.806383

The simple regression model shows:

$$Y_t = -9.59 + 9.11\ X_t \qquad R^2 = 89.46\%$$
$$(1.11)*$$

*Standard error of regression coefficient S_b.

The multiple regression model with advertising budgets for two previous years is:

$$Y_t = -37.88 + 4.97\ X_{t-1} + 6.93\ X_{t-2} \qquad R^2 = 94.1\%$$
$$\quad\ (1.52)\quad (1.82)$$

This model has two advantages:

1. The explanatory power has increased from 89.46% to 94.1%.

2. Using only lagged variables does not require any assumptions about actual future budgets.

Example 5.2

The Los Alamitos Equipment Company wants to identify trends in demand for its heavy equipment so that funds available for investment, and related expenditures, can be efficiently allocated. The company collected data on real GDP and the Treasury-bill rate (Table 5.2). Using popular statistical software, *MINITAB*, the company obtained one simple (trend) equation and one multiple regression model that incorporates explanatory factors besides trend.

The results from *MINITAB* (Figure 5.2) are as follows:

Simple regression (trend) equation

$$Y = 821 + 4.07\ X_1 \qquad\qquad R^2 = 54.6\%$$
$$\qquad\ (0.7019)$$

Multiple regression equation

$$Y = 221.7 + 1.99\ X_1 + 0.504\ X_2 - 8.93\ X_3 \qquad R^2 = 78.0\%$$
$$\qquad\ (1.855)\quad (0.1308)\quad (2.821)$$

where X_1 = time, X_2 = real GDP, and X_3 = 90-day T-bill rate

Table 5.2—LOS ALAMITOS EQUIPMENT COMPANY

Year	Sales (mil. $) (Y)	Time (X_1)	GNP (X_2)	T-Bill Rate (X_3)
2000	921.58	30	1489.3	12.42
1999	913.01	29	1485.8	12.81
1998	934.99	28	1506.9	11.75
1997	913.17	27	1525.8	15.05
1996	903.33	26	1512.5	14.90
1995	906.66	`25	1510.1	14.39
1994	891.65	24	1477.9	13.61
1993	922.27	23	1464.2	9.15
1992	915.71	22	1461.4	9.62
1991	897.52	21	1496.2	13.35
1990	904.71	20	1489.3	11.84
1989	922.57	19	1486.6	9.67
1988	912.60	18	1469.2	9.38
1987	913.99	17	1472.6	9.38
1986	916.93	16	1468.4	8.57
1985	916.26	15	1448.8	7.31
1984	918.31	14	1437.0	6.48
1983	809.61	13	1400.0	6.39
1982	977.15	12	1388.4	6.11
1981	892.60	11	1385.8	5.50
1980	886.17	10	1363.3	4.84
1979	875.18	9	1341.3	4.63
1978	858.59	8	1315.4	4.67
1977	847.57	7	1303.3	5.15
1976	840.74	6	1295.8	5.16
1975	837.22	5	1287.2	4.92
1974	814.76	4	1259.7	5.63
1973	799.99	3	1248.4	6.33
1972	791.62	2	1221.0	5.39
1971	777.73	1	1206.3	5.75

Figure 5.2—MINITAB REGRESSION RESULTS

Regression Analysis
1. Simple (trend) regression:
  The regression equation is: Sales = 821 + 4.07 Time

Predictor	Coef	Stdev	t-ratio	p
Constant	821.32	12.46	65.91	0.000
Time	4.0744	0.7019	5.80	0.000

s = 33.27   R-sq = 54.6%   R-sq (adj) = 53.0%

Analysis of Variance

Source	DF	SS	MS	F	p
Regression	1	37310	37310	33.70	0.000
Error	28	31002	1107		
Total	29	68312			

Unusual Observations

Obs.	Time	Sales	Fit	Stddev Fit	Residual	St Resid
19	12.0	977.15	870.21	6.55	106.94	3.28R*

Durbin-Watson statistic = 1.65

2. Multiple regression:
The regression equation is: Sales = 222 + 1.99 Time + 0.504 GNP – 8.93 T-bill

Predictor	Coef	Stdev	t-ratio	p
Constant	221.7	164.3	1.35	0.189
Time	1.989	1.855	1.07	0.293
GNP	0.5041	0.1308	3.85	0.001
T-bill	-8.928	2.821	-3.16	0.004

s = 24.02   R-sq = 78.0%   R-sq (adj) = 75.5%

Analysis of Variance

Source	DF	SS	MS	F	p
Regression	3	53315	17772	30.81	0.00
Error	26	14997	577		
Total	29	68312			

Source	DF	SEQ SS
Time	1	37310
GNP	1	10228
T-bill	1	5777

Unusual Observations

Obs	Time	Sales	Fit	Stddev Fit	Residual	St Resid
18	13.0	809.61	896.21	6.34	-86.60	-3.74R*
19	12.0	977.15	890.87	6.30	86.28	3.72R*

Durbin-Watson statistic = 3.03

*R denotes an observation with a large standard residual.

NONLINEAR REGRESSION

Thus far we have assumed a linear relationship. In some cases, however, a nonlinear form may be more appropriate. For example, in Example 5.1, it may sometimes be difficult to assume a linear relationship between lagged advertising budgets and sales because of the diminishing returns effect of accumulated advertising.

In addition to the nonlinearity that might be associated with such decay, it is often postulated that the sales-advertising relationship is S-shaped; that is, at lower levels of advertising the ability of ads to reach the audience is at best limited. At moderate spending levels, audience reach expands and sales grow relatively faster. At higher and higher spending levels, sales response slows and eventually the market is oversaturated.

A popular formulation to account for this phenomenon is:

$$Y_t = b_o + b_1 \, 1/X_{t-1} + b_2 \, 1/X_{t-2} \qquad\qquad b_1, b_2 < 0$$

This specification represents a hyperbola describing an S-shaped relationship. Example 5.3 illustrates this, using data from Table 5.3.

Table 5.3—ANNUAL DATA FOR TOOTHPASTE SALES WITH CURRENT AND PREVIOUS ADVERTISING BUDGETS (in millions of dollars)

Year	Sales(Y_t)	Advertising Budget(X_t)	X_{t-1}	X_{t-2}	$1/X_{t-1}$	$1/X_{t-2}$
1990	113.750	15.000				
1991	124.150	14.000	15.000		0.067	
1992	133.000	15.400	14.000	15.000	0.071	0.067
1993	126.000	18.250	15.400	14.000	0.065	0.071
1994	162.000	17.300	18.250	15.400	0.055	0.065
1995	191.625	23.000	17.300	18.250	0.058	0.055
1996	189.000	19.250	23.000	17.300	0.043	0.058
1997	210.000	23.056	19.250	23.000	0.052	0.043
1998	224.250	26.000	23.056	19.250	0.043	0.052
1999	245.000	28.000	26.000	23.056	0.038	0.043

Figure 5.3—EXCEL REGRESSION OUTPUT

SUMMARY OUTPUT

Regression Statistics

Multiple R	0.98301631
R-square	0.96632107
Adjusted R-square	0.9528495
Standard error	9.19034396
Observations	8

ANOVA

	Df	SS	MS	F	Significance F
Regression	2	12117.04531	6058.52266	71.730392	0.00020816
Residual	5	422.3121109	84.4624222		
Total	7	12539.35742			

	Coefficients	Standard Error	t Stat	P-value
Intercept	413.935303	19.50573694	21.22121	4.31E-06
X Variable 1	-1614.3547	448.4473008	-3.59988	0.015545
X Variable 2	-2514.2279	487.7338655	-5.15492	0.0036

	Lower 95%	Upper 95%	Lower 95.0%	Upper 95.0%
Intercept	363.7943	464.0763	363.7943	464.0763
X Variable 1	-2767.12	-461.586	-2767.12	-461.586
X Variable 2	-3767.99	-1260.47	-3767.99	-1260.47

Example 5.3

Using the nonlinear form specified above yields:

$$Y_t = 413.94 - 1614.35 \ 1/X_{t-1} - 2514.22 \ 1/X_{t-2} \qquad R^2 = 96.63\%$$
$$\quad (448.45) \qquad\qquad (487.73)$$

USING DUMMY VARIABLES

Forecasting with qualitative (dummy) variables can help in many practical business situations. Suppose you need to predict monthly sales based on advertising expenditures and such variables as indicators of the local economy or sales of a complementary product. Your company plans a price change. Add a qualitative-variable column containing 0s for all months before the price change and 1s for all months thereafter. The X coefficient for this variable estimates the effect of the price change on sales.

Dummy variables can be used to represent:

1. Temporal effects, such as shifts in relations between:
   a. War time and peace time years
   b. Different seasons

2. Qualitative (or categorical) variables such as
   a. Sex
   b. Marital status
   c. Occupational or social status
   d. Age
   e. Location
   f. Product features
   g. Race

Adding these qualitative variables to regression models can improve accuracy whenever nonnumeric factors affect the outcomes. Thus far, we have assumed that any independent variable that is to be used in an estimating equation has values that can be measured on at least a cardinal scale (e.g., 1, 2, 3, etc.). However, there are many instances where a relationship may not be described on such a refined measurement scale. For example, we may believe that sex can influence the level of salary. Sex may be treated as a dummy variable that has only two values—a 1 when its influence is to be included in the estimating equation, and a 0 otherwise. To illustrate, suppose our salary equation is

$$Y = b_0 + b_1 X_1 + b_2 X_2$$

where X_1 = experience in years

$$X_2 = \left\{ \begin{array}{l} 1 \text{ for males} \\ 0 \text{ for females} \end{array} \right\} = \text{dummy variable}$$

That is, X_2 is a dummy variable representing the gender. Note that this dummy variable merely shifts the intercept of our estimating equation by the amount of its coefficient, b_2, whenever $X_2 = 1$.

The single equation is equivalent to the following two equations:

$$Y = b_0 + b_1 X_1 + b_2 \qquad \text{for males}$$
$$Y = b_0 + b_2 X_2 \qquad \text{for females}$$

Note that b_2 represents the effect of a male on salary and b_1 represents the effect of experience differences (the b_2 value is assumed to be the same for males and females). The important point is that one multiple regression equation will yield both estimated lines. One line is the estimate for males and the other is the estimate for females. Dummy variables provide a useful technique for taking into account the influence of unusual factors.

Example 5.4

Assume the following data:

Salary (Y)	Experience (X_1)	Gender (X_2)
$50,000	5	1
45,000	4	1
52,000	8	0
35,000	2	0
55,000	12	1
38,000	2	1
25,000	1	0
40,000	2	1
43,000	6	0
36,000	2	0
26,000	1	0

Figure 5.4 shows the *MicroTSP* input procedure and a variety of regression output. The estimated multiple regression equation is:

$$Y = 28692 + 2243\ X_1 + 5696\ X_2 \qquad R^2 = 83.02\%$$
$$(429) \qquad (2835)$$

Figure 5.4—MICROTSP DATA INPUT AND REGRESSION OUTPUT

Sample Data:

OBS	Salary	Experience	Sex
1	50000.00	5.000000	1.000000
2	45000.00	4.000000	1.000000
3	52000.00	8.000000	0.000000
4	35000.00	2.000000	0.000000
5	55000.00	12.000000	1.000000
6	38000.00	2.000000	1.000000

Figure 5.4—MICROTSP DATA INPUT AND REGRESSION OUTPUT, *con't.*

7	25000.00	1.000000	0.000000
8	40000.00	2.000000	1.000000
9	43000.00	6.000000	0.000000
10	36000.00	2.000000	0.000000
11	26000.00	1.000000	0.000000

Running Least-Squares Regression on MicroTSP:

>LS
Dependent variable//SALARY
List may include D, AR, SAR, MA, SMA, and PDL items.
Independent variable List ? c experien sex

Descriptive Statistics and Correlative Matrix:

SMPL range: 1 - 11   Number of observations: 11

Variable	Mean	SD	Maximum	Minimum
SALARY	40454.545	9832.2290	55000.000	25000.000
EXPERIEN	4.0909091	3.4483197	12.000000	1.0000000
SEX	0.4545455	0.5222330	1.0000000	0.0000000

	Covariance	Correlation
SALARY, SALARY	87884298.000	1.0000000
SALARY, EXPERIEN	26595.041	0.8628471
SALARY, SEX	2338.8430	0.5010459
EXPERIEN, EXPERIEN	10.809917	1.0000000
EXPERIEN, SEX	0.4132231	0.2524094
SEX, SEX	0.2479339	1.0000000

Regression Output:

LS / / Dependent variable is SALARY
Date: 1-11-1998 / Time: 23.07
SMPL range: 1 - 11
Number of observations: 11

Variable	Coefficient	Std. Error	T-STst.	2-Tail Sig.
C	28691.617	2338.2987	12.270296	0.0000
EXPERIEN	2242.5150	429.30467	5.2235979	0.0008
SEX	5695.8084	2834.7115	2.0093080	0.0794

R-squared	0.830198	Mean of dependent variable	40454.55
Adjusted R-squared	0.787748	SD of dependent variable	9832.229
SE of regression	4529.792	Sum of dependent variable	1.64E+08
Log likelihood	-106.4596	F-statistic	19.55687
Durbin-Watson statistic	1.639067	Probability (F-statistic)	0.000831

Residual Plot, Actual, and Filled Values

Residual Plot	obs	RESIDUAL	ACTUAL	FITTED
. I * * ▲	1	4400.00	50000.0	45600.0
. I . * ▲	2	1642.52	45000.0	43357.5
. I * . ▲	3	5368.26	52000.0	46631.7
* . I . ▲	4	1823.35	35000.0	33176.6
. * I . ▲	5	-6297.60	55000.0	61297.6
* I . ▲	6	-8724.55	38000.0	38872.5
. I * . ▲	7	-5934.13	25000.0	30934.1
. I * . ▲	8	1127.54	40000.0	38872.5
. I * . ▲	9	8532.93	43000.0	42146.7
* . I . ▲	10	2823.35	36000.0	33176.6
* . I . ▲	11	-4934.13	26000.0	30934.1

The explanatory power of the model (R^2) is 83.02 percent, which suggests that both experience and gender make a contribution to the salary level. The computed t values, 5.22 (2243/429) and 2.01 (5695/2835), indicate that both variables are statistically significant at the 10 percent significance level. (Again, in multiple regressions, look beyond these statistics [R^2 and t values], which will be discussed in greater detail later in this Chapter.)

For the two values (0 and 1) of X_2, the equation provides

$$Y = 28692 + 2243\ X_1 + 5696\ (1)$$
$$= 34388 + 2243\ X_1 \qquad \text{for males}$$

and

$$Y = 28692 + 2243\ X_1 + 5696\ (0)$$
$$= 28692 + 2243\ X_1 \qquad \text{for females}$$

These two equations may be interpreted as follows:

1. The regression coefficient, $b_1 = 2243$, which is the slope of each of the regression lines, represents the estimated increase in salary for each year in experience. This value applies to both males and females.

2. The other regression coefficient, $b_2 = 5696$, applies only to males. This means that males receive $5,696 more in salary than females for the same years of experience.

WEIGHTED (DISCOUNTED) REGRESSION

The problem with using the ordinary least-squares model is that the line fits early data points more closely than it fits later ones. The *weighted (or discounted) least-squares model* gets around this problem. With this method we use weights that decline from recent to older data.

With standard regression, the computed line minimizes the squared distances from the points to the line. In discounted regression, the line minimizes weighted squared distances. Because earlier values are discounted, they have less influence on the final forecast; the more weight placed on particular data, the more the line reflects those data.

Table 5.4 shows the four sets of weights for eight periods ($t = 0,...,7$) that are generated by four different discount factors. Weights are computed using the following formula:

$$W_t = \sqrt{(\text{discount factor})}$$

Table 5.4—DISCOUNT FACTOR

t	0.70	0.80	0.90	1.00
7	0.29	0.46	0.69	1.00
6	0.34	0.51	0.73	1.00
5	0.41	0.57	0.77	1.00
4	0.49	0.64	0.81	1.00
3	0.59	0.72	0.85	1.00
2	0.70	0.80	0.90	1.00
1	0.84	0.89	0.95	1.00
0	1.00	1.00	1.00	1.00

Note: When the discount factor is 1.00, all data get equal weight and the result is the same as with the traditional least-squares method. As the discount factor is reduced, the weights on older data fall off substantially.

Example 5.5

To illustrate the method, we use quarterly sales and the number of warranty claims of a refrigerator maker, as given in Table 5.5. The company believes that warranty claims in a given quarter (C_t) are closely related to sales from the previous quarter (S_{t-1}). (This example is adapted from Gardner Jr., E., "When The Recent Past Counts More," Lotus, May 1990.)

Table 5.5—DISCOUNTED LEAST-SQUARES REGRESSION

				Actual Data			Discounted Data		
				PrvQtr				Pred	
			Weight	Sales	Claims	Weight	Sales x Wt	Claims xW$_T$	Claims
Year	Qtr	T	Wt	X	Y	X1	X2	Y	Y
1996	4	7	0.46	397.00	33.00	0.46	182.62	15.18	36.48
1997	1	6	0.51	408.00	36.00	0.51	208.08	18.36	37.66
	2	5	0.57	427.00	38.00	0.57	243.39	21.66	39.69
	3	4	0.64	430.00	39.00	0.64	275.20	24.96	40.01
	4	3	0.72	433.00	42.00	0.72	311.76	30.24	40.33
1998	1	2	0.80	445.00	44.00	0.80	356.00	35.20	41.62
	2	1	0.89	465.00	45.00	0.89	413.85	40.05	43.75
	3	0	1.00	507.00	47.00	1.00	507.00	47.00	48.24
	4			520.00					49.63

Discount factor 0.80

Regression Output:

Constant	0.00
Std Err of Y Est	1.44
R-Squared	0.99
No. of Observations	8.00
Degrees of Freedom	6.00
X Coefficient(s)	-5.95 0.11
Std Err of Coef	9.40 0.02

Without proof, using the discounted data, the multiple regression equation to be fitted becomes:

$$Y_t = aX_1 + bX_2$$
where $Y_t = W_t \times C_t$, $X_1 = W_t$, and $X_2 = W_t \times S_t$

The bottom section of Table 5.5 shows regression output with predicted warranty claims:

$$Y = -5.95 \, X_1 + 0.11 \, X_2 \qquad R^2 = 99\%$$
$$(9.40) \qquad (0.02)$$

Figure 5.5 reveals that the solid line labeled Discounted fits later data points more closely than the broken line of the standard model and better reflects changes in claims experience. As you can see from Figure 5.5, the discounted prediction for the fourth quarter of 1998 is lower than the standard prediction for the same quarter.

Figure 5.5—REGRESSION MODEL COMPARISONS

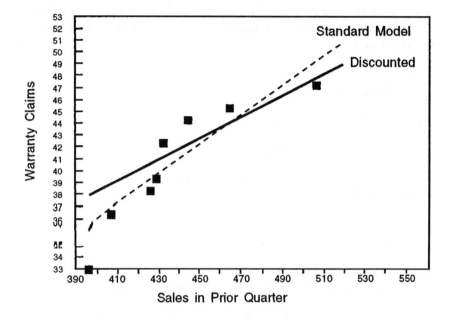

STATISTICS TO LOOK FOR

In multiple regressions that involve more than one independent (explanatory) variable, managers must look for the following statistics:

- t-statistics
- R-bar squared and F-statistic
- Multi-collinearity
- Auto-correlation (or serial correlation)

t-STATISTICS

The t-statistic is taken up again here because it is more valid in multiple than in simple regressions. Because the t-statistic shows the significance of each explanatory variable in predicting the dependent variable, it is desirable to have as large (either positive or negative) a t-statistic as possible for each independent variable. Generally, a t-statistic greater than +2.0 or less than -2.0 is acceptable. Explanatory variables with low t-value can usually be eliminated from the regression without substantially decreasing R^2 or increasing the standard error of the regression. In a multiple regression:

$$\text{t-statistic} = \frac{b_i}{S_{b_i}}$$

where   i = the independent variable

R-BAR SQUARED AND F-STATISTIC

A more appropriate test for goodness of fit for multiple regressions is R-bar squared ($\bar{R}^2$):

$$\bar{R}^2 = 1 - (1 - R^2)\frac{n-1}{n-k}$$

where   n = the number of observations
               k = the number of coefficients to be estimated

An alternative test of the overall significance of a regression equation is the F-test. Virtually all computer programs for regression analysis show an F-statistic.

The F-statistic is defined as:

$$F = \frac{(Y' - \bar{Y})^2/k}{(Y - Y')^2/n - k - 1} = \frac{\text{Explained variation} / k}{\text{Unexplained variation} / n-k-1}$$

If the F-statistic is greater than the table value, it is concluded that the regression equation is statistically significant in overall terms.

MULTI-COLLINEARITY

When using more than one independent variable in a regression equation, there is sometimes a high correlation among the independent variables themselves. Multi-collinearity occurs when these variables interfere with each other. It is a pitfall because equations with multicollinearity may produce spurious forecasts.

Multi-collinearity can be recognized when:

- The t-statistics of two seemingly important independent variables are low.
- The estimated coefficients on explanatory variables have the opposite sign from what would logically be expected.

There are two ways to get around the problem of multi-collinearity:

- One of the highly correlated variables may be dropped from the regression.
- The structure of the equation may be changed using one of the following methods:
  - Divide both the left and right-hand side variables by some series that will leave the basic economic logic but remove multi-collinearity.
  - Estimate the equation on a first-difference basis.
  - Combine the collinear variables into a new variable, which is their weighted sum.

AUTO-CORRELATION (SERIAL CORRELATION)

Auto-correlation is another major pitfall often encountered in regression analysis. It occurs where there is a correlation between successive errors. The Durbin-Watson statistic provides the standard test for auto-correlation. Table A.4 in the Appendix provides values for the Durbin-Watson statistic for specified sample sizes and explanatory variables. The table gives the significance points for dL and dU for tests on the auto-correlation of residuals (when no explanatory variable is a lagged endogenous variable). The number of explanatory variables, K, excludes the constant term.

Generally speaking,

Durbin-Watson Statistic	Auto-correlation
Between 1.5 and 2.5	No auto-correlation
Below 1.5	Positive auto-correlation
Above 2.5	Negative auto-correlation

Auto-correlation usually indicates that an important part of the variation of the dependent variable has not been explained. The best solution to this problem is to search for other explanatory variables to include in the regression equation.

CHECKLISTS

Choosing among alternative forecasting equations basically involves two steps. The first step is to eliminate the obvious losers. The second is to select the winner among the remaining contenders.

HOW TO ELIMINATE LOSERS

1. Does the equation make sense? Equations that do not make sense intuitively or from a theoretical standpoint must be eliminated.

2. Does the equation have explanatory variables with low t-statistics? These equations should be re-estimated or dropped in favor of equations in which all independent variables are significant. This test will eliminate equations where multi-collinearity is a problem.

3. How about a low R^2? The R^2 can be used to rank the remaining equations in order to select the best candidates. A low R^2 could mean:
   - A wrong functional was fitted.
   - An important explanatory variable is missing.
   - Other combinations of explanatory variables might be more desirable.

HOW TO CHOOSE THE BEST EQUATION

1. *Best Durbin-Watson statistic:* Given equations that have survived all previous tests, the equation with the Durbin-Watson statistic closest to 2.0 can be a basis for selection.

2. *Best forecasting accuracy:* Examining the forecasting performance of equations is essential for selecting one equation from those that have not been eliminated. The equation whose prediction accuracy is best in terms of measures of forecasting errors, such as MAD, MSE, RMSE, or MPE (to be discussed in detail in Chapter 9), generally provides the best basis for forecasting.

It is important to note that neither *Lotus 1-2-3* nor *Quattro Pro* calculates many statistics such as R-bar squared ($\overline{R}^2$), F-statistic, and Durbin-Watson statistic. For these you need regression packages such as *Statistical Analysis System (SAS)*, *STATPACK*, or *Statistical Packages for*

Social Scientists (SPSS), to name a few. These packages all have PC versions.

USING A COMPUTER STATISTICAL PACKAGE

Example 5.6

Stanton Consumer Products Corporation wishes to develop a forecasting model for its dryer sales by using multiple regression analysis. The marketing department has prepared the following sample data.

Month	Sales of Washers (X_1)	Disposable Income (X_2)	Savings (X_3)	Sales of Dryers (Y)
January	$45,000	$16,000	$71,000	$29,000
February	42,000	14,000	70,000	24,000
March	44,000	15,000	72,000	27,000
April	45,000	13,000	71,000	25,000
May	43,000	13,000	75,000	26,000
June	46,000	14,000	74,000	28,000
July	44,000	16,000	76,000	30,000
August	45,000	16,000	69,000	28,000
September	44,000	15,000	74,000	28,000
October	43,000	15,000	73,000	27,000

The computer statistical package SPSS was employed to develop the regression model. Figure 5.6 contains the input data and output that results using three explanatory variables. To help you understand the listing, illustrative comments are added whenever applicable.

Figure 5.6—SPSS REGRESSION OUTPUT

Variables Entered/Removed[b]

Model	Variables Entered	Variables Removed	Methods
1	SAVINGS, sales, INCOME[a]		Enter

[a]All requested variables entered.
[b]Dependent variables: SALESDRY

Model Summary[b]

Model	R	R-square	Adjusted R-square	Std. Error of the Estimate	Durbin-Watson
1	0.992[a]	0.983	0.975	286.1281	2.094

[a] Predictors: (Constant), SAVINGS, sales, INCOME
[b]Dependent variable: SALESDRY

ANOVA[b]

Model		Sum of Squares	df	Mean Square	F	Sig.
1	Regression	29108784.1	3	9702928.03	118.517	.000[a]
	Residual	491215.904	6	81869.317		
	Total	29600000.0	9			

[a]Predictors: (Constant), SAVINGS, sales, INCOME
[b]Dependent variable: SALESDRY

Coefficients[a]

Model		Understandardized Coefficients		Standardized Coefficients		
		B	Std. Error	Beta	t	Sig.
1	(Constant)	-45796.35	4877.651		-9.389	0.000
	sales	0.597	0.081	0.394	7.359	0.000
	INCOME	1.177	0.084	0.752	13.998	0.000
	SAVINGS	0.405	0.042	0.508	9.592	0.000

[a]Dependent variable: SALESDRY

Residual Statistics[a]

	Minimum	Maximum	Mean	Std. Dev.	N
Predicted value	24109.801	30088.072	27200.000	1798.4186	10
Residual	-280.7998	444.5215	5.457E-12	233.6227	10
Std. predicted value	-1.718	1.606	0.000	1.000	10
Std. residual	-1.016	1.554	.000	.816	10

[a]Dependent variable: SALESDRY

1. *The forecasting equation:* From the SPSS output we see that:

$$Y' = -45,796.35 + 0.597X_1 + 1.177X_2 + 0.405X_3$$

Suppose that in November the company expects:

X_1 = sales of washers = $43,000
X_2 = disposable income = $15,000
X_3 = savings = $75,000

The forecast sales for the month of November would then be:

$$Y' = -45,796.35 + 0.597(43,000) + 1.177(15,000) + 0.405(75,000)$$
$$= -45,796 + 25,671 + 17,655 + 30,375$$
$$= \$27,905.35$$

2. *The coefficient of determination:* Note that the SPSS output gives the value of R, R², and R² adjusted. In our example, R = 0.992 and R² = 0.983. In the case of multiple regression, we know that R² is more appropriate:

$$\bar{R}^2 = 1 - (1 - R^2)\ \frac{(n-1)}{(n-k)}$$

$$= 1 - (1 - 0.983)\ \frac{10-1}{10-3} = 1 - 0.017\ (9/7)$$
$$= 1 - 0.025 = 0.975$$

This tells us that 97.5 percent of total variation in sales of dryers is explained by the three explanatory variables. The remaining 2.2 percent is not explained by the equation.

3. *The standard error of the estimate* (S_e): This is a measure of dispersion of actual sales around the equation. The output shows $S_e = 286.1281$.

4. *Computed t:* We read from the output:

	t-Statistic
X_1	7.359
X_2	13.998
X_3	9.592

All t values are greater than a rule-of-thumb table t value of 2.0. (With n − k − 1 = 10 − 3 − 1 = 6 degrees of freedom and a level of significance of, say, 0.01, we see from Table A.2 in the Appendix that the table t value is 3.707.) For a two-sided test, the level of significance to look up was .005. In any case, we conclude that all three of the explanatory variables we have selected were statistically significant.

5. *F-test:* From the output, we see that:

$$F = \frac{\text{Explained variance}/k}{\text{Unexplained variance}/(n - k - 1)} = \frac{29.109/3}{0.491/6}$$
$$= 9.703/0.082 = 118.517 \text{ (which is given in the printout)}$$

At a significance level of 0.01, our F-value is far above the value of 9.78 given in Table A.3 in the Appendix, so we conclude that the regression as a whole is highly significant.

6. *Conclusion*: Based on statistical considerations, we see that:

- The equation had a good fit.
- All three variables are significant explanatory variables.
- The regression as a whole is highly significant.
- The model developed can be used as a forecasting equation with great confidence.

CONCLUSION

Multiple regression analysis is the examination of the effect of a change in several explanatory variables on the dependent variable. For example, various financial ratios bear on the market price of a firm's stock. Many important statistics that are unique to multiple regression analysis were explained with computer illustrations. The emphasis was on how to pick the best forecasting equation.

CHAPTER 6
TIME SERIES
ANALYSIS AND
CLASSICAL
DECOMPOSITION

A time series is a sequence of data points at constant time intervals such as a week, month, quarter, or year. *Time series analysis* breaks data into components and projects them into the future. The four commonly recognized components are trend, seasonal, cycle, and irregular variation.

1. The *trend component* (T) is the general upward or downward movement of the average over time. It may require many years of data to determine or describe these movements. The basic forces underlying a trend include technological advances, productivity changes, inflation, and population change.

2. The *seasonal component* (S) is a recurring fluctuation of data points above or below the trend value that repeats with a usual frequency of one year, e.g., Christmas sales.

3. *Cyclical components* (C) are recurrent upward and downward movements that repeat with a frequency longer than a year. Because this type of movement is attributed to business cycles (such as recession, inflation, unemployment, and prosperity), its periodicity (recurrent rate) does not have to be constant.

4. The *irregular* (or *random*) *component* is a series of short, erratic movements that follow no discernible pattern. It is caused by unpredictable or nonrecurring events such as floods, wars, strikes, elections, environmental changes, and new legislation.

TREND ANALYSIS

Trend analysis is a special type of simple regression. This method involves a regression whereby a trend line is fitted to a time series of data. In practice, however, one typically finds linear and nonlinear curves used for business forecasting. Thus, trends can be described by a straight line or a curve.

LINEAR TREND

The *linear* trend line equation can be shown as

$$Y = a + b\,t$$

where   t = time.

The formula for the coefficients a and b is essentially the same as in simple regression. For regression purposes, a time period can be given a number so that $\Sigma t = 0$. When there is an odd number of periods, the period in the middle is assigned a zero value. If there is an even number, then -1 and +1 are assigned the two periods in the middle, so that again $\Sigma t = 0$.

With $\Sigma t = 0$, the formula for b and a reduces to the following:

$$b = \frac{n\,\Sigma tY}{n\,\Sigma t^2}$$

$$a = \frac{\Sigma Y}{n}$$

Example 6.1

Case 1 (odd number)

	19X5	19X6	19X7	19X8	19X9
t =	-2	-1	0	+1	+2

Case 2 (even number)

	19X5	19X6	19X7	19X8	19X9	20X0
t =	-3	-2	-1	+1	+2	+3

In each case $\Sigma t = 0$.

Example 6.2

Consider the historical sales of ABC Company:

Year	Sales (in millions of dollars)
20X1	10
20X2	12
20X3	13
20X4	16
20X5	17

Since the company has data for five years, an odd number, the year in the middle is assigned a zero value.

Year	t	Sales(Y)	tY	t^2	Y^2
20X1	-2	10	-20	4	100
20X2	-1	12	-12	1	144
20X3	0	13	0	0	169
20X4	+1	16	16	1	256
20X5	+2	17	34	4	289
	0	68	18	10	958

$$b = \frac{(5)(18)}{(5)(10)} = \frac{90}{50} = 1.8$$

$$a = \frac{68}{5} = 13.6$$

The estimated trend equation is therefore:

$$Y' = \$13.6 + \$1.8\ t$$

To project sales in 20X6 sales, we assign +3 to the t value for the year 20X6.

$$Y' = \$13.6 + \$1.8\ (3)$$
$$= \$19$$

NONLINEAR TREND

A typical example of nonlinear trend is a constant growth model. A model structure that captures the increasing growth pattern is described in Table 6.1. Los Al sales data show the constant growth rate, or constant rate of change over time, by a proportional rather than a constant amount. Other common nonlinear trends described by the *modified exponential growth curve* and the *logistic growth curve* are discussed in a later chapter.

Table 6.1—TOTAL SALES REVENUE FOR LOS AL, INC. (1990-1999)

Year	Sales	Time	ln(Sales)
1990	2000.1	1	7.6009525
1991	2308.9	2	7.7445265
1992	2645.0	3	7.8804263
1993	2909.4	4	7.9757022
1994	3243.0	5	8.0842541
1995	3745.0	6	8.2281769
1996	4170.3	7	8.3357433
1997	4852.4	8	8.4872287
1998	5312.1	9	8.5777425
1999	5550.8	10	8.6216973

Regression Output

Constant	7.5110692
Std Err of Y Est	0.0291502
R-squared	0.9939996
No. of observations	10
Degrees of freedom	8

X Coefficient(s)	0.11683
Std Err of Coef	0.00321

In the constant rate of change, or proportional change, model, the average historical rate of change in a variable is determined and projected into the future. (This is essentially identical to the compounding of value model used in finance.) If a firm is projecting its sales for five years into the future and if it has determined that sales are increasing at an annual rate of 10 percent, the forecaster would simply multiply the 10 percent compound value interest factor for five years by current sales.

Assuming current sales are \$1 million, the forecast of sales five years from now would be:

Sales in Year 5 = Current Sales x $(1 + \text{Growth Rate})^5$

= \$1,000,000 x $(1.10)^5$
= \$1,000,000 x 1.61
= \$1,610,000.

More generally, the constant rate of change projection model can be stated as follows:

Value t Years in the Future = Current Value x $(1 + \text{Rate of Change})^t$

Just as the constant annual change in a business time series can be estimated by fitting historical data to a linear regression model of the form $Y = a + bt$, so too can the annual growth rate in a constant rate of change projection model be estimated using the same technique. In this case, the growth rate is estimated using linear regression by fitting historical data to the logarithmic transformation of the basic model. For example, formulating a constant growth rate model for firm sales would take the form:

$$S_t = S_o (1 + g)^t \qquad (1)$$

Here sales t years in the future (S_t) are assumed to be equal to current sales, S_o, compounded at a growth rate, g, for a period of t years. Taking logarithms of both sides of equation (1) results in the expression:

$$\ln S_t = \ln S_o + \ln (1 + g) \times t \qquad (2)$$

Note that equation (2) is an expression of the form:

$$Y_t = a + bt,$$

where $Y_t = \ln S_t$, $a = \ln S_o$, and $b = \ln (1 + g)$; hence, its coefficients, $\ln S_o$ and $\ln (1 + g)$, can be estimated using the least squares regression technique.

Applying this technique to the Los Al sales data for the 1990-1999 period shown in Table 6.1 results in the regression (standard error in parenthesis):

$$\ln S_t = 7.51 + 0.117t \quad R^2 = 99.4\%,$$
$$(0.003)$$

or, equivalently, by transforming this estimated equation back to its original form:

$$S_t = [\text{Antilog } 7.51] \times [\text{Antilog } 0.117]^t = 1{,}826.21 \ (1.124)^t$$

(*Note:* Most scientific calculators have a key to antilog.)

   In this model, $1,826.21 million is the adjusted sales figure for t = 0 (which would be 1989, since the first year of data used in the regression estimation [t=1] was 1990); and 1.124 is equal to one plus the average annual rate of growth, meaning that Los Al sales have increased by 12.4 percent annually over the 1990-1999 period.
   To forecast sales in any future year using this model, we subtract 1990 from the year being forecast to determine t. Thus, a constant growth model forecast of sales in 2006 is:

$$t \qquad = 2006 - 1990 \ = 17$$
$$S_{2006} \quad = 1{,}826.21 \ (1.124)^{17}$$
$$\qquad = \$13{,}322.26.$$

DECOMPOSITION OF TIME SERIES

When sales exhibit seasonal or cyclical fluctuation, we use a method called *classical decomposition* for dealing with seasonal, trend, and cyclical components together. The classical decomposition model is a time series model. This means that the method can only be used to fit time series data, whether monthly, quarterly, or annually. The types of time series data the company deals with include sales, earnings, cash flows, market share, and costs.

We assume that a time series is combined into a model that consists of all four components—trend (T), cyclical (C), seasonal (S), and random (R). We assume the model is of a multiplicative type, i.e.,

$$Y_t = T \times C \times S \times R$$

In this section, we illustrate step by step how the classical decomposition method works with quarterly sales data.

The approach basically takes the following four steps:

1. Determine seasonal indices, using a four-quarter moving average.

2. Deseasonalize the data.

3. Develop the linear least squares equation in order to identify the trend component of the forecast.

4. Forecast sales for each of the four quarters of the coming year.

The data we are going to use are the quarterly sales data for video sets over the past four years (Table 6.2). We begin our analysis by showing how to identify the seasonal component of the time series.

Table 6.2—QUARTERLY SALES DATA FOR VCRs OVER THE PAST FOUR YEARS

Year	Quarter	Sales
1	1	5.8
	2	5.1
	3	7.0
	4	7.5
2	1	6.8
	2	6.2
	3	7.8
	4	8.4
3	1	7.0
	2	6.6
	3	8.5
	4	8.8
4	1	7.3
	2	6.9
	3	9.0
	4	9.4

Step 1: Use a moving average to measure the combined trend-cyclical

(TC) components of the time series. This way we eliminate the seasonal and random components, S and R. To do this:

a) Calculate the fourth quarter moving average for the time series as discussed. However, the moving average values computed will not correspond directly to the original quarters of the time series.

b) We resolve this difficulty by using the midpoints between successive moving-average values. For example, since 6.35 corresponds to the first half of quarter 3 and 6.6 corresponds to the last half of quarter 3, we use $(6.35+6.6)/2 = 6.475$ as the moving average value of quarter 3. Similarly, we associate $(6.6+6.875)/2 = 6.7375$ with quarter 4. A complete summary of the moving-average calculation is shown in Table 6.3.

Table 6.3—MOVING AVERAGE CALCULATIONS FOR THE VCR SALES TIME SERIES

Year	Quarter	Sales	4-Quarter Moving Average	Centered Moving Average
1	1	5.8		
	2	5.1		
			6.35	
	3	7.0		6.475
			6.6	
	4	7.5		6.7375
			6.875	
2	1	6.8		6.975
			7.075	
	2	6.2		7.1875
			7.3	
	3	7.8		7.325
			7.35	
	4	8.4		7.4
			7.45	
3	1	7.0		7.5375
			7.625	
	2	6.6		7.675
			7.725	
	3	8.5		7.7625
			7.8	
	4	8.8		7.8375

Table 6.3—MOVING AVERAGE CALCULATIONS FOR THE VCR SALES
TIME SERIES, *con't.*

Year	Quarter	Sales	4-Quarter Moving Average	Centered Moving Average
			7.875	
4	1	7.3		7.9375
			8.0	
	2	6.9		8.075
			8.15	
	3	9.0		
	4	9.4		

c) Next, we calculate the ratio of the actual value to the moving average value for each quarter in the time series having a four-quarter
moving average entry. This ratio in effect represents the seasonal-
random component, SR=Y/TC. The ratios calculated this way
appear in Table 6.4.

Table 6.4—SEASONAL RANDOM FACTORS FOR THE SERIES

Year	Quarter	Sales	4-Quarter Moving Average	Centered Moving Average TC	Each Random SR = Y/TC
1	1	5.8			
	2	5.1			
			6.35		
	3	7.0		6.475	1.081
			6.6		
	4	7.5		6.738	1.113
			6.875		
2	1	6.8		6.975	0.975
			7.075		
	2	6.2		7.188	0.863
			7.3		
	3	7.8		7.325	1.065
			7.35		
	4	8.4		7.400	1.135
			7.45		
3	1	7.0		7.538	0.929

Table 6.4—SEASONAL RANDOM FACTORS FOR THE SERIES, *con't.*

Year	Quarter	Sales	4-Quarter Moving Average	Centered Moving Average TC	Each Random SR = Y/TC
			7.625		
	2	6.6		7.675	0.860
			7.725		
	3	8.5		7.763	1.095
			7.8		
	4	8.8		7.838	1.123
			7.875		
4	1	7.3		7.938	0.920
			8.0		
	2	6.9		8.075	0.854
			8.15		
	3	9.0			
	4	9.4			

d) Arrange the ratios by quarter and then calculate the average ratio by quarter in order to eliminate random influence.

For example, for quarter 1

$$(0.975+0.929+0.920)/3 = 0.941$$

e) The final step adjusts the average ratio slightly (for example, for quarter 1, 0.941 becomes 0.940), which will be the seasonal index (Table 6.5).

Table 6.5—SEASONAL COMPONENT CALCULATIONS

Quarter	Seasonal Random SR	Seasonal Factor S	Adjusted S
1	0.975		
	0.929		
	0.920	0.941	0.940
2	0.863		
	0.860		

Table 6.5—SEASONAL COMPONENT CALCULATIONS, *con't.*

Quarter	Seasonal Random SR	Seasonal Factor S	Adjusted S
	0.854	0.859	0.858
3	1.081		
	1.065		
	1.095	1.080	1.079
4	1.113		
	1.135		
	1.123	1.124	1.123
		4.004	4.000

Step 2: After obtaining the seasonal index, we must first remove the effect of season from the original time series. This process is referred to as deseasonalizing the time series. For this, we must divide the original series by the seasonal index for that quarter.

Step 3: Looking at the graph in Figure 6.1, we see that the time series seems to have an upward linear trend. To identify this trend, we develop the least squares trend equation. This procedure is shown in Table 6.6.

Table 6.6—DESEASONALIZED DATA

Year	Quarter	Sales	Seasonal S	Deseasonal Data	t	tY	t^2
1	1	5.8	0.940	6.17	1	6.17	1
	2	5.1	0.858	5.94	2	11.89	4
	3	7.0	1.079	6.49	3	19.46	9
	4	7.5	1.123	6.68	4	25.72	16
2	1	6.8	0.940	7.23	5	36.17	25
	2	6.2	0.858	7.23	6	43.35	36
	3	7.8	1.079	7.23	7	50.59	49
	4	8.4	1.123	7.48	8	59.86	64
3	1	7.0	0.940	7.45	9	67.01	81
	2	6.6	0.858	7.69	10	76.91	100
	3	8.5	1.079	7.88	11	86.64	121
	4	8.8	1.123	7.84	12	94.07	144
4	1	7.3	0.940	7.76	13	100.94	169
	2	6.9	0.858	8.04	14	112.57	196

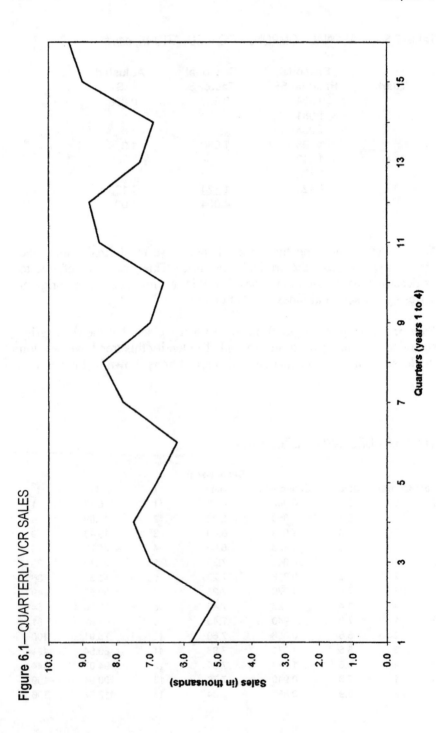

Figure 6.1—QUARTERLY VCR SALES

Table 6.6—DESEASONALIZED DATA, *con't.*

Year Quarter	Sales	Seasonal S	Deseasonal Data	t	tY	t²
3	9.0	1.079	8.34	15	125.09	225
4	9.4	1.123	8.37	16	133.98	256
			117.82	136	1,051.43	1,496

t-bar = 8.5   y-bar = 7.3638
b = 0.1469
a = 6.1147

which means y = 6.1147 + 0.1469 t for the forecast periods:

t = 17
    18
    19
    20

Step 4: Develop the forecast using the trend equation and adjust it to account for the effect of season (Figure 6.2). The quarterly forecast (Table 6.7) can be obtained by multiplying the trend forecast by the seasonal factor.

Table 6.7—QUARTER-TO-QUARTER FORECAST FOR YEAR 5

Year	Quarter	Trend Forecast	Seasonal Factor	Quarterly Forecast
5	1	8.6120 (a)	0.940	8.0953
	2	8.7589	0.858	7.1514
	3	8.9058	1.079	9.6094
	4	9.0527	1.123	10.1662

Note: (a) y = 6.1147 + 0.1469 t = 6.1147 + 0.1469 (17) = 8.6120

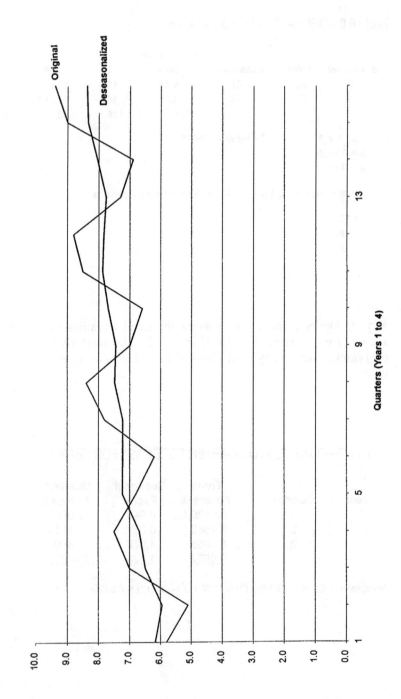

Figure 6.2—QUARTERLY VCR SALES: ORIGINAL VERSUS DESEASONALIZED

CONCLUSION

A time series is a chronological sequence of data on a particular variable. Several methods are available to analyze time series data, among them trend analysis and decomposition of time series. Trend analysis—linear and curvilinear—can be used effectively when a company has no data. The classical decomposition method is used for seasonal and cyclical situations.

CHAPTER 7
FORECASTING WITH
NO DATA*

An electronics manufacturer develops a new CD-ROM player. A pharmaceutical firm targets people at risk of AIDS for the first time in an ad campaign for its vaccine.

The life cycle of a typical new product is divided into four major stages: introduction, growth, maturity, and saturation. How can these firms forecast future sales of new products? Most quantitative forecasting models are designed to detect patterns (trends, cycles, seasonality, etc.) in past time-series data and to project those patterns into the future.

If you have no past data available, you can still develop a model that projects future growth without data. Trend models fall into this category. There is no doubt that forecasting with such a model involves a certain amount of guesswork. At best, the model projects long-term trends based on reasonable assumptions about the immediate future. Fortunately, trend analysis (linear or nonlinear) and spreadsheet models such as *Microsoft's Excel, Lotus 1-2-3*, and Quattro Pro are handy tools for analyzing those assumptions.

The basic idea is to assume data values for the first period in the future and for some later period, usually the time when you think the market will stabilize. Then you use forecasting models to fill in the data between these two periods, using a variety of possible growth patterns. Once you have some actual data, you'll be able to arrive at a final forecast. Although not as reliable as forecasts based on historical data, this procedure makes the forecasting process more objective than operating with no model.

Growth models widely in use include:

1. The linear model (constant change growth)

2. The exponential model (constant percentage growth)

*This chapter draws heavily on E. Gardner, Jr., "Forecast with No Data," *Lotus*, August 1991.

3. The logistic growth model

4. The modified exponential model

We will illustrate each of the four models using the Peters Company as an example. The company is about to introduce a new VCR player, Model 310. Using its years of experience with other VCR players (their own and others'), the company:

- Predicts that it will sell 1.05 million units by the end of 2003.
- Expects annual sales to hit 3.15 million units in 10 years.
- Foresees a saturation level of 6.5 million units sold each year.

Table 7.1 calculates forecasts using the four models. Figure 7.1 plots and compares the predictions of these models.

As can be seen from Figure 7.1, all the growth curves start at the same point, the first-year data assumption of 1.05 million, and run through the target value of 3.15 million in the year 2012. Their routes to that target, however, differ significantly.

THE LINEAR MODEL—CONSTANT CHANGE GROWTH

The linear (constant change growth) model assumes that growth is constant.

The *linear* trend line equation can be shown as

$$Y = a + b\,t$$

where t = time.

As was discussed in Chapter 6 on time series analysis, the formula for the coefficients a and b are essentially the same as those for simple regression. The linear trend equation used in this example is:

$$Y = 816.667 + 233.333\,t$$

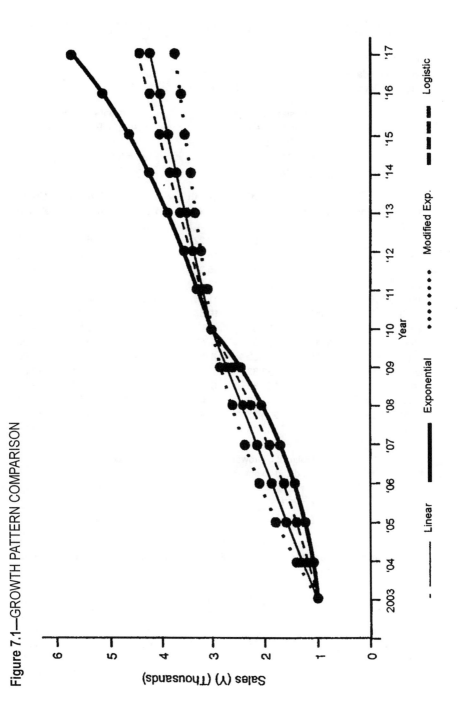

Figure 7.1—GROWTH PATTERN COMPARISON

Table 7.1—SALES OF NEW VCR-GROWTH PATTERN COMPARISONS

INPUTS
First -period data	1050	Target sales	3150
Saturation level	6500	Target period	10

	Constant Change Growth–Linear		Constant Percentage Growth–Exponential
	a = 816.667		a = 929
	b = 233.333		b = NA
	g = NA		g = 0.1298

Year	Period	Forecast	Growth Amount	Growth Percent	Forecast	Growth Amount	Growth Percent
1993	1	1050			1050		
1994	2	1283	233.33	22.22	1186	136.32	12.98
1995	3	1517	233.33	18.18	1340	154.02	12.98
1996	4	1750	233.33	15.38	1514	174.02	12.98
1997	5	1983	233.33	13.33	1711	196.61	12.98
1998	6	2217	233.33	11.76	1933	222.14	12.98
1999	7	2450	233.33	10.53	2184	250.98	12.98
2000	8	2683	233.33	9.52	2468	283.56	12.98
2001	9	2917	233.33	8.70	2788	320.38	12.98
2002	10	3150	233.33	8.00	3150	361.97	12.98
2003	11	3383	233.33	7.41	3559	408.97	12.98
2004	12	3617	233.33	6.90	4021	462.06	12.98
2005	13	3850	233.33	6.45	4543	522.05	12.98
2006	14	4083	233.33	6.06	5133	589.83	12.98
2007	15	4317	233.33	5.71	5799	666.41	12.98

	Optimistic Growth Modified Exponential		Average Growth Logistic
	a = 6500		a = 0.0002
	b = 5753		b = 0.0010
	g = 0.9474		g = 0.8385

Year	Period	Forecast	Growth Amount	Growth Percent	Forecast	Growth Amount	Growth Percent
1993	1	1050			1050		
1994	2	1337	286.87	27.32	1214	164.45	15.66
1995	3	1609	271.77	20.33	1398	183.60	15.12
1996	4	1866	257.47	16.01	1601	202.95	14.52
1997	5	2110	243.91	13.07	1823	221.88	13.86
1998	6	2351	231.07	10.95	2063	239.69	13.15
1999	7	2560	207.39	9.35	2318	255.58	12.39
2000	8	2767	196.47	8.10	2587	268.79	11.60

Table 7.1—SALES OF NEW VCR-GROWTH PATTERN COMPARISONS, *con't.*

Year	Period	Forecast	Growth Amount	Growth Percent	Forecast	Growth Amount	Growth Percent
2001	9	2964	186.13	7.10	2866	278.60	10.77
2002	10	3150	176.33	6.28	3150	284.45	9.93
2003	11	3326	167.33	5.60	3436	285.99	9.08
2004	12	3493	167.05	5.02	3719	283.13	8.24
2005	13	3652	158.26	4.53	3995	276.04	7.42
2006	14	3802	149.93	4.11	4260	265.14	6.64
2007	15	3944	142.04	3.74	4511	251.05	5.89

In Table 7.1, we see that the linear model predicts that sales of Model 310 will increase by some 233,333 units each year. Even though unit growth remains fixed, percentage growth declines more rapidly than in the other models (to be discussed later in this chapter).

THE EXPONENTIAL MODEL—CONSTANT PERCENTAGE GROWTH

A typical example of nonlinear trend is a constant percentage growth model. A model structure here is the constant growth rate, or constant rate of change over time by a proportional rather than constant amount. (Other common nonlinear trends described by the *S-type curves* such as *modified exponential growth curve* and the *logistic growth curve* are discussed later.)

As discussed in Chapter 6, the growth rate is estimated using linear regression by fitting historical data to the logarithmic transformation of the basic model. The exponential model takes the following form:

$$S_t = a (1 + g)^t,$$

where a is the starting point for the growth curve, the point at which the straight line that represents this growth pattern intersects the Y axis of the graph, and g is the rate of growth.

For this example, the model gives us $S_t = 929 (1 + 0.1298)^t$. Note that the value of a (929) is multiplied by 1.1298 for the first-period forecast, by $(1.1298)^2 = 1.2764$ for the second-period forecast, by $(1.1298)^3 = 1.4421$ for the third-period forecast, and so forth. Thus, the forecasts become larger until they exceed the target sales level.

The exponential model projects a 12.98 percent increase in sales of VCRs each year, which means that the number of units will increase by a larger amount each year.

Many people mistakenly believe that the simple exponential model is too optimistic because it predicts constant percentage growth. How, they ask, can sales of any product consistently grow at a certain percentage year after year?

Admittedly, exponential growth gets out of hand and reaches impossible saturation levels after passing the target level. Note, however, that since it takes time for exponential growth to build up steam, its predictions of early growth are actually pessimistic compared with other models.

MODIFIED EXPONENTIAL GROWTH

The modified exponential model is the most optimistic. It projects early growth of about 27.32 percent from 2003 to 2004. The curve that got this model (Figure 7.1) runs well above the other curves for every year until it reaches the target value. After that, growth slows dramatically as sales approach the saturation level.

Of the four models shown in Table 7.1, the modified exponential model always produces the most optimistic growth pattern between any two data values. If you expect your data to show strong early growth, use the modified exponential model as a planning tool.

The modified exponential growth model takes the following form:

$$Y_t = a - bg^t$$

In this equation, a is the saturation level (SL), and b and g are parameters that determine the shape of the growth curve. Note that:

(1) g is computed by subtracting a from the target level, dividing that difference between a and the first period forecast, then raising that ratio to the power of 1 over the target period minus 1. g is always less than 1.

(2) b is simply the difference between a and the first-period forecast divided by g. When multiplied by g, it is the difference between a and the first-period forecast.

In the example, a is 6,500, b is 5,753, and g is 0.9474. For the first period, the forecast value is the same as the first period data, because 0.9474 to the first power is 0.9474. Therefore, b x g is 5,450, and a - (b x g) is 1,050. For the second period, $g^2 = (0.9474)^2 = 0.8976$, so b x g^2 is 5,163, and a - (b x g^2) is 1,337. In subsequent periods, g is raised to larger powers and therefore decreases, so smaller and smaller amounts are subtracted from a, and the forecast gets closer to the saturation level.

LOGISTIC GROWTH

The logistic model should be used when you expect growth to follow an S-shaped curve. That is, you expect slow growth at first, followed by a period of rapid expansion, then a decline in growth as sales approach the saturation level.

This type of forecasting model is typically used to fit the life cycle of a new product. Examples were Sony's Betamax and Texas Instrument's electronic calculator. The logistic curve is a middle-ground assumption falling between the exponential curve and the modified exponential curve.

The logistic-curve growth model is determined with the following equation:

$$Y_t = 1/(a - bg^t)$$

where a = 1/SL. The behavior of this fraction is more complicated than you would expect. In Figure 7.1, notice that the amount of growth each period increases for a time and then begins to decrease. In terms of percentage growth, the logistic curve always starts out somewhere below the modified exponential curve. It gradually catches up as sales approach the saturation point.

A WORD OF CAUTION

Forecasting with no data can be a problem. If you choose too pessimistic a model, you may underestimate early sales and fail to meet customer demand. If you bank on too optimistic a model, initial revenues may not meet expectations and the entire project could sour.

Nevertheless, it is better than going forward with no model of the future. The trend and growth models presented here should at least give you a starting point.

CHECKLISTS

CHOOSING THE RIGHT GROWTH MODEL

The big question is how to choose the right model. The following questions can be helpful:

1. Think of the area between the exponential and the modified exponential curves as the range of likely values for actual data. The modified exponential model generates the best-case scenario; the exponential model generates the worst-case scenario; the linear and logistic models represent middle-ground possibilities.

2. Examine your assumptions about first-period data, target sales data, and saturation level. The size of the range among the models depends on these assumptions.

3. Estimate these numbers carefully but do "what-if" on the effects of alternative values.

4. In a new product environment, models must work hand-in-hand with solid marketing experience and expert judgment. Combine your marketing experience with these models.

5. Computer models are useful for testing hypotheses. Before basing business plans on any forecasting model, compare the model's projected growth patterns against the growths of products that you believe would receive a similar reception in the marketplace.

CHAPTER 8
THE BOX-JENKINS
APPROACH TO
FORECASTING

If forecasting is the sole purpose of the model, time series analysis has certain advantages over regression and econometric models. One advantage is that it is easier to gather other explanatory variables; time series analysis requires only past series of the variable of interest.

Time series models used in the Box-Jenkins methodology are autoregressive (AR) and moving average (MA) models. They are commonly called ARIMA (Auto Regressive Integrated Moving Average) models. ARIMA models use either past values (the autoregressive model), past errors (the moving average model), or combinations of past values and past errors (the ARIMA model). The Box-Jenkins method is well suited to handling complex time series and other forecasting situations in which the basic pattern is not readily apparent. It uses the iterative approach of identifying a possible useful model from a general class of models. The chosen model is then checked against the actual data to see if it accurately describes the series. If the model does not fit well, the process is repeated until a satisfactory model is found.

The Box-Jenkins method is known to be very powerful for short-range forecasts. Applications include:

1. Forecasting stock prices daily

2. Forecasting earnings

3. Forecasting different categories of quality assurance

4. Analyzing a large number of energy time series for a utility company

5. Sales forecasting

6. Forecasting employment

MAJOR TIME SERIES TOOLS USED

Box-Jenkins modeling relies heavily on three familiar time series tools:

DIFFERENCING

Differencing is done to change from non-stationary series to stationary ones. The first condition that justifies the use of the ARIMA models for forecasting is whether the time-series data satisfy *stationary* conditions. Stationarity means that data fluctuate around a constant mean or variance with no trend over time. Note the following guidelines:

Stationary Data	Nonstationary Data
(1) No trend	(1) Trend
(2) No seasonality	(2) Seasonality
(3) Constant variance	(3) Varying variance

For example, the first differencing of $Y_t = Y_t - Y_{t-1}$ can be shown as follows:

t	Y_t	ΔY_{t-1}	$Y_t = Y_t - Y_{t-1}$
1	55	—	—
2	56	55	1
3	58	56	2
4	60	58	2
5	61	61	1

The original series shows an upward trend, while the differenced series are stationary. Sometimes a second round of diffferencing may be necessary before new data become stationary.

AUTO-CORRELATIONS (ACs)

Auto-correlation measures the relationship between two values (such as ones in period t and period t-4). It is computed to determine (1) whether AR terms are needed and (2) what the appropriate order (or number) of a moving average (MA) model is.

Caution: In Box-Jenkins the term *moving average* has a different meaning from the moving average forecasting method discussed in Chapter 2.

PARTIAL AUTO-CORRELATIONS (PACs)

Partial auto-correlations measure the residual relationship between values in period t and values in periods t-1, t-2, t-3, etc. It is used to determine (1) whether MR terms are needed and (2) what the appropriate order of an autoregressive (AR) model is.

THE MODELS

If Y_t is a stationary series, the ARIMA models look like this:

1. The AR model is the lagged model of Y_t. For example, an autoregressive model of order 1—termed AR(1):

   $$= b_0 + b_1 Y_{t-1} + e_t$$

where Y_t = dependent variable
Y_{t-1} = independent variable that is the dependent variable with one period lag
b_0 and b_1 = constant term and regression coefficient
e_t = residual (or error) term that represents random events not explained by the model (white noise)

2. The MA model forecasts Y_t on the basis of the past performance of its forecasting errors. For example, a moving average model of order 1—termed MA(1):
   $$Y_t = e_t - W_1 e_{t-1} + b_0$$
where Y_t = dependent variable
W_1 = weight
e_t and e_{t-1} = residual (or error) and one with one period time lag
b_0 = constant term

3. The ARIMA model combines the AR and MA models. For example, ARIMA(1,0,1)
   $$Y_t = b_0 + b_1 Y_{t-1} - W_1 e_{t-1} + e_t$$

BOX-JENKINS NOTATION

Before discussing the Box-Jenkins approach, some explanation of Box-Jenkins terminology is called for. An ARIMA is identified in the Box-Jenkins approach using p's, d's, and q's. Small letters signify ordinary autoregressive (p), moving average (q), or differencing (d) factors; capital letters signify a seasonal (quarterly [lag 4] or monthly [lag 12]) autoregressive (P), seasonal moving average (Q), or seasonal differencing (D) factors. That is, ARIMA(p,d,q)(P,D,Q).

For example,

1. ARIMA(100)(000) is a simple autoregressive model based on the original series with no seasonality; it is the same as AR(1).

2. ARIMA(001)(000) represents a simple moving average model, with no seasonality, based on the original series; it is the same as MA(1).

3. ARIMA(011)(000) represents a simple moving average model, with no seasonality, based on the differences or changes in the original data series.

4. ARIMA(011)(001) is a moving average model on the first differences, but also contains a seasonal moving average. This is often called SARIMA where S stands for seasonality.

Note: When neither difference nor seasonality takes place, the appropriate model is ARIMA(p,q).

THE STEP-BY-STEP APPROACH

A step-by-step approach to the Box-Jenkins methodology is outlined primarily to structure the exposition. As shown in Figure 8.1, the Box-Jenkins approach involves five separate stages. These stages are (1) plotting the data, (2) identifying the model, (3) model estimation, (4) diagnostic testing, and (5) forecasting with the model.

STEP 1: PLOT THE DATA.

This step is needed to check for evidence of possible nonstationarity in the series. Nonstationarity occurs when a series exhibits no affinity for a mean value. The sales series of most firms and many macroeconomic series exhibit nonstationarity due to an upward drift over time. When estimating a Box-Jenkins model, it is first necessary to derive a stationary series. If nonstationarity is evidenced in the raw series, a technique such as taking the first differences of the raw series (or log transformation) of the original is employed to obtain a stationary series.

Figure 8.1—FLOW DIAGRAM OF THE BOX-JENKINS METHOD

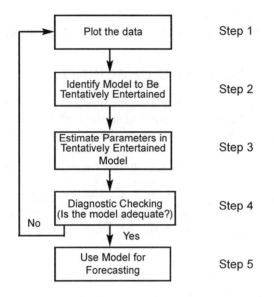

Source: Adapted from G.P. Box and G.M. Jenkins, *Time Series Analysis Forecasting and Control* (San Francisco: Holden-Day, 1970).

STEP 2: IDENTIFYING THE MODEL.

This step involves identifying possible Box-Jenkins models consistent with the data being analyzed. You must first determine whether AR and MA terms are needed by looking at the plots of ACs and PACs. Then you look at the opposite plot to determine the order (or number) of the AR and MA terms. The rules are as follows:

1. If the ACs trail off exponentially to zero, an AR process is indicated; if the PACs trail off, an MA process is indicated; and if both trail off, a mixed ARIMA process is indicated.

2. In order to determine the order of the MA and AR processes, count the number of AC and PAC coefficients that are significantly different from zero.

STEP 3: MODEL ESTIMATION.

For the preliminary models identified in Step 2, obtain estimates of their parameters. This can be readily accomplished by using a Box-Jenkins software.

STEP 4: DIAGNOSTIC CHECKING.

Several checks need to be made on the adequacy of the model estimated in Step 3. One check is the statistical strength of the model. This involves (1) the t-test for the significance of the regression coefficients and (2) RMSE (Root Mean Square Error) for *ex ante* forecasting performance. Another check on the estimated models is whether their residuals are white (random) noise. If this series is not uncorrelated, additional information in the past sequence of the series can be exploited in forecasting. For the purpose of this step, we do a chi-square (χ^2) test, known as the *Box-Pierce Q statistic*, on the auto-correlations of the residuals. The test statistic is:

$$Q = (N - d)\sum_{j=1}^{k} r^2_k$$

which is approximately chi-square distributed with $k - p - q$ degrees of freedom. In this formula:

- N = length of the data series
- d = degree of differencing to obtain a stationary series
- k = first k auto-correlations being checked
- r_k = sample auto-correlation function of the kth residual term
- p = number of AR terms
- q = number of MA terms

If the calculated Q value is larger than the χ^2 for $k - p - q$ degrees of freedom (see Table A.5 in the Appendix), the model is judged "misspecified."

As a rule of thumb, the model is misspecified (1) if the Q statistic is greater than 18.0, or (2) if the lag 1 auto-correlation is larger than 2 divided by the square root of the number of observations in the time series (e.g., 0.25 (2/64) for 64 observations). If this happens, the analyst must try an alternative model.

STEP 5: FORECASTING WITH THE MODEL.

Ex post forecasts are made for the period of data that were withheld from the model estimation sample to illustrate the use of Box-Jenkins models for forecasting. The earnings data of Zyland Corporation provide an example to illustrate the steps in using this methodology.

Example 8.1 Quarterly Earnings of Zyland Corporation

Figure 8.2 details this earnings series for the sample period of the first quarter of 1985 to the second quarter of 1998.

Step 1: Plot the data.

Figure 8.2 contains a plot of the earnings data showing an increasing trend over time. Figure 8.3 plots the first differences of the original (non-stationary) data that appear to be stationary.

Step 2: Identifying the model.

To identify possible Box-Jenkins models consistent with the data being analyzed, first, ACs for the sample period were computed to check whether the earnings series is stationary. As shown in Figure 8.4, the ACs are decreasing very slowly, indicating that the series is nonstationary.

Next, the first difference of the data series was used to compute sample ACs. As shown in Figure 8.5, the sample ACs approach very quickly to zero, indicating that the first difference is stationary.

The sample ACs shows that the population AC (r_1) is significantly different from zero. Hence, the model is the first-order moving average type – MA(1).

Figure 8.6 shows the partial auto-correlations (PACs) of the 1st differenced series.

Figure 8.2—EARNINGS DATA FOR THE ZYLAND CORPORATION

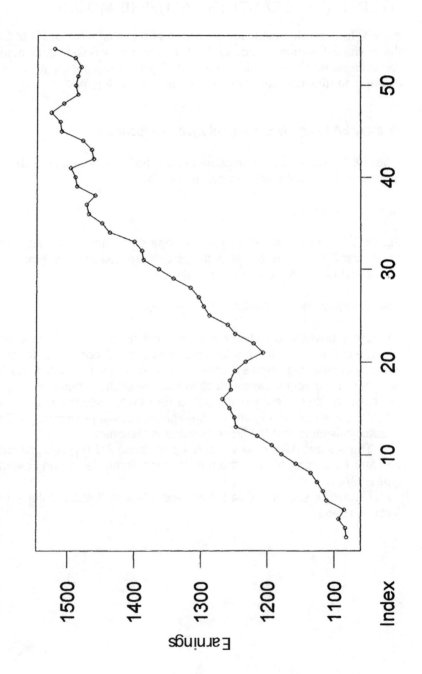

Figure 8.3—PLOTS OF FIRST DIFFERENCES

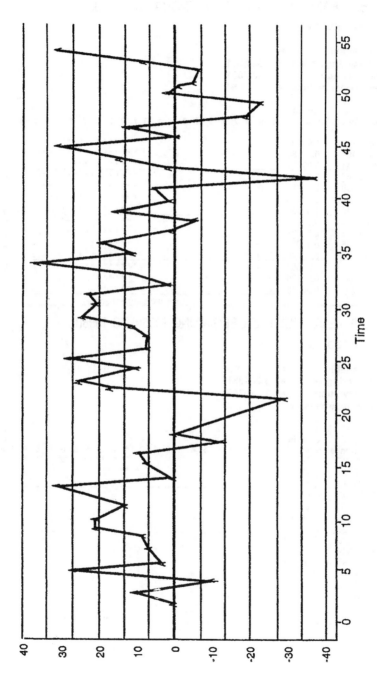

Figure 8.4—EARNINGS DATA, BEGINNING 1985(I) TO 1998 (I)

ARIMA PROCEDURE

Name of variable   =   X
Mean of working series =   1329.311
Standard deviation   =   1.43.7001
Number of observations =   54

Lag	Covariance	Correla-tion	-1 9 8 7 6 5 4 3 2 1 0 1 2 3 4 5 6 7 8 9 1	Std.
0	20649.711	1.00000	****************	0
1	19592.493	0.94880	• ****************	0.136083
2	18528.344	0.89727	• ****************	0.227728
3	17452.587	0.84517	• ****************	0.285794
4	16259.568	0.78740	• ****************	0.328838
5	15114.588	0.73195	• ****************	0.362074
6	13957.440	0.67591	• ************** •	0.388510
7	12702.354	0.61513	• ************* •	0.409708
8	11364.842	0.55036	• ************ •	0.426469
9	10167.655	0.49239	• *********** •	0.439425
10	9032.281	0.43740	• ********** •	0.49526
11	8022.430	0.38850	• ********* •	0.457340
12	7107.686	0.34420	• ******* •	0.463411
13	6350.776	0.30755	• ****** •	0.468121

• = two standard errors

Figure 8.5—EARNINGS DATA, BEGINNING 1985(I) TO 1998(II)

ARIMA PROCEDURE

Name of variable   =   XD
Mean of working series =   8.301887
Standard deviation   =   15.15245
Number of observations =   53

Lag	Covariance	Correlat-lation	-1 9 8 7 6 5 4 3 2 1 0 1 2 3 4 5 6 7 8 9 1	(more accurate) Std. Error
0	229.597	1.00000	******************	0
1	62.918879	0.27404	*****	0.137361
2	30.791442	0.13411	• *** •	0.147315
3	-5.586803	-0.02433	• •	0.149601
4	-1.014870	-0.00442	• •	0.149676
5	-13.944956	-0.06074	• * •	0.149678
6	-3.036928	-0.01323	• •	0.150143
7	-9.401620	-0.04095	• * •	0.150165
8	-58.855867	-0.25634	• ***** •	0.150375
9	-18.292251	-0.07968	• ** •	0.158406
10	0.456034	0.00199	• •	0.159160
11	-0.050286	-0.00022	• •	0.159161
12	-48.751891	-0.21234	• **** •	0.159161
13	-31.512710	-0.13725	• *** •	0.163319

• = two standard errors

Auto-correlations (ACs)

	1	2	3	4	5	6	7	8	Standard Error
				Lag					
r_j	.27	.13	-.02	-.00	-.06	-.01	-.04	-.26	1/n = 1/53 =.137

Figure 8.6—EARNINGS DATA, BEGINNING 1985(I) TO 1998(I)

First Differenced Series
ARIMA Procedure
Partial Auto-correlations

Lag	Correlation	-1 9 8 7 6 5 4 3 2 1 0 1 2 3 4 5 6 7 8 9 1
1	0.27404	• *****
2	0.06380	• * •
3	-0.08275	• ** •
4	0.01446	• •
5	-0.05455	• * •
6	0.01342	• •
7	-0.03097	• * •
8	-0.26896	***** •
9	0.07003	• * •
10	0.06710	• * •
11	-0.05681	• * •
12	-0.24883	***** •
13	-0.05887	• * •

Autocorrelation Check for White Noise

To Lag	Chi Square	DF	Prob	Auto-correlations							
6	5.51	6	0.480	0.274	0.134	-0.024	-0.004	-0.061	-0.013
12	13.50	12	0.334	-0.041	-0.256	-0.080	-0.002	-0.000	-0.212

Partial Auto-correlations (PACs)

	1	2	3	4	5	6	7	8	Standard Error
				Lag					
r_j	.27	.06	-.08	.01	-.05	.01	-.03	-.27	1/n = 1/53 =.137

The population PAC (r1) shows that it is significantly different from zero. The first differenced series is also of the first-order autoregressive type - AR(1).

Step 3: Model estimation.

Estimates of the parameters of the preliminary models identified in Step 2 are next obtained. By combining AR(1) and MA(1) models, the following models are suggested.

1.   ARIMA (1,1,0)
2.   ARIMA (0,1,1)
3.   ARIMA (1,1,1)

The estimation was done using Box-Jenkins computer software. The SAS ARIMA output is shown in Figure 8.7. The parameter estimates for the models and key statistics for diagnostic testing are summarized in Figure 8.8.

Figure 8.7—SAS EXAMPLE OF THE ARIMA MODEL

DATA EARNINGS;
INPUT EARNINGS;
TITLE EARNINGS SERIES, BEGINNING 1985 I TO 1998 II

1081.4	1083.0	1093.3	1084.7	1111.5	1116.9	1125.7	1135.4
1157.2	1178.5	1193.1	1214.8	1247.1	1249.0	1256.8	1267.0
1254.7	1256.3	1248.6	1232.4	1206.3	1221.0	1248.4	1259.7
1287.2	1295.8	1303.3	1315.4	1341.2	1363.3	1385.8	1388.5
1400.0	1437.0	1448.8	1468.4	1672.0	1459.2	1486.5	1489.4
1496.2	1461.4	1464.2	1477.9	1510.1	1512.5	1525.8	1506.9
1485.8	1489.3	1485.7	1480.7	1490.1	1521.4		

PROC ARIMA;
IDENTIFY VAR = EARNINGS;
IDENTIFY VAR = EARNINGS 85 (I);
ESTIMATE P=1 Q=1;
ESTIMATE P=1;
ESTIMATE Q=1;
FORECAST LEAD = 10 PRINTALL;

Figure 8.7—SAS EXAMPLE OF THE ARIMA MODEL *con't.*

ARIMA (1, 1, 0) MODEL OF EARNINGS SERIES
ARIMA PROCEDURE

Conditional Least Squares Estimation

Parameter	Estimate	Approx. Std. Error	T Ratio	Lag
MU	8.40311	2.83133	2.97	0
AR, 1	0.28655	0.13749	2.08	1

Constant Estimate = 5.99519029
Variance Estimate = 219.862332
Std. Error Estimate = 14.8277555
AIC = 438.197856*
SBC = 442.13844*
Number of Residuals = 53
* Does not include log determinant.

Correlations of the Estimates

Parameter	MU	ARI, 1	Note:
			$B^1 Y_t = Y_{t-1}$
MU	1.000	0.036	$B^2 Y_{t-1} = Y_{t-2}$
ARI, 1	0.036	1.000	$B^2 Y_t = Y_{t-2}$

Auto-correlation Check of Residuals

To Lag	Chi Square	DF	Prob	Auto-correlations					
6	1.00	5	0.963	-0.017	0.083	-0.075	0.015	-0.064	0.003
12	8.78	11	0.642	0.019	-0.260	-0.022	0.040	0.069	-0.202
18	10.75	17	0.869	-0.084	-0.062	-0.092	0.049	-0.059	0.026
24	15.46	23	0.878	-0.134	0.060	0.140	0.097	0.030	-0.030

Model for Variable Earnings

Estimated Mean = 8.40310865
Period(s) of Differencing = 1

Autoregressive Factors
Factor 1:1 - 0.28655 8**(1)

$(1 - .2865 B^1) (Y_t - Y_{t-1}) = 8.4031 + e_t$
$Y_t = 8.4031 + 1.2866 Y_{t-1} - .2866 e_{t-2} + e_t$

Figure 8.7—SAS EXAMPLE OF THE ARIMA MODEL *con't.*

ARIMA (0, 1, 1) Model of Earnings Series
ARIMA Procedure

Conditional Least Squares Estimation

Parameter	Estimate	Approx. Std. Error	T Ratio	Lag
MU	8.35102	2.51748	3.32	0
AR, 1	-0.23122	0.13901	-1.66	1

Constant Estimate = 8.35102142
Std. Error Estimate = 223.364625
AIC = 439.035465*
SBC = 442.976048*
Number of Residuals = 53
*Does not include log determinant.

Correlations of the Estimates

Parameter	MU	ARI, 1
MU	1.000	-0.019
ARI, 1	-0.019	1.000

Auto-correlation Check of Residuals

To Lag	Chi Square	DF	Prob	Auto-correlations					
6	1.79	5	0.878	0.037	0.143	-0.066	0.019	-0.065	-0.013
12	9.16	11	0.607	0.005	-0.252	-0.030	0.009	0.046	-0.207
18	11.60	17	0.824	-0.096	-0.076	-0.102	0.035	-0.069	0.025
24	16.26	23	0.844	-0.122	0.067	0.138	0.103	0.047	-0.023

Model for Variable Earnings

Estimated Mean = 8.35102142
Period(s) of Differencing = 1

Moving Average Factors
Factor 1:1 + 0.23122B** (1)

$(Y_t - Y_{t-1}) = 8.3510 + (1 = 0.2312 \ B') \ e_t$
$Y_t = 8.3510 + Y_{t-1} + 0.2312 \ e_{t-1} + e_t$

Figure 8.7—SAS EXAMPLE OF THE ARIMA MODEL *con't.*

ARIMA (1, 1, 1) Model of Earnings Series
ARIMA Procedure

Conditional Least Squares Estimation

Parameter	Estimate	Approx. Std. Error	T Ratio	Lag
MU	8.41760	2.98274	2.82	0
MA1, 1	0.13054	0.49341	0.26	1
AR1, 1	0.40763	0.45377	0.90	1

Constant Estimate = 4.98633646
Variance Estimate = 223.740305.
Std. Error Estimate = 14.9579512
AIC = 440.074992*
SBC = 445.985868*
Number of Residuals = 53
*Does not include log determinant.

Correlations of the Estimates

Parameter	MU	MA1, 1	ARI, 1
MU	1.000	0.025	0.035
MA1, 1	0.025	1.000	0.957
AR1, 1	0.035	0.957	1.000

Auto-correlation Check of Residuals

To Lag	Chi Square	DF	Prob			Auto-correlations			
6	0.81	4	0.938	-0.005	0.051	-0.084	0.007	-0.062	0.012
12	8.82	10	0.549	0.017	-0.264	-0.024	0.056	0.077	-0.199
18	10.63	16	0.831	-0.085	-0.061	-0.086	0.051	-0.050	0.020
24	15.62	22	0.834	-0.139	0.057	0.145	0.101	0.027	-0.033

Model for Variable Earnings

Estimated Mean = 8.41760103
Period(s) of Differencing = 1

Autoregressive Factors
Factor 1:1 - 0.40763 B**(1)

$(1 - 0.4076 \, B') \, (Y_t - Y_{t-1}) = 8.4176 + (1 - 0.1305 \, B') \, e_t$
$Y_t = 8.4176 + 1.4076 \, Y_{t-1} - 0.4076 \, Y_{t-2} - 0.1305$

Figure 8.8—DIAGNOSTIC TESTING SUMMARIZED

1) ARIMA (1, 1, 0) MODEL:
- $(1 - .2866B') (Xt - Xt-1) = 8.4031 + et$
  - (2.08) (2.97) t statistics

- Auto-correlation check of residuals

To Lag	Chi Square	DF	Prob	
6	1.00	5	0.963	Since Q values < 18,
12	8.78	11	0.642	the residuals are white noise,
18	10.75	17	0.869	The model is useful
24	15.46	23	0.878	

Box-Pierce Statistics

- ex ante-forecast error for the sample estimation period
  RMSE = 14.5453

2) ARIMA (0, 1, 1) model:
- $X_t - X_{t-1} = 8.3510 + 0.2312 e_{t-1} + e_t$
  - (3.32) (-1.66)
  - $X_t = 8.3510 + X_{t-1} + .2312 e_{t-1} + e_t$

- Auto-correlation check of residuals

To Lag	Chi Square	DF	Prob	
6	1.79	5	0.878	Since Q values < 18,
12	9.16	11	0.607	the residuals are white noise,
18	11.60	17	0.824	The model is useful
24	16.26	23	0.844	

- ex ante-forecast error
  RMSE = 14.6607

3) ARIMA (1, 1, 1) model:
- $(1 - .4076B) (X_t - X_{t-1}) = 8.4176 + (1 - .1305B) e_t$
  - (0.90) (2.82) (0.26)
  - $X_t = 8.4176 + 1.4076X_{t-1} - 0.4076X_{t-2} - 0.1305e_{t-1} + e_t$

- Auto-correlation check of residuals

To Lag	Chi Square	DF	Prob	
6	0.81	4	0.938	Since Q values < 18,
12	8.82	10	0.549	the residuals are white noise,
18	10.63	16	0.831	The model is useful
24	15.62	22	0.834	

- ex ante-forecast error
  RMSE = 14.5284

Step 4: Diagnostic checking.

Several checks need to be made on the adequacy of the model estimated in Step 3. As shown in Figure 8.8, all three models appear to have statistical strength in terms of large t-values and low RMSEs.

Also, they all show that residuals are random (i.e., white noise, or serially uncorrelated), as indicated by the Box-Pierce Q statistic. (Using a rule of thumb, we note that the Q statistic is less than 18.0 in all three models. Therefore, the residuals of all three models are white noise.)

Given this evidence, though all three models appear to be correctly specified, we chose ARIMA(1,1,0) as the final model for forecasting due to (1) the larger t-statistics of its parameter estimates and (2) a higher probability of the residuals being serially uncorrelated. Its RMSE of 14.5453 was as good as those of the other two.

Step 5: Forecasting with the model.

The *ex post* forecasts made by using the ARIMA(1,1,0) for the period from the third quarter of 1998 to the fourth quarter of 2000 are shown in Figure 8.9.

Figure 8.9—FORECASTS OF VARIABLE EARNINGS

		Obs	Forecast	Std Error	Lower 95%	Upper 95%	Actual	Residual
		54	1498.7888	14.8278	1469.7269	1527.8506	1521.4000	22.6112
			--------------Forecast Begins------------------				
3rd	1998	55	1536.3642	14.8278	1507.3024	1565.4261		
4th	1998	56	1246.6474	24.1616	1499.2916	1594.0032		
1st	1999	57	1555.5893	31.5537	1493.7452	1617.4334		
2nd	1999	58	1564.1468	37.7064	1490.2436	1638.0499		
3rd	1999	59	1572.5941	43.0354	1488.2463	1656.9420		
4th	1999	60	1581.0099	47.7861	1487.3509	1674.6689		
1st	2000	61	1589.4166	52.1087	1487.2855	1691.5478		
2nd	2000	62	1597.8208	56.1001	1487.8667	1707.7749		
3rd	2000	63	1606.2242	59.8260	1488.9675	1723.4809		
4th	2000	64	1614.6274	63.3331	1490.4968	1738.7580		

A SEASONAL ISSUE

Seasonal patterns make Box-Jenkins forecasting more difficult because on top of the periodic pattern there is a longer, repetitive pattern occurring every Sth period, where S is the length of seasonality. To estimate the seasonal pattern, seasonal parameters need to be included in the model, now called SARIMA.

SARIMA is beyond the scope of this book and reserved for an advanced text. However, virtually all Box-Jenkins software can handle this situation.

COMPUTER SOFTWARE

Many statistical and forecasting packages, including *Minitab*, *SAS*, *Systat*, *SPSS*, *MicroTSP*, and *Sibyl/Runner*, contain programs that perform Box-Jenkins analysis. Computer software that specializes in handling Box-Jenkins models includes the *Pack System*, *AFSTAT*, and *AUTOJB*. PC packages specifically designed to perform Box-Jenkins techniques include *ARIMA* and *Micro-BJ*.

CONCLUSION

The Box-Jenkins approach is well suited to time-series forecasting problems. This chapter discussed the method, step by step, using an example and a computer program. However, the approach is not without shortcomings:

1. The method is relatively expensive, although the computer run time has been significantly reduced.

2. A large amount of data, at least 72 observations, are required. The model cannot be updated; new data mean complete refitting.

CHAPTER 9
MODELS BASED ON LEARNED BEHAVIOR— MARKOV MODEL AND INDIRECT METHODS

The forecasting methods we have discussed to date were for the most part based on the use of historical data. They did not consider how consumers behave in making purchase decisions in the marketplace. In this section, we will present a model based on learned behavior, the *Markov model*, along with indirect methods of sales forecasting, the use of economic indicators, input-output analysis, survey techniques, and econometric forecasting.

THE MARKOV MODEL

We operate on the thesis that consumption is a form of learned behavior; that is, consumers tend to repeat their past consumption activities. Some consumers become loyal to certain product types as well as specific brands. Others seek other brands and products.

In general, there is a great degree of regularity about such behavior. The Markov model was developed to predict market share by considering consumer brand loyalty and switching behaviors.

The model has the following objectives:

1. To predict the market share that a firm will attain at some point in the future.

2. To predict whether some constant or level market share will be obtained in the future. Most Markov models result in a final constant market share where changes in market share will no longer result with the passage of time.

3. To investigate the impact of a company's marketing strategies and promotional efforts such as advertising on gain or loss in market share.

To meet these objectives, we must compute what is called transition probabilities for all the companies in the market. Transition probabilities are nothing more than the probabilities that a certain seller will retain, gain, and lose customers. To develop this, we need sample data for past consumer behavior.

Let us assume that there are three battery manufacturers, A, B, and C. Each knows that consumers switch from one firm to another over time because of dissatisfaction with service, advertising, and other sales promotion efforts. We assume that each firm maintains records of consumer movements for a specified time, like one month. We further assume that no new customers enter and no old customers leave the market during this period.

Table 9.1 provides data on the flows among all the firms.

Table 9.1—FLOW OF CUSTOMERS

Firms	Jan. 1 Customers	Gains From A	B	C	Losses To A	B	C	Feb.1 Customers
A	300	0	45	35	0	30	30	320
B	600	30	0	20	45	0	15	590
C	400	30	15	0	35	20	0	390

This table can be converted into a matrix form, as shown in Table 9.2.

Table 9.2—RETENTION, GAIN, AND LOSS

	Firms	Retention and Loss to A	B	C	Total
Retention	A	240	30	30	300
And	B	45	540	15	600
Gain	C	35	20	345	400
	Total	320	590	390	1,300

Table 9.3 is a matrix of the same size as the one in Table 9.2 illustrating exactly how each probability was determined.

Table 9.3—TRANSITION PROBABILITY MATRIX

	Firms	Probability of Customers Being Retained or Lost		
		A	B	C
Probability of	A	240/300 =.80	30/300 =.10	30/300 =.10
Customer being	B	45/600 =.75	540/600 =.9	15/600 =.025
Retained or Gained	C	35/400 =.0875	20/400 =.05	345/400 =.8625

The rows in this matrix show the probability of the retention of customers and the loss of customers; the columns represent the probability of retention of customers and the gain of customers. For example, row 1 indicates that A retains .8 of its customers and loses .1 to B and .1 to C (30 each). Also, column 1, for example, indicates that A retains .8 of its customers (240), gains .075 of B's customers (45), and gains .0875 of C's customers (35).

The original market share on January 1 was:

(300A 600B 400C) = (.2308A .4615B .3077C)

With this we will be able to calculate market share, using the transition matrix we developed in Table 9.3.

To illustrate: Company A held 23.08 percent of the market at January 1. Of this, it retained 80 percent; it gained 10 percent of Company B's 46.15 percent of the market, and picked up 10 percent of Company C's 30.77 percent. The February 1 market share of Company A is, therefore, calculated to be:

Retention	.8 x .2308 = .1846
Gain from B	.1 x .4615 = .0462
Gain from C	.1 x .3077 = .0308
	.2616*

Company B's market share is as follows:

Gain from A	.075 x .2308 = .0173
Retention	.9 x .4615 = .4154
Gain from C	.025 x .3077 = .0077
	.4404*

Company C's market share is:

Gain from A	.0875 x .2308 = .0202
Gain from B	.05 x .4615 = .0231
Retention	.8625 x .3077 = .2654
	.3087*

*These numbers do not add up to exactly 100 percent due to rounding errors.

Thus market share on February 1 came out to be approximately:

- 26% for Company A
- 44% for Company B
- 30% for Company C

Market share forecasts may be used to generate a specific forecast of sales. For example, if industry sales are forecast to be, say, $10 million (obtained through regression analysis, input-output analysis, or some other technique), the forecast of sales for A is $2.6 million ($100 million x .26).

If the company wishes to forecast market share for March, then, procedure is exactly the same as before except that it uses the February 1 forecasted market share as a basis. The forecaster must be careful when using the Markov model: Distant forecasts by this method, after many time periods, generally are not very reliable. Even in short-term forecasts, the transition matrix must be constantly updated for accuracy of projection.

At least in theory, most Markov models will result in a final constant market share in which market share will no longer change with the passage of time. However, this market share and its derivation will not be discussed here. In effect, this model has little practical application because the constant or level condition assumes no changes in competitive efforts of the firms within the industry.

INDIRECT METHODS

Indirect methods include techniques in which forecasts can be based on projections of national or regional economic activity (such as GDP or leading economic indicators), industry sales, or market surveys.

Typically, the indirect method involves the following three steps:

1. Forecast the level of economic indicators like GDP.

2. Translate the forecast into an industry forecast.

3. Translate the industry sales forecast into a company forecast.

INDEXES OF ECONOMIC INDICATORS

There are three types of economic indicators: leading, coincident, and lagging.

Leading Indicators

The Index of Leading Economic Indicators, officially called the *Composite Index of 11 Leading Indicators,* is the economic series that tends to predict future changes in economic activity. It was designed to reveal the direction of the economy in the next six to nine months. If the Index is consistently rising, even only slightly, the economy is chugging along and a setback is unlikely. If the indicator drops for three or more consecutive months, look for an economic slowdown and possibly a recession in the next year or so.

The eleven indicators in the Index are subject to revision. For example, petroleum and natural gas prices were found to distort the data for crude material prices and were dropped.

This series is the government's main barometer for forecasting business trends. Each of the series has shown a tendency to change before the economy makes a major turn—hence, the term "leading indicators." The Index is designed to forecast economic activity six to nine months ahead (1982 = 100). The indicators published monthly by the U.S. Department of Commerce are:

1. Average workweek of production workers in manufacturing. Employers find it a lot easier to increase the number of hours worked in a week than to hire more employees.

2. Initial claims for unemployment insurance. The number of people who sign up for unemployment benefits signals changes in present and future economic activity.

3. Change in consumer confidence. This is based on the University of Michigan's survey of consumer expectations. The index measures consumer optimism about the present and future state of the economy (1966=100). Note: Consumer spending buys two-thirds of

GDP (all goods and services produced in the economy), so any sharp change may be an important factor in an overall turnaround.

4. Percent change in prices of sensitive crude materials. Rises in prices of such critical materials as steel and iron usually mean factory demands are going up, which means factories plan to step up production.

5. Contracts and orders for plant and equipment. Heavier contracting and ordering usually lead to economic upswings.

6. Vendor performance. Vendor performance represents the percentage of companies reporting slower deliveries. As the economy grows, firms have more trouble filling orders.

7. Stock prices. A rise in the common stock index indicates expected profits and lower interest rates. Stock market advances usually precede business upturns by three to eight months.

8. Money supply. A rising money supply means easy money that sparks brisk economic activity. This usually leads recoveries by as much as 14 months.

9. New orders for manufacturers of consumer goods and materials. New orders mean more workers hired, more materials and supplies purchased, and increased output. Gains in this series usually lead recoveries by as much as four months.

10. Residential building permits for private housing. Gains in building permits signal business upturns.

11. Factory backlogs of unfilled durable goods orders. Backlogs signify business upswings.

The components of the Index are adjusted for inflation. Rarely do these components all go in the same direction at once. Each factor is weighted. The composite figure is designed to tell only in which direction business will go. It is not intended to forecast the magnitude of future ups and downs.

Coincident Indicators

Coincident indicators tend to move up and down in line with the aggregate economy and therefore are measures of current economic activity. They are intended to gauge current economic conditions. Examples are gross domestic product (GDP), employment, retail sales, and industrial production.

Lagging Indicators

Lagging indicators follow or trail behind aggregate economic activity. The government currently publishes six lagging indicators: unemployment rate, labor cost per unit, loans outstanding, average prime rate charged by banks, ratio of consumer installment credit outstanding to personal income, and ratio of manufacturing and trade inventories to sales. Figure 9.1 depicts these three types of economic indicators.

INPUT-OUTPUT ANALYSIS

Another indirect forecasting method is input-output analysis. This method of analysis is concerned with the inter-industry flows of goods or services in the economy or inter-departmental flow in a company.

Input-output analysis focuses on the sales of each industry to firms in that industry, other industries, and other sectors such as governmental units and foreign purchasers. The data are set forth in a matrix table that depicts each industry as a row and a column. Each industry's row indicates its sales to firms in that industry, to other industries, and to other sections of the economy, such as governmental units and foreign firms. Some tables set forth the dollar volume or percent of total sales of the industry to the other sectors. The table most applicable to business sales forecasting presents indexes representing expected increases in sales of the companies in the industries. The tables that have been prepared to date depict a large number of industries.

For illustrative purposes, Table 9.4 presents an abridged, hypothetical input-output table involving only four industries. The coefficients reflect the impact of a dollar increase in sales in each industry on the expected sales of the industries in row 1. For instance, a $1.00 increase in sales of paper and allied products (column 3) is expected to produce a $0.06 increase in sales of lumber and wood products. Thus, it indicates to firms in the lumber and wood products industry the impact of changes in sales in the paper and allied products industry. Similar conclusions can be drawn from data in the other rows.

Note: Forecasts are limited, however, to industrial products and to very large companies with broad product groupings.

Figure 9.1—LEADING, COINCIDENT, AND LAGGING INDICATORS

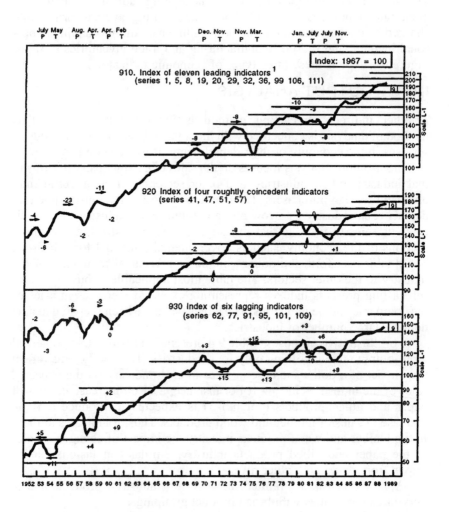

Source: Business Conditions Digest (U.S. Department of Commerce Bureau of Economic Analysis).

Table 9.4—INPUT-OUTPUT TABLE

	Lumber and Wood Products	Household Furniture	Paper and Allied Products	Plastics and Synthetic Materials
Lumber and wood products	1.00	0.08	0.06	0.001
Household furniture	0.002	1.00	0.001	0.002
Paper and allied products	0.04	0.002	1.00	0.001
Plastic and synthetic materials	0.003	0.008	0.02	1.00

MARKET SURVEY TECHNIQUES

Market survey techniques constitute another important forecasting tool, especially for short-term projections. Designing surveys that provide unbiased and reliable information is costly and difficult. Properly carried out, however, survey research can provide managers with valuable information that would be unobtainable otherwise.

Surveys generally involve the use of interviews or mailed questionnaires asking business firms, government agencies, and individuals about their future plans. Business firms plan and budget virtually all their expenditures in advance of actual purchases. Budgets can thus provide much useful information for forecasting. Government units also prepare formal budgets well before the actual spending is done, and surveys of budget material, congressional appropriations hearings, and the like can provide a wealth of information to the forecaster. Finally, even individual consumers usually plan expenditures for such major items as automobiles, furniture, housing, vacations, and education well ahead of the purchase date, so surveys of consumer intentions often accurately predict future spending on consumer goods.

While surveys provide an alternative to quantitative forecasting techniques (survey information may be all that is obtainable in certain forecasting situations, e.g., when a firm is attempting to project demand for a new product), they are frequently used to supplement rather than replace quantitative analysis. The value of survey techniques as a supplement to quantitative methods stems from two factors. First, surveys and other qualitative methods are especially well suited to picking up the non-quantifiable psychological element that is inherent in most economic behavior. Second, quantitative models generally assume stable consumer tastes; if these are actually changing, survey data may reveal such changes.

ECONOMETRIC FORECASTING

This approach uses a system of simultaneous equations (mainly through regression) to describe the operation of the economy—of a nation or the particular market within which a company operates—and the relationships among variables. The equations are then solved simultaneously to obtain a forecast for key variables such as GDP and consumer spending.

For example, assume that sales are a function of price, advertising, disposable income, and GDE. While variables such as disposable income and GDP are exogenous to (determined outside) the forecasting system, others are interdependent. For example, the advertising budget will affect the price of the product, since manufacturing and selling expenses influence the per-unit price. The price, in turn, is influenced by the number of sales which can also affect the level of advertising. All of this points to the interdependence of all variables in the system, which justifies a system of simultaneous equations, as follows:

1   Sales = r(price, advertising, disposable income, GDP)
2   Manufacturing costs = f(volume, technology)
3   Selling expenses = f(advertising, sales, and others)
4   Price = f(manufacturing costs, selling expenses)

As in regression analysis, the forecaster must (1) determine the functional form of each of the equations, (2) estimate the values of their coefficients, and (3) test for the statistical significance of the results and the validity of the assumptions.

Keep in mind that though econometric models are usually quite complex and expensive to construct, they can give very accurate forecasts.

CONCLUSION

This chapter has been concerned with forecasting based on consumer behavior—the Markov model—and with several popular indirect forecasting methods, those that begin with analysis of an aggregate economic variable, such as GDP, and produce industry or company sales as a component of that aggregate. In many cases, these forecasts are conducted by an outside source, such as a private consultant or a governmental agency. The forecaster then translates this forecast first into one for the industry and then into company sales forecasts.

CHAPTER 10
EVALUATION OF
FORECASTS

The cost of a prediction error can be substantial. The forecaster must always find ways to improve his forecasts. One way is to examine some objective evaluations of alternative forecasting techniques. This section presents guidelines for such evaluations. Two evaluation techniques are presented here. The first is in the form of a checklist. A forecaster could use it to evaluate either a new model being developed or an existing model. The second is a statistical technique for evaluating a model.

COST OF PREDICTION ERRORS

There is always a cost to failure to predict a certain variable accurately. It is important to determine the cost of the prediction error in order to minimize the potential detrimental effect on the future profitability of the company. The cost of a prediction error can be substantial, depending upon the circumstances. For example, failure to make an accurate projection on sales could result in poor production planning, too much or too little purchase of labor, and so on, eventually resulting in potentially huge financial losses.

The cost of a prediction error is basically the contribution or profit lost on an inaccurate prediction. It can be measured in terms of lost sales, disgruntled customers, and idle machines.

Example 10.1

Assume that a company has been selling a toy doll costing $0.60 for $1.00 each. Fixed costs $300. The company does not allow unsold dolls to be returned. It has predicted sales of 2,000 units. However, unforeseen competition has reduced sales to 1,500 units. The cost of its prediction error—that is, its failure to predict demand accurately—would be calculated as follows:

1. Initial predicted sales = 2,000 units.
   Optimal decision: purchase 2,000 units.
   Expected net income = $500 [(2,000 units x $.40 contribution) − $300 fixed costs]

2. Alternative parameter value =1,500 units.
   Optimal decision: purchase 1,500 units.
   Expected net income = $300 [(1,500 units x $.40 contribution) − $300 fixed costs]

3. Results of original decision under alternative parameter value:
   Expected net income = Revenue (1,500 units x $1.00) - Cost of Dolls (2,000 units x $.60) − $300 fixed costs = $1,500 − $1,200 − $300 = $0.

4. Cost of prediction error, (2) − (3), = $300.

CHECKLIST

Two main items to be checked are the data and the model with its accompanying assumptions. The questions to be raised are the following:

1. Is the source reliable and accurate?

2. If there is more than one source that is reliable and accurate, is the source used the best?

3. Are the data the most recent available?

4. If the answer to question 3 is yes, are the data subject to subsequent revision?

5. Is there any known systemic bias in the data that should be dealt with?

The model and its accompanying assumptions should be similarly examined. Among other things, the model has to make sense from a theoretical standpoint. The assumptions should be clearly stated and tested as well.

MEASURING THE ACCURACY OF FORECASTS

The performance of a forecast should be checked against its own record or against that of other forecasts. There are various statistical measures that can be used to measure performance of the model. Of course, performance is measured in terms of forecasting error, where error is defined as the difference between a predicted value and the actual result.

Error (e) = Actual (A) – Forecast (F)

MAD, MSE, RMSE, and MAPE

Popular measures for summarizing historical errors include the *mean absolute deviation* (MAD), the *mean squared error* (MSE), the *root mean squared error* (RMSE), and the *mean absolute percentage error* (MAPE). The formulas used to calculate MAD, MSE, and RMSE are:

$$\text{MAD} = \Sigma \,|e| \,/\, n$$

$$\text{MSE} = \Sigma \, e^2 \,/\, (n - 1)$$

$$\text{RMSE} = \sqrt{(\Sigma \, e^2/n\,)}$$

Sometimes it is more useful to compute forecasting errors in percentages rather than in amounts. The MAPE is calculated by finding the absolute error in each period, dividing it by the actual value for that period and then averaging these absolute percentage errors:

$$\text{MAPE} = \frac{\Sigma |e|/A}{n}$$

The following example illustrates the computation of MAD, MSE, and RMSE, and MAPE.

Example 10.2

Sales data of a microwave oven manufacturer are given in Table 10.1.

Table 10.1—CALCULATION OF ERRORS

Period	Actual(A)	Forecast(F)	e(A - F)	|e|	e²	Absolute Percent Error |e|/A
1	217	215	2	2	4	.0092
2	213	216	-3	3	9	.0014
3	216	215	1	1	1	.0046
4	210	214	-4	4	16	.0190
5	213	211	2	2	4	.0094
6	219	214	5	5	25	.0023
7	216	217	-1	1	1	.0046
8	212	216	-4	4	16	.0019
			-2	22	76	.0524

Using these figures,

MAD $\quad = \Sigma|e| /n = 22/8 = 2.75$

MSE $\quad = \Sigma\, e^2 / (n - 1) = 76/7 = 10.86$

RMSE $\quad = \sqrt{e^2 / n} = \sqrt{76/8} = \sqrt{9.5} = 3.08$

MAPE $\quad = \Sigma\, |e|/A / n = .0524/8 = .0066$

One way these measures are used is to evaluate the forecasting ability of alternative forecasting methods. For example, using either MAD or MSE, a forecaster could compare the results of exponential smoothing with alphas and elect the one that performed best, the one that produces the lowest MAD or MSE for a given set of data. Also, they can help select the best initial forecast value for exponential smoothing.

THE U STATISTIC AND TURNING POINT ERRORS

In measuring the accuracy of a forecast, two standards may be identified. First, one could compare the forecast being evaluated with a naive forecast to see if there are vast differences. The naive forecast can be perhaps the same as last year, a moving average, or the output of an exponential smoothing technique. Second, the forecast may be compared against the outcome when there is enough data to do so. The comparison may be actual versus forecast for a variable, or the change observed may be compared with the change forecast.

The Theil U Statistic is based on a comparison of the predicted change with the observed change. The calculation is:

$$U = \frac{(1/n) \sum (F - A)^2}{(1/n) \sum F^2 + (1/n) \sum A^2}$$

The smaller the value of U, the more accurate the forecast. Clearly, U=0 is a perfect forecast, since the forecast would equal actual and F - A = 0 for all observations. At the other extreme, U=1 would be a case of all forecasts being incorrect. If U is greater than or equal to 1, the predictive ability of the model is lower than a naive no-change extrapolation. (Many computer software packages routinely compute the U statistic.)

Still other evaluation techniques consider the number of *turning point* errors based on the total number of reversals of trends. The turning point error is also known as "error in the direction of prediction." In certain cases such as interest rate forecasts, the turning point error is more important than the accuracy of the forecast, i.e., the ability to anticipate reversals of interest rate trends is more important—perhaps substantially more important—than the precision of the actual forecast. Substantial gains or losses may arise from a move from generally upward moving rates to downward rate trends (or vice versa), while gains or losses from under- or over-estimating the extent of a continued increase or decrease in rates may be much more limited.

CONTROL OF FORECASTS

It is important to monitor forecast errors to insure that the forecast is performing well. If the model is performing poorly, the forecaster might either run the existing model again or switch to another forecasting model or technique. Forecasting can be controlled by comparing forecasting errors to predetermined values or limits. Errors that fall within the limits are judged acceptable while errors outside the limits signal that corrective action is desirable (see Figure 10.1).

Forecasts can be monitored using either tracking signals or control charts.

TRACKING SIGNALS

A tracking signal is based on the ratio of cumulative forecast error to the corresponding value of MAD:

Tracking signal = $\sum (A - F) / MAD$

Figure 10.1—MONITORING FORECAST ERRORS

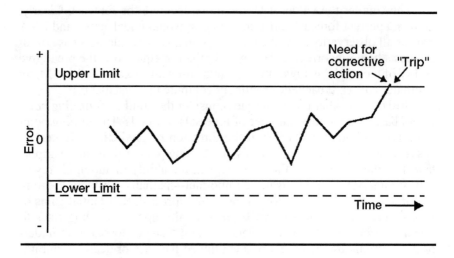

The resulting tracking signal values are compared to predetermined limits. These, which are based on experience and judgment, often range from plus or minus 3 to plus or minus 8. Values within the limits suggest that the forecast is performing adequately. When the signal goes beyond the range, corrective action is appropriate.

Example 10.3

Going back to Example 10.1, the deviation and cumulative deviation have already been computed:

$$MAD = \Sigma|A - F| / n = 22 / 8 = 2.75$$

$$\text{Tracking signal} = \Sigma(A - F) / MAD = -2 / 2.75 = -0.73$$

A tracking signal as low as -0.73 is well within the limit (-3 to -8). It would not suggest any action at this time. Note: After an initial value of

MAD has been computed, the estimate of the MAD can be continually updated using exponential smoothing:

$$MAD_t = \alpha\,(A - F) + (1 - \alpha)\,MAD_{t-1}$$

CONTROL CHARTS

The control chart approach involves setting upper and lower limits for individual forecasting errors rather than cumulating errors. The limits are multiples of the estimated standard deviation of forecast, S_f, which is the square root of MSE. Control limits are often set at 2 or 3 standard deviations.

$$\pm\,2(\text{or } 3)\,S_f$$

(*Note*: Plot the errors and see if all errors are within the limits, so that the forecaster can visualize the process and determine if the method being used is in control.)

Example 10.4

For the sales data in Table 10.2, using the naive forecast we will determine if the forecast is in control. For illustrative purposes, we will use two sigma control limits.

Table 10.2—ERROR CALCULATIONS

Year	Sales	Forecasts	Error	Error^2
1	320			
2	326	320	6	36
3	310	326	-16	256
4	317	310	7	49
5	315	317	-2	4
6	318	315	3	9
7	310	318	-8	64
8	316	310	6	36
9	314	316	-2	4
10	317	314	3	9
			-3	467

First, compute the standard deviation of forecast errors:

$$S_f = \sqrt{e^2 / (n-1)} = \sqrt{467/(9-1)} = 7.64$$

Two sigma limits are then plus or minus $2(7.64) = -15.28$ to $+15.28$.

Note that the forecast error for year 3 is below the lower bound, so the forecast is not in control (Figure 10.2). The use of other methods such as moving average, exponential smoothing, or regression would possibly achieve a better forecast.

It is important to develop a system for monitoring forecasts. Computers may be programmed to print a report showing the past history whenever the tracking signal "trips" a limit. For example, when exponential smoothing is used, the system may try a different value of α (so the forecast will be more responsive) to continue forecasting.

Figure 10.2—CONTROL CHART FOR FORECASTING ERRORS

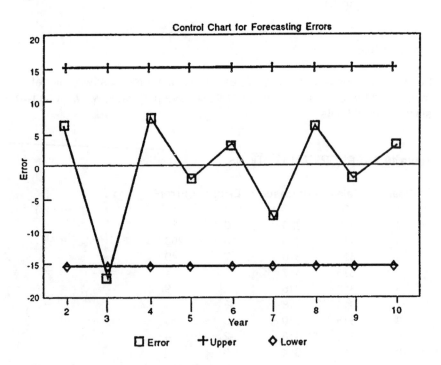

CONCLUSION

There is always a cost associated with failure to predict a certain variable accurately. Because all forecasts tend to be off the mark, it is important to provide a measure of accuracy for each forecast. Several measures of forecast accuracy and a measure of turning point error can be calculated.

These quite often are used to help managers evaluate the performance of a given method as well as choose among alternative forecasting techniques. Control of forecasts requires deciding whether a forecast is performing adequately, using either a control chart or a tracking signal. Selecting a forecasting method means choosing a technique that will serve its intended purpose at an acceptable level of cost and accuracy.

CHAPTER 11
WHAT ARE THE RIGHT
FORECASTING TOOLS
FOR YOU?

The life cycle of a typical new product has four major stages: introduction, growth, maturity, and saturation (decline). The proper choice of forecasting methodology depends on where the market is. Figure 11.1 shows the effects of product life cycle on forecasting methodologies. Table 11.1 summarizes the forecasting methods that have been discussed in this book, in the following sequence:

1. Description

2. Accuracy

3. Identification of turning point

4. Typical application

5. Data required

6. Cost

7. Time required to develop an application and make forecasts

Figure 11.1—PRODUCT LIFE CYCLE EFFECTS ON FORECASTING METHODOLOGY

Introduction

Data:	No data available; rely on qualitative methods.
Time:	Need long horizon.
Methods:	Qualitative (judgment), such as market surveys and Delphi.

Figure 11.1—PRODUCT LIFE CYCLE EFFECTS ON FORECASTING
METHODOLOGY, *con't.*

Growth
Data: Some data available for analysis.
Time: Still need long horizon; trends and cause-effect relationships
             important.
Methods: Market surveys still useful. Regression, time series, and growth
             models justified.

Maturity
Data: Considerable data available for analysis.
Time: More uses of short-term forecasts; still need long-term
             projections, but trends change only gradually.
Methods: Quantitative methods more useful. Time series helpful for
             trend, seasonal. Regression and exponential smoothing very useful.

Decline
Data: Abundant data.
Time: Short horizon.
Methods: Continue use of maturity methods as applicable. Judgment and
             market surveys may signal changes.

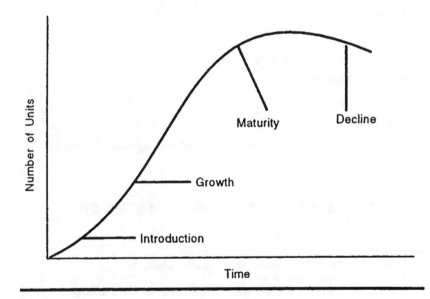

Table 11.1—SUMMARY OF COMMONLY USED FORECASTING METHODS
Qualitative (Judgmental) Techniques

Technique	Delphi Method	Expert Opinions
Description:	A panel of experts is interrogated by a sequence of questionnaires in which the responses to one questionnaire are used to produce the next questionnaire. Any information available to some experts and not to the others is thus passed on to the others, enabling all the experts to have access to all the information for forecasting.	Based on the assumption that several experts can arrive at a better forecast than can one person. There is no secrecy, and communication is encouraged. Forecasts are sometimes influenced by social factors and may not reflect a true consensus.
Accuracy:		
Short-term (0-3 mon):	Fair to very good	Poor to fair
Medium-term (3 mon-2 yr):	Fair to very good	Poor to fair
Long-term (2 yr and over):	Fair to very good	Poor
Identification of turning point:	Fair to good	Poor to fair
Typical application:	Forecasts of long-range and new product sales; technological forecasting.	Forecasts of long-range and new product sales; technological forecasting.
Date required:	A coordinator issues the sequence of questionnaires, editing and consolidating the responses.	Information from a panel of experts is presented openly in group meetings to arrive at a consensus forecast. Minimum is two sets of reports over time.
Cost of forecasting with a computer:	Expensive	Minimal
Time required to develop an application and make forecasts:	1 month	Two weeks

Table 11.1—SUMMARY OF COMMONLY USED FORECASTING METHODS, *con't.*
Qualitative (Judgmental) Techniques

Technique	PERT-Derived	Sales Force Polling	Consumer Surveys
Description:	Based on three esimates provided by experts: pessimistic, most likely, and optimistic.	Based on sales force opinions; tends to be too optimistic.	Based on market surveys regarding specific consumer purchases.
Accuracy:			
Short-term (0-3 mon):	Fair	Fair to good	Fair to good
Medium-term (3 mon-2yr):	Poor	Poor	Poor
Long-term (2yr and over):	Poor	Poor	Poor
Identification of turning point:	Poor to fair	Poor to good	Poor
Typical application:	Same as expert opinions.	Forecasts of short-term sales forecasts.	Forecasts of short-term sales forecasts.
Dates required:	Same as expert opinions.	Data by regional and product line breakdowns.	Telephone contacts, personal interviews or questionnaires.
Cost of forecasting with a computer:	Minimal	Minimal	Expensive
Time required to develop an application and make forecasts:	Two weeks	Two weeks	More than a month

Table 11.1—SUMMARY OF COMMONLY USED FORECASTING METHODS, *con't.*
Indirect Methods

Technique	Input-Output Model	Leading Indicator	Lifecycle Analysis
Description:	Concerned with the interindustry or interdepartmental flow of goods or services in the economy or a company and its markets. It shows what flow of inputs must occur to obtain outputs.	Time series of an economic activity whose movement in a given direction precedes the movement of some other time series in the same direction.	Analysis and forecasting new product growth rates based on S-curves.
Accuracy:			
Short-term (0-3 mon):	Not applicable	Poor to good	Poor
Medium-term (3 mon-2yr):	Good to very good	Poor to good	Poor to good
Long-term (2yr and over):	Good to very good	Very poor	Poor to good
Identification of turning point:	Fair	Good	Poor to good
Typical application:	Forecasts of company sales and division sales for industrial sectors and subsectors.	Forecasts of sales by product class.	Forecasts of new product sales.
Data application:	Ten or fifteen years' history. Considerable amounts of information on product and service flows within a corporation (or economy) for each year for which an input-output analysis is desired.	The same as an intention-to-buy survey plus 5 to 10 years' history.	As a minimum, the annual sales of the product being considered or a similar product are sometimes necessary.
Cost of forecasting with a computer:	Expensive	Varies with application	Varies with application
Time required to develop an application and make forecasts:	More than a month	One month	One month

Table 11.1—SUMMARY OF COMMONLY USED FORECASTING METHODS, *con't.*
Quantitative Methods

Technique *Description:*	Regression Analysis Functionally relates sales to other economic, competitive, or internal variables and estimates an equation using the least-squares technique.	Econometric Model A system of interdependent regression equations that describes some sector of economic sales or profit activity. The parameters of the regression equations are usually estimated simultaneously.	Markov Analysis Models based on learned behavior: Consumers tend to repeat their past brand loyalty.
Accuracy:			
Short-term (0-3 mon):	Good to very good	Good to very good	Excellent
Medium-term (3 mon-2yr):	Good to very good	Very good to excellent	Poor
Long-term (2yr and over):	Poor	Good	Poor
Identification of turning point:	Good	Excellent	Good
Typical application:	Forecasts of sales by product classes, forecasts of earnings, and other financial data.	Forecasts of sales by product classes, forecasts or earnings.	Forecasts of sales and cash collections.
Data required:	At least 30 observations are recommended for acceptable results.	The same as for regression.	Data required for transaction probabilities.
Cost of forecasting with a computer:	Varies with application	Expensive	Expensive
Time required to develop an application and make forecasts:	Depends on ability to identify relationships	More than a month	More than a month

Table 11.1—SUMMARY OF COMMONLY USED FORECASTING METHODS, *con't.*
Time Series Methods

Technique	Moving Average	Exponential Smoothing	Trend Analysis
Description:	Averages are updated as the latest information is received; weighted average of a number of consecutive points of the series.	Similar to moving average, except that more recent data points are given more weight. Effective when there is random demand and no seasonal fluctuation in the data series.	Fits a trend line to time-series data. There are two variations, linear and nonlinear.
Accuracy:			
Short-term (0-3 mon):	Poor to good	Fair to very good	Very good
Medium-term (3 mon-2yr):	Poor	Poor to good	Good
Long-term (2yr and over):	Very poor	Very poor	Good
Identification of turning point:	Poor	Poor	Poor
Typical application:	Inventory control for low-volume items and sales with no data.	Production and inventory control, forecasts of sales, and financial data.	New product forecasts and products in the growth and maturity stages of the life cycle; inventory control.
Data required:	A minimum of two years of sales history if seasonals are present; otherwise, fewer data. (Of course, the more history the better.) The moving average must be specific.	The same as for a moving average.	Varies with the technique used. However, a good rule of thumb is to use a minimum of five years' annual data to start and, thereafter, the complete history.
Cost of forecasting with a computer:	Very minimal	Minimal	Varies with application
Time required to develop an application and make forecasts:	One day	One day	One day

Table 11.1—SUMMARY OF COMMONLY USED FORECASTING METHODS, *con't.*
Time Series Methods

Technique	Classical Decomposition	Box-Jenkins
Description:	Decomposes a time series into seasonals, trend cycles, and irregular elements. Primarily used for detailed time-series analysis (including estimating seasonals).	Iterative procedure that produces an autoregressive, integrated moving average model, adjusts for seasonal and trend factors, estimates appropriate weighting parameters, tests the model, and repeats the cycle as appropriate.
Accuracy:		
Short-term (0-3 mon):	Very good to excellent	Very good to excellent
Medium-term (3 mon-2yr):	Good	Poor to good
Long-term (2yr and over):	Very poor	Very poor
Identification of turning point:	Very good	Fair
Typical application:	Tracking and warning, forecasts of sales and financial data.	Production and inventory control for large volume items, forecasts of cash balances and earnings.
Data required:	A minimum of three years' history to start; thereafter, the complete history.	Production and inventory control for large volume items, forecasts of cash balances and earnings.
Cost of forecasting with a computer:	Minimal	Expensive
Time required to develop an application and make forecasts:	One day	Two days

Source: Heavily adapted from John Chambers, S. Mullick, and D. Smith, *"How to Choose the Right Forecasting Technique."* Harvard Business Review. Vol. 49, no. 4, July-August 1971.

In an effort to help forecasters choose the right methodology, Figure 11.2 ranks forecasting methodologies by:

1. Accuracy: Why do you need the forecast?
2. Cost: How much money is involved?
3. Timing: When will the forecast be used?
4. Form: Who will use the forecast?
5. Data: What data are available?

Figure 11.2—FORECASTING DECISION MATRIX

Techniques	Accuracy: Why Do You Need the Forecast?	Rankings
Qualitative or Judgmental	High Accuracy ↕ Low Accuracy	Delphi Market Surveys Consensus Opinion Sales Force Polling Expert Opinion
Time Series	High Accuracy ↕ Low Accuracy	Box-Jenkins Classical Decomposition Exponential Smoothing Moving Average Trend Analysis
Causal, Markov and Indirect	High Accuracy ↕ Low Accuracy	Input-Output Analysis Econometric Leading Indicator Regression Surveys Life Cycle Analysis

Techniques	Cost: How Much Money Is Involved?	Rankings
Qualitative or Judgmental	Low Cost ↕ High Cost	Expert Opinion Sales Force Polling Market Surveys
Time Series	Low Cost ↕ High Cost	Trend Analysis Moving Average Exponential Smoothing Classical Decomposition Box-Jenkins
Causal, Markov and Indirect	Low Cost ↕ High Cost	Regression Leading Indicator Life Cycle Analysis Econometric Input-Output Analysis

Figure 11.2—FORECASTING DECISION MATRIX, *con't.*

Techniques	Timing: When Will the Forecast Be Used?	Rankings
Qualitative or Judgmental	Short Lead Time ↕ Long Lead Time	Expert Opinion Consensus Opinion Sales Force Polling Market Surveys Delphi
Time Series	Short Lead Time ↕ Long Lead Time	Trend Analysis Moving Average Exponential Smoothing Classical Decomposition Box-Jenkins
Causal, Markov, and Indirect	Short Lead Time ↕ Long Lead Time	Markov Regression Leading Indicator Life Cycle Analysis Surveys Econometric Input-Output Analysis

Techniques	Form: Who Will Use the Forecast?	Rankings
Qualitative or Judgmental	Precise Forecast ↕ Imprecise Forecast	Market Surveys Expert Opinion Sales Force Polling Delphi
Time Series	Precise Forecast ✕ Imprecise Forecast	All Similar, Giving Precise Forecasts
Causal, Markov, and Indirect	Precise Forecast ✕ Imprecise Forecast	All Similar, Giving Precise Forecasts

Techniques	Data: What Data Are Available?	Rankings
Qualitative or Judgmental	Considerable Data Required ↕ Little Data Required	Generally All Similar, Little Historical Data Needed
Time Series	Considerable Data Required ↕ Little Data Required	All Similar, At Least Two Years' Data Usually Required

Figure 11.2—FORECASTING DECISION MATRIX, *con't.*

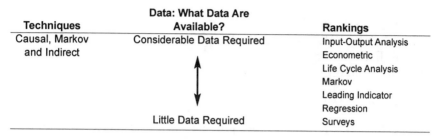

Techniques	Data: What Data Are Available?	Rankings
Causal, Markov and Indirect	Considerable Data Required	Input-Output Analysis
		Econometric
		Life Cycle Analysis
		Markov
		Leading Indicator
		Regression
	Little Data Required	Surveys

FORECASTING AND STATISTICAL SOFTWARE

There are numerous computer software programs that are used for forecasting purposes, including both specialized forecasting software and general purpose statistical software. Some programs are stand-alone; others are spreadsheet add-ins. Still others are templates. Some of the more popular programs are:

Forecast Pro

Forecast Pro, a stand-alone forecasting software program, uses artificial intelligence. A built-in expert system first examines your data, then guides you to state-of-the-art forecasting techniques (exponential smoothing, Box-Jenkins, dynamic regression, Croston's model, event models, and multiple level models)—whichever method suits the data best.

Business Forecast Systems, Inc.
68 Leonard St.
Belmont, MA 02178
617/484-5050, 617/484-9219 (fax)
http://ourworld.compuserve.com/homepages/ForecastPro

Easy Forecaster Plus I and II

Easy Forecaster Plus I and II are stand-alone forecasting programs developed by the Institute of Business Forecasting. The models they incorporate include naive, moving averages, exponential smoothing (single, double, and Holt's), linear trend line, and multiple regression. The program selects the optimal model automatically and prepares monthly/quarterly forecasts using seasonal indices.

Institute of Business Forecasting
P.O. Box 670159, Station C
Flushing, NY 11367-9086
718/463-3914, 718/544-9086 (fax)
E-mail: IBF@ibf.org
http://www.ibf.org

LifeCast Pro

LifeCast Pro is a new stand-alone product that allows quick integration of different marketing assumptions, prices, market research, competitive intelligence, historical similarities, and expert judgment, all within a graphically based product life cycle framework. Using *LifeCast Pro* will help you "sell" your forecasts as believable because it merges statistical diffusion theory with your own assumptions in a way that is easy to explain to management. Features include:

- Data availability options (high/medium/ or none)
- Incorporation of price scenarios and elasticities
- Jackknife stability analysis
- Automatic search for best saturation
- Search area analysis and precision estimates
- Life cycle analysis for mature products
- Statistical forecasting equations
- Ease of use

LifeCast Pro
6516 Wedgewood Way
Tucker, GA 30084
E-mail: huntertec@mindspring.com
http://www.mindspring.com/~jimstrick/hunter.htm

Sales & Market Forecasting Toolkit

Sales & Market Forecasting Toolkit is a spreadsheet template that produces sales and market forecasts even for new products with limited historical data. It has eight powerful methods for more accurate forecasts, and offers spreadsheet models, complete with graph, ready-to-use with your numbers. The Toolkit offers a variety of forecasting methods to help you generate accurate business forecasts even in new or changing markets with limited historical data, including customer polling, whole market penetration, chain method, strategic modeling, and moving averages, exponential smoothing, and linear regressions.

Built-in macros allow you to enter data into your forecast automatically. For example, enter values for the first and last months of a 12-month forecast. The compounded-growth-rate macro will automatically compute and enter values for the other ten months.

Lotus Selects
P.O. Box 9172
Cambridge, MA 02139-9946
800/635-6887
617/693-3981

Forecast! GFX

Forecast! GFX is a stand-alone system that can perform five time-series analyses: seasonal adjustment, linear and nonlinear trend analysis, moving-average analysis, exponential smoothing, and decomposition. Trend analysis supports linear, exponential, hyperbolic, S-curve, and polynomial trends. Hyperbolic trend models are used to analyze data that indicate a decline toward a limit, such as the output of an oil well or the price of a particular model of personal computer. *Forecast! GFX* can perform multiple-regression analysis with up to ten independent variables.

Intex Solutions
35 Highland Cir.
Needham, MA 01294
617/449-6222
617/444-2318 (fax)

ForeCalc

ForeCalc, a spreadsheet add-in, features nine forecasting techniques and includes both automatic and manual modes, eliminating the need to export or re-enter data. In automatic mode, when you highlight the historical data in your spreadsheet, such as sales, expenses, or net income, *ForeCalc* tests several exponential-smoothing models and picks the one that best fits the data.

Forecast results can be transferred to your spreadsheet with upper and lower confidence limits. *ForeCalc* generates a line graph showing the original data, the forecasted values, and confidence limits.

ForeCalc can automatically choose the most accurate forecasting technique from simple one-parameter smoothing, Holt's two-parameter smoothing, Winters' three-parameter smoothing, trendless seasonal models, and dampened versions of Holt and Winters' smoothing.

The manual mode lets you select the type of trend and seasonality, yielding nine possible model combinations. You can vary the type of trend (constant, linear, or dampened), as well as the seasonality (non-seasonal, additive, or multiplicative).

Business Forecast Systems, Inc.
68 Leonard St.
Belmont, MA 02178
617/484-5050

StatPlan IV

StatPlan IV is a stand-alone program for those who understand how to apply statistics to business analysis. You can use it for market analysis, trend forecasting, and statistical modeling. *StatPlan IV* lets you analyze data by range, mean, median, standard deviation, skewness, kurtosis, correlation analysis, one- or two-way analysis of variance (ANOVA), cross tabulations, and t-test. Its forecasting methods include multiple regression, stepwise multiple regression, polynomial regression, bivariate curve fitting, auto-correlation analysis, trend and cycle analysis, and exponential smoothing.

The data can be displayed in X-Y plots, histograms, time-series graphs, auto-correlation plots, actual vs. forecast plots, or frequency and percentile tables.

Lotus Selects
P.O. Box 9172
Cambridge, MA 02139-9946
800/635-6887
617/693-3981

Geneva Statistical Forecasting

Geneva Statistical Forecasting, a stand-alone program, can batch-process forecasts for thousands of data series, if the series are all measured in the same time units (days, weeks, months, and so on). The software automatically tries out as many as nine different forecasting methods, including six linear and nonlinear regressions and three exponential-smoothing techniques, in order to pick the one that best fits your historical data. *Geneva Statistical Forecasting* tries as many as nine forecasting methods for each line item.

The program incorporates provisions that simplify and accelerate the process of re-forecasting data items. Once you complete the initial forecast, you can save a data file which records the forecasting method assigned to each line item. When it is time to update the data, simply retrieve the file and reforecast, using the same methods as before.

Pizzano & Co.
800 W. Cummings Park
Woburn, MA 01801
617/935-7122

SmartForecasts

SmartForecasts, a stand-alone forecasting program, automatically chooses the right statistical method; and lets you manually adjust forecasts to reflect your business judgment before producing forecast results.

SmartForecasts combines the benefits of statistical and judgmental forecasting. It can determine which statistical method will give you the most accurate forecast, and handle all the math. Forecasts can be modified using the program's EYEBALL utility if, for instance, you need to adjust a sales forecast to reflect an anticipated increase in advertising or a decrease in price. *SmartForecasts* summarizes data with descriptive statistics, plots the distribution of data values with histograms, plots variables in a scattergram, and identifies leading indicators.

You can forecast using single- and double-exponential smoothing, and simple- and linear-moving averages. It can build seasonality into your forecasts using Winters' exponential smoothing, or you can eliminate seasonality by using times series decomposition and seasonal adjustment.

SmartForecasts also features simultaneous multiseries forecasting of up to 60 variables and 150 data points per variable and offers multivariate regression to let you relate business variables.

Smart Software, Inc.
4 Hill Rd.
Belmont, MA 02178
800/762-7899
617/489-2748 (fax)

Tomorrow

Tomorrow, a stand-alone forecasting program, uses an optimized combination of linear regression, single exponential smoothing, adaptive rate response single exponential smoothing, Brown's one-parameter double exponential smoothing, Holt's two-parameter exponential smoothing, Brown's one-parameter triple exponential smoothing, and Gardner's three-parameter damped trend.

There's no need to reformat your existing spreadsheets. *Tomorrow* recognizes and forecasts formula cells (totals and subtotals, for example). It handles both horizontally and vertically oriented spreadsheets. It accepts historical data in up to thirty separate ranges. It also:

- Allows you to specify seasonality manually or calculates seasonality automatically.

- Allows you to do several forecasts of different time series (for example, sales data from   different regions) at once.

- Recognizes and forecasts time series headings (names of months, etc.).

- At your option, makes forecasts a normal part of your spreadsheet.

- Allows you to look at any part of the spreadsheet (including the forecast) without leaving *Tomorrow.*

- Checks for and prevents accidental overlaying of nonempty or protected cells.

- With an optional annotation mode, labels forecast cells, calculates MAPE, and, when seasonality is automatically determined, describes the seasonality.

Isogon Corp.
330 Seventh Ave.
New York, NY 10001
212/967-2424

MicroTSP

MicroTSP is stand-alone software that provides the tools used most often in practical econometric and forecasting work. It covers descriptive statistics and a wide range of single equation estimation techniques including ordinary least squares (multiple regression), two-stage least squares, nonlinear least squares, and probit and logit.

Its forecasting tools include exponential smoothing including single exponential, double exponential, and Winters' smoothing, and Box-Jenkins methodology.

Quantitative Micro Software
4521 Campus Dr., Suite 336
Irvine, CA 92715
949/856-3368

SIBYL/RUNNER

Sibyl/Runner is an interactive, stand-alone forecasting system. In addition to allowing usage of all major forecasting methods, the package permits analysis of the data, suggests available forecasting methods, compares results, and provides several accuracy measures in a way that makes it easier for the user to select an appropriate method and forecast needed data under different economic and environmental conditions. (For details, see S. Makridakis, Hodgsdon, and S. Wheelwright, "An Interactive Forecasting System," *American Statistician*, November 1974.)

Applied Decision Systems
Lexington, MA 02173
617/424-9820

Forecast Plus

Forecast Plus, stand-alone forecasting software, uses artificial intelligence. A built-in expert system examines your data, then guides you to 13 forecasting methods including exponential smoothing, Box-Jenkins, or regression—whichever method suits the data best.
The software features:

- A simple menu system
- High resolution graphic capability
- Ability to choose an appropriate forecasting technique
- Ability to handle all phases of forecasting analysis
- Optimization of smoothing constants

StatPac, Inc.
3814 Lyndale Ave., South
Minneapolis, MN 55409
612/822-8252

OTHER FORECASTING SOFTWARE

There are many other forecasting software programs, among them:

Autocast II and 4 Cast

Delphus, Inc.
103 Washington St. #348
Morristown, NJ 07960
201/267-9269

Trendsetter Expert Version

Concentric Data Systems
110 Turnpike Rd.
Westborough, MA 01581
800/325-9035

GENERAL PURPOSE STATISTICAL SOFTWARE

There are numerous widely used statistical software programs that can be used in order to build a forecasting model. Some of the more popular ones include:

1. *SPSS*

2. *Minitab*
   Minitab, Inc.
   3081 Enterprise Dr.
   State College, PA 16801-3008
   814/231-2682
   http://www.minitab.com

3. *MathSoft's S-Plus*
   MathSoft Inc.
   1700 Westlake Ave., Suite 500
   Seattle, WA 98109
   800/569-0123
   206/283-8802
   http://www.mathsoft.com/splus

For example, the *Minitab* statistical program, *Release 11 for Windows*, includes numerous forecasting tools such as: (a) time series methods (trend analysis, decomposition, moving average, single and double smoothing, Winters' Method, and ARIMA), and (b) regression analysis.

WHAT IS THE RIGHT PACKAGE FOR YOU?

Since different software packages choose different techniques for many of the same tasks, it is a good idea to select a package that explains which method it is using and why, so you can learn the most appropriate technique for your specific forecasting task. Figure 11.3 spells out your options in choosing the right package.

Figure 11.3—WHICH FORECASTING SOFTWARE IS RIGHT FOR YOU? SOME OPTIONS

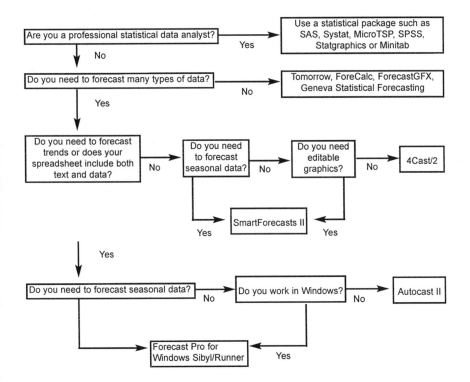

CONCLUSION

Today's managers have some powerful tools at hand to simplify the forecasting process and increase its accuracy. The automated versions of forecasting models should be considered by any manager who is regularly
called upon to provide forecasts. A personal computer with a spreadsheet
is a good beginning, but the stand-alone packages currently available provide the most accurate forecasts and are the easiest to use. In addition,
they can automatically select the best of several forecasting models for a
particular data set.

PART III
APPLICATIONS

CHAPTER 12
FINANCIAL AND
EARNINGS
FORECASTING

Financial forecasting, an essential element of planning, is the basis for budgeting activities. It is also needed when estimating future financing requirements.

The company may look either internally or externally for financing. Internal financing refers to cash flow generated by the company's normal operating activities. External financing refers to capital provided by parties external to the company. Forecasts of future sales and related expenses provide the firm with the information to project future external financing needs. The Chapter discusses (1) the *percent-of-sales method* to determine the amount of external financing needed, (2) the CPA's involvement in prospective financial statements, and (3) earnings forecast.

THE PERCENT-OF-SALES METHOD

Percentage of sales is the most widely used method for projecting a company's financing needs. This method involves estimating expenses, assets, and liabilities for a future period as a percent of the sales forecast and then using these percentages, together with the projected sales, to construct pro forma balance sheets.

The basic steps in projecting financing needs are:

1. Project the firm's sales. The sales forecast is the initial, most important step. Most other forecasts (budgets) follow the sales forecast.

2. Project additional variables such as expenses.

3. Estimate the investment in current and fixed assets necessary to support the projected sales.

4. Calculate the firm's financing needs.

The following example illustrates how to develop a pro forma balance sheet and determine the amount of external financing needed.

Example 12.1

Assume that sales for 20x0 = $20, projected sales for 20x1 = $24, net income = 5% of sales, and the dividend payout ratio = 40%. Figure 12.1 illustrates the method, step by step. All dollar amounts are in millions.

Figure 12.1—PRO FORMA BALANCE SHEET (in Millions of Dollars)

	Present (20x0)	% of Sales (20x0 Sales = $20)	Projected (20x1 Sales = $24)
ASSETS			
Current assets	2	10	2.4
Fixed assets	4	20	4.8
Total assets	6		7.2
LIABILITIES AND STOCKHOLDERS' EQUITY			
Current liabilities	2.0	10	2.4
Long-term debt	2.5	n.a.	2.5
Total liabilities	4.5		4.9
Common stock	0.1	n.a.	0.1
Paid-in capital	0.2	n.a.	0.2
Retained earnings	1.2		1.92[a]
Total equity	1.5		2.22
Total liabilities and Stockholders' equity	6.0		7.12 Total internal financing
			0.08[b] Total external financing
			7.20 Total financing

[a] 20 x 2 retained earnings = 20.1 retained earnings + projected net income – cash dividends paid
= $ 1.2 + 5%($24) - 40% [5%($24)]
= $1.2 + $1.2 - $0.48 = $2.4 - $$0.48 = $1.92

[b] External financing needed = projected total assets – (projected total liabilities + projected equity)
= $7.2 - ($4.9 + $2.22) = $7.2 - $7.12 = $0.08

The steps for the computations are:

Step 1.
Express those balance sheet items that vary directly with sales as a percentage of sales. Any item such as long-term debt that does not vary directly with sales is designated n.a., or not applicable.

Step 2.
Multiply these percentages by the 20x1 projected sales = $24 to obtain the projected amounts as shown in the last column.

Step 3.
Insert figures for long-term debt, common stock and paid-in-capital from the 20x0 balance sheet.

Step 4.
Compute 20x1 retained earnings as shown in (b).

Step 5.
Sum the asset accounts, obtaining total projected assets of $7.2 million, and also add the projected liabilities and equity to obtain $7.12 million, the total financing provided. Since liabilities and equity must total $7.20 million, but only $7.12 million is projected, we have a shortfall of $0.08 million, which is the external financing needed.

Although the additional funds required can be forecast by setting up pro forma balance sheets, it is often easier to use the following formula:

External funds needed (EFN)	=	Required increase in assets	-	Spontaneous increase in liabilities	-	Increase in retained earnings

$$\text{EFN} = (A/S)\,\Delta S - (L/S)\,\Delta S - (PM)(PS)(1\text{-}d)$$

where A/S = Assets that increase automatically as a percentage of increases in sales
      L/S = Liabilities that similarly increase automatically as a percentage of sales
      ΔS = Change in sales
      PM = Profit margin on sales
      PS = Projected sales
      d = Dividend payout ratio

Example 12.2

In Example 12.1,

A/S	=	$6/$20	=	30%
L/S	=	$2/$20	=	10%
ΔS	=	($24 - $20)	=	$4
PM	=	5% on sales		
PS	=	$24		
d	=	40%		

Plugging these figures into the formula yields:

$$EFN = 0.3(\$4) - 0.1(\$4) - (0.05)(\$24)(1 - 0.4)$$
$$= \$1.2 - \$0.4 - \$0.72 = \$0.08$$

Thus, the amount of external financing needed is $800,000, which can be raised by issuing notes payable, bonds, stocks, or any combination of these financing sources.

The major advantage of the percent-of-sales method of financial forecasting is that it is simple and inexpensive to use. One important assumption behind the method is that the firm is operating at full capacity. This means that the company does not have sufficient productive capacity to absorb a projected increase in sales and thus requires additional investment in assets. The method must be used with extreme caution if there is excess capacity in certain asset accounts.

To obtain a more precise projection of the firm's future financing needs, however, it may be necessary to prepare a cash budget.

THE CERTIFIED PUBLIC ACCOUNTANT'S ROLE

The American Institute of Certified Public Accountants (AICPA) in *Statement of Position 45-4* provides guidelines for business enterprises that publish financial forecasts. Improved financial forecasting should be of concern to the AICPA and the Securities and Exchange Commission (SEC) in terms of financial decision-making, security analysis, and in affecting the future market value of securities through investor expectations. Figure 12.2 presents an excerpt from the 1983 Annual Report of Masco Corporation that contains (1) a five-year cash flow forecast, (2) five-year forecasts for growth in sales, and (3) key assumptions used in the forecasts.

Figure 12.2—MANAGEMENT FORECAST DISCLOSURE BY MASCO CORPORATION

FIVE-YEAR FORECAST

We have included in this annual report a sales forecast for each of our major product lines and operating groups for 1988.

While we recognize that long-term forecasts are subject to many variables and uncertainties, our experience has been that our success is determined more by our own activities than by the performance of any industry or the economy in general. In addition, the balance and diversity of our products and markets have been such that a shortfall in expected performance in one area has been largely offset by higher than anticipated growth in another.

Although variations may occur in the forecast for any individual product line, we have a relatively high level of confidence that our overall five-year growth forecast is achievable.

ASSUMPTIONS USED IN FORECAST

1. Average 2-3 percent annual real growth in GNP.
2. Average inflation 5-7 percent.
3. Present tax structure to continue.
4. No change in currency exchange rates.
5. No acquisitions.
6. No additional financing.
7. Dividend payout ratio 20 percent.
8. Four percent after-tax return on investment of excess cash.
9. No exercise of stock options.

FIVE-YEAR CASH FLOW FORECAST

(In Thousands)	1984-1988
Net Income	$ 850,000
Depreciation	280,000
	1,130,000
Working Capital	(230,000)
Note Payments	(280,000)
Capital Expenditures	(260,000)
Dividends	(170,000)
Net Cash Change	190,000
Beginning Cash, 1-1-84	210,000
Cash, 12-31-88	$ 400,000

SALES GROWTH BY PRODUCTS

(In Thousands)

	Sales Forecast		Actual Sales		
	5-Year Growth Rate 1984-1988	1988	5-Year Growth Rate 1979-1983	1983	1978
Products for the Home and Family	14%	$1,225,000	16%	$ 638,000	$308,000
Products for Industry	16%	875,000	9%	421,000	278,000
Total Sales	15%	$2,100,000	13%	$1,059,000	$586,000

SALES GROWTH BY SPECIFIC MARKETS AND PRODUCTS[1][2]

(In Thousands)

	Forecast		Actual		
	5-Year Growth Rate 1984-1988	1988	5-Year Growth Rate 1979-1983	1983	1978
Masco Faucet Sales [3]	15%	$490,000	9%	$243,000	$155,000
Faucet Industry Sales-Units	7%	35,000	(5)%	25,000	32,000
Masco Market Share-Units	2%	38%	5%	34%	27%
Housing Completions	4%	1,700	(4)%	1,400	1,700
Independent Cold Extrusion Industry Sales	13%	$580,000	1%	$310,000	$290,000
Masco Cold Extrusion Sales [3]	14%	$170,000	5%	$ 88,000	$ 70,000
Truck Production	7%	3,400	(8)%	2,400	3,700
Auto Production	4%	8,200	(6)%	6,800	9,200
Masco Auto Parts Sales	13%	$210,000	8%	$113,000	$ 76,000

(1) Excludes foreign sales.   (2) Industry data Masco estimates.   (3) Includes foreign sales.

Source: 1983 Annual Report of Masco Corporation.

There are two kinds of prospective financial statements, forecasts and projections.

A *financial forecast* presents management's expectations, including the expectation that all assumptions will take place. Though it reflects what management expects to occur, its assumptions are not necessarily the most probable. A financial forecast may be most useful to general users, since it presents the client's expectations; it is thus most appropriate to passive users, those not negotiating directly with the client.

A financial forecast may give a single monetary amount based on the best estimate, or it may give a reasonable range. Caution: This range must not be chosen in a misleading manner.

Although an accountant is involved, sole responsibility for the presentation is management's, because only management knows how it plans to run the business and accomplish its plans.

A *financial projection* presents a "what-if" scenario, one that management does not necessarily expect to occur, although a given assumption may actually occur if management moves in that direction. A financial projection may be most beneficial for limited users seeking answers to hypothetical questions based on varying assumptions. These users may wish to alter scenarios based on anticipated changing situations. A financial projection, like a forecast, may contain a range.

A financial projection may be presented to general users only when it supplements a financial forecast. Financial projections are not permitted in tax shelter offerings and other general-use documents.

FUNCTIONS OF THE CPA

CPAs can perform three functions with respect to prospective financial statements that will be relied upon by third parties: examination, compilation, and application of agreed procedures. CPAs must prepare prospective financial statements according to AICPA standards (see below).

Prospective financial statements may be for general or limited use. General use is for those not directly dealing with the client. The general user may take the deal or leave it. Limited use is for those having a direct relationship with the client.

Both forecasts and projections may be presented as a complete set of financial statements (balance sheet, income statement, and statement of cash flows). However, it is usually more practical to present them in summarized or condensed form. At a minimum, the financial statement items to be presented are:

- Sales
- Gross margin
- Nonrecurring items
- Taxes
- Income from continuing operations
- Income from discontinued operations
- Net income
- Primary and fully diluted earnings per share
- Material changes in financial position

Not considered prospective financial statements are pro-forma financial statements and partial presentations.

The AICPA's Code of Professional Ethics says members preparing prospective financial statements:

- Cannot vouch for the achievability of prospective results.
- Must disclose assumptions.
- Must report/state the nature of the work performed and the degree of responsibility assumed.

CPAs are not permitted to furnish services on prospective financial statements if the statements are appropriate only for limited use but are distributed to parties not involved directly with the issuing company.

TYPES OF ENGAGEMENTS

CPAs may perform five types of engagements in connection with prospective financial statements:

Plain paper

The CPA's name is not associated with the prospective statements. This service can only be conducted if all of the following conditions are satisfied:

- The CPA is not reporting on the presentation.
- The prospective statements are on paper not identifying the accountant.

- The prospective financial statements are not shown with historical financial statements that have been audited, reviewed, or compiled by the CPA.
- Plain paper services are not allowed on prospective financial statements for third-party use.

Internal use

The prospective financial statements are simply assembled, meaning mathematical and clerical functions are performed. Assembling financial data is permitted if:

- Third parties will not use the statements, and
- The CPA's name is associated with the statement.

Note that assembling prospective financial statements is for internal use only, and the statements should be so marked.

Compilation

This is the lowest level of service performed for prospective financial statements directed to third parties. The compilation engagement involves:

- Assembling prospective data.
- Using procedures to ascertain whether the presentation and assumptions are appropriate.
- Preparing a compilation report.

With a compilation, no assurance is given regarding the presentation or assumptions; it serves mainly to identify obvious matters for further investigation. Working papers have to be prepared to show there was proper planning and supervision of the work, as well as compliance with required compilation procedures. The CPA must also obtain a management letter from the client regarding representations given to him.

Warning: A compilation should not be made when the forecasted financial statements do not disclose significant assumptions or when the financial projections exclude the hypothetical assumptions.

Agreed-upon procedures

Here the CPA applies procedures agreed to or requested by specific users and issues a report. The report identifies the procedures used, gives the accountant's findings, and restricts distribution of the report to particular parties. The specified users must participate in establishing the procedures. Also, the procedures must be more than a simple reading of the prospective data.

Examination

The CPA appraises the preparation underlying the supporting assumptions and the presentation of prospective financial information in accordance with AICPA standards. A report is then issued on whether AICPA guidelines have been adhered to and whether the assumptions are reasonable. Examination is the highest level of assurance. An adverse opinion must be given if there is a failure to disclose a material assumption or if disclosed assumptions are unreasonable. For example, there may not be a reasonable expectation that the actual figure will fall within the range of assumptions presented in a forecast having a range. A disclaimer opinion is necessary if the scope of the examination is limited, such as when a required examination procedure cannot be performed because of client restrictions or inappropriate circumstances.

EARNINGS FORECASTS

For many years financial analysts have predicted earnings per share and stock price performance. Such forecasts are given consideration emphasis in providing guidance to investors. Recently, management disclosures in financial statements have placed greater emphasis on the development of forecasting methodology in this area. The accuracy of these earnings forecasts has been given much attention recently, primarily because of the SEC's position on financial forecasts and the AICPA's issuance of a Statement of Position.

SECURITY ANALYSTS VERSUS TIME-SERIES MODELS

Forecasts of earnings per share (EPS) for business firms are published by both management and security analysts. Unfortunately, however, the accuracy of EPS forecasts by security analysts has been shown to be little better than that produced by naive models such as extrapolating the past trend of earnings (see Chapter 6). Indeed, it increasingly appears that the change in EPS may be a random variable.

Examples of EPS forecast sources by independent security analysts include (1) Value Line Investment Survey, (2) Lynch, Jones and Ryan's Institutional Brokers Estimate System (IBES), (3) Standard & Poor's Earnings Forecaster, and (4) Zacks Investment Research's Icarus Service. Figure 12.3 presents an excerpt from the monthly report from the Icarus Service.

Figure 12.4 summarizes the pros and cons of both approaches.

Table 12.1 shows sources of earnings forecasting data preferred by financial analysts.

Table 12.1—What Are Your Present Sources of Earnings Forecasting Data?

Rank	1	2	3	4	5
Company contacts	56	28	24	8	9
Own research	55	15	5	1	
Industry statistics	19	14	14	7	
Other analysis	12	17	2	8	11
Historical financial data	8	12	8	5	4
Economic forecasts	7	7	10	3	
Competition	1	7	2	6	1
Computer simulation					2
Field trips		1			
Government agencies			2		
Industry & trade sources	1	7	17	3	5
Public relations of a promotional nature					1
Retired directors					1
Rumor					2
Wall Street sources	1	4	9	3	4

Rank   1 = most preferred
        5 = least preferred

Source: Brent W. Carper, Frank M. Barton Jr., and Haroldene F. Wunder, "The Future of Forecasting," *Management Accounting*, August, 1979. pp. 27-31.

Figure 12.3—EXTRACT FROM MONTHLY SUMMARY REPORT OF THE ICARUS SERVICE

A. Description of Data

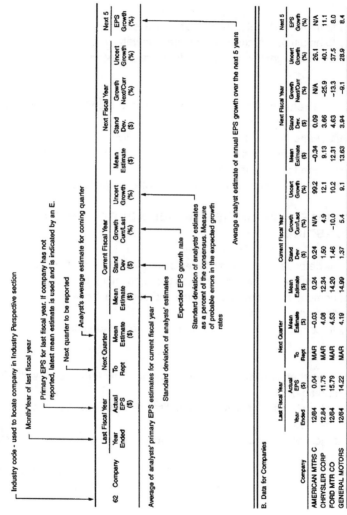

B. Data for Companies

	Last Fiscal Year		Next Quarter		Current Fiscal Year				Next Fiscal Year				Next 5
Company	Year Ended	Actual EPS ($)	To Rept	Mean Estimate ($)	Mean Estimate ($)	Stand Dev ($)	Growth Curr/Last (%)	Uncert Growth (%)	Mean Estimate ($)	Stand Dev. ($)	Growth Next/Curr (%)	Uncert Growth (%)	EPS Growth (%)
AMERICAN MTRS C	12/84	0.04	MAR	-0.03	0.24	0.24	N/A	99.2	-0.34	0.09	N/A	26.1	N/A
CHRYSLER CORP	12/84	11.75	MAR	4.08	12.34	1.50	4.9	12.1	9.13	3.66	-25.9	40.1	11.1
FORD MTR CO	12/84	15.79	MAR	4.53	14.20	1.46	-10.0	10.2	12.31	4.63	-13.3	37.5	8.0
GENERAL MOTORS	12/84	14.22	MAR	4.19	14.99	1.37	5.4	9.1	13.63	3.94	-9.1	28.9	8.4

Source: Zacks Investment Research, Inc. *The Icarus Service* (Chicago, Illinois).

Figure 12.4—PROS AND CONS OF SECURITY ANALYST AND UNIVARIATE
TIME-SERIES MODEL APPROACHES TO FORECASTING

SECURITY ANALYST APPROACH TO FORECASTING
Pros
1. Ability to incorporate information from many sources.
2. Ability to adjust to structural change immediately.
3. Ability to update continually as new information becomes available.

Cons
1. High initial setup cost and high ongoing cost to monitor numerous variables, make company visits, and so on.
2. Heavy dependence on the skills of a single individual.
3. Analyst may have an incentive not to provide an unbiased forecast (e.g., pressure to conform to consensus forecasts).
4. Analyst may be manipulated by company officials (at least in the short run).

UNIVARIATE TIME SERIES MODEL APPROACH TO FORECASTING
Pros
1. Ability to detect and exploit systematic patterns in the past series.
2. Relatively low degree of subjectivity in the forecasting (specially given the availability of computer algorithms to identify and estimate modes).
3. Low cost and ease of updating.
4. Ability to compute confidence intervals around the forecasts.

Cons
1. Limited number of observations available for new firms, firms with structural change, and so on.
2. Financial statement data may not satisfy distributional assumptions of time series model used.
3. Inability to update forecasts between successive interim or annual earnings releases.
4. Difficulty of communicating approach to clients (especially the statistical methodology used in identifying and estimating univariate models).

Source: George Foster, *Financial Statement Analysis*, 2nd ed., Prentice-Hall, Englewood Cliffs, N.J., 1986, p. 278.

This section compares various forecasting methods using a sample drawn from the Standard and Poor's (S&P) 400. It also examines the ability of financial analysts to forecast earnings per share performance based on the relationship of past forecasts of future earnings by financial analysts and through the use of recent univariate time-series models.

Our EPS sample was drawn from the 1984-1988 time period using the quarterly *Compustat Industrial* data tapes available from S&P. Included in our sample are figures for 30 firms randomly selected from the S&P 400 index for manufacturing firms over the period January 1984 to July 1988, using monthly data as reported to the public security markets. To collect data on financial analyst forecasts, we selected the *Value Line Forecasting Survey*, one of several reporting agencies that employ financial analysts and report their forecasts weekly.

In order to compare the forecasting ability of financial analysts with extrapolative models, seven time-series models were used to forecast earnings per share. The popular computer forecasting software RATS was used to estimate the models.

Data for the resulting sample of firms were used over the five-year time period studied (January, 1993 - June, 1997) to estimate the models. A relatively short period was chosen to avoid the possibility of structural changes in the economy affecting the results of the study.

Next, forecasts were derived from July 1997 to June 1998 using monthly data. The accuracy of the forecasts from each of the models for the period was evaluated using the two measures: (1) MAPE (mean absolute percentage error) and (2) MSE (mean square error).

FORECASTING METHODOLOGY

The models used are based on those proposed by earnings forecasters in the accounting, finance, and forecasting literature and discussed in earlier chapters:

1. Exponential smoothing model with additive seasonal effect.

2. Single exponential smoothing model.

3. Exponential smoothing model with linear trend and seasonal additive effects.

4. Exponential smoothing model with exponential trend and seasonal additive effects.

5. Box-Jenkins analysis, **SARIMA**$(1,0,0)$ $(0,1,0)$ s $= 12$. A seasonal autoregressive integrated moving average (**SARIMA**) model is

identified with first order autoregressive parameters and a 12-month seasonal adjustment.

6. Box-Jenkins analysis, **SARIMA**(1,0,0) (0,1,1) s = 12. A seasonal autoregressive integrated moving average (**SARIMA**) model is identified with first order autoregressive parameters and a 12-month seasonal adjustment. It also contains a seasonal moving average.

7. Linear trend analysis.

8. Value Line forecast.

FORECASTING ACCURACY

In Table 12.2, the sample average forecast error was estimated for each of 12 months based on earlier data. From July 1997 through June 1998, the monthly forecast errors are presented using the MAPE measure. From this analysis there is some variation in forecasting accuracy. Exponential forecasting methods (1, 2, and 3) performed well. The Box-Jenkins approaches (5 and 6) and the linear trend analysis (7) were reasonably successful. The monthly Value Line forecast resulted in the largest forecast errors overall.

Table 12.2 presents the MAPE results. Generally, the MSE reflected similar conclusions (Table 12.3).

CONCLUSION

Financial forecasting, an essential element of planning, is needed whenever future financing needs are being estimated. Basically, forecasts of future sales and their related expenses provide the firm with the information needed to project its financing requirements. Furthermore, earnings forecasts provide useful information concerning the expectations of a firm's future total market return that is of interest to security analysts and investors. Different methods for forecasting earnings were compared in terms of their accuracy, and the role of the CPA in prospective financial statements was discussed.

Table 12.2—SAMPLE AVERAGE FORECAST ERRORS FROM 30
COMPANIES MEAN ABSOLUTE PERCENTAGE ERROR (MAPE)

	Method 1	Method 2	Method 3	Method 4	Method 5	Method 6	Method 7	Method 8
1997:7	0.28	0.30	0.39	1.54	0.42	0.64	0.57	1.77
1997:8	0.24	0.23	0.29	1.51	0.72	0.95	0.58	1.39
1997:9	0.19	0.22	0.16	1.51	1.00	1.23	0.56	0.70
1997:10	0.19	0.22	0.16	1.55	1.28	1.54	0.56	0.70
1997:11	0.24	0.43	0.46	1.48	1.72	1.98	0.56	1.73
1997:12	0.27	0.71	0.71	1.48	2.09	2.35	0.69	4.28
1998:1	0.42	0.83	1.11	1.46	2.47	2.60	0.55	4.97
1998:2	0.42	0.83	1.11	1.46	2.47	2.60	0.55	4.97
1998:3	0.67	2.15	2.10	2.00	3.31	3.45	0.73	6.01
1998:4	0.78	3.17	1.48	1.72	3.53	3.65	0.73	9.00
1998:5	0.81	1.44	1.44	1.80	0.86	0.99	0.68	8.62
1998:6	0.81	1.44	1.44	1.80	0.86	0.99	0.68	8.62

Table 12.3—SAMPLE AVERAGE FORECAST ERRORS FROM 30
COMPANIES MEAN SQUARE ERROR (MSE)

	Method 1	Method 2	Method 3	Method 4	Method 5	Method 6	Method 7	Method 8
1997:7	0.42	0.34	0.39	6.27	0.12	0.12	1.21	1.59
1997:8	0.31	0.23	0.40	6.17	0.13	0.13	1.26	1.63
1997:9	0.31	0.23	0.33	5.93	0.14	0.14	1.31	1.69
1997:10	0.31	0.21	0.33	5.93	0.14	0.14	1.31	1.69
1997:11	0.32	0.64	0.76	6.22	0.48	0.47	1.47	2.19
1997:12	0.34	0.78	0.87	5.93	0.55	0.53	1.62	2.39
1998:1	0.71	1.32	1.38	5.91	0.97	0.95	1.45	0.99
1998:2	0.71	1.32	1.38	5.91	0.97	0.95	1.45	0.99
1998:3	1.40	5.48	1.81	5.68	3.89	3.86	2.28	0.85
1998:4	1.20	6.10	1.40	5.33	3.45	3.43	1.95	0.82
1998:5	1.21	7.29	1.41	5.21	3.35	3.34	2.03	0.74
1998:6	1.21	7.29	1.41	5.21	3.35	3.34	2.03	0.74

CHAPTER 13
CASH FLOW
FORECASTING

A forecast of cash collections and potential write-offs of accounts receivable is essential in cash budgeting and in judging the appropriateness of current credit and discount policies. The critical step in making such a forecast is estimating the cash collection and bad debt percentages to be applied to sales or accounts receivable balances. This chapter discusses several methods of estimating *cash collection rates* (or *payment proportions*) and illustrates how these rates are used for cash budgeting purposes.

The first approach, which is based on the Markov model, uses a probability matrix based on the estimates of what are referred to as transition probabilities. The second approach uses a simple average. The third approach, empirically tested and improved by the author, offers a more pragmatic method of estimating collection and bad debt percentages by relating credit sales to collection data. This method employs regression analysis. Using these approaches, a financial planner should be able to

- Estimate future cash collections from accounts receivable.

- Establish an allowance for doubtful accounts.

- Provide valuable insight into better methods of managing accounts receivable.

THE MARKOV APPROACH

The Markov (probability matrix) approach has been around for a long time. It has been successfully applied by Cyert and others to accounts receivable analysis, specifically to estimating that portion of accounts receivable that will eventually become uncollectible. The method requires classification of outstanding accounts receivable according to age categories that reflect the stage of account delinquency, e.g., current accounts, accounts one month past due, accounts two months past due, and so forth.

Consider the following example: XYZ department store divides its accounts receivable into two classifications: 0 to 60 days old and 61 to 120 days old. Accounts that are more than 120 days old are declared uncollectible. XYZ currently has $10,000 in accounts receivable: $7,000 in the 0-60 category and $3,000 in the 61-120 category. An analysis of past XYZ records provides us with the matrix of transition probabilities (Table 13.1).

Table 13.1—PROBABILITY MATRIX

From/To	Collected	Uncollectible	0-60 Days Old	61-120 Days Old
Collected	10	0	0	0
Uncollectible	0	10	0	0
0-60 days old	.3	0.0	.5	.2
61-120 days old	.5	.1	.3	.1

Transition probabilities are nothing more than the probability that an account receivable will move from one age stage to another. We noted three basic features of this matrix. First, notice the bracketed element, 0 , in the matrix. This indicates that $1 in the 0-60 category cannot become a bad debt in one month's time. Now look at the two elements in parenthesis. Each of these is 1, indicating that, in time, all the accounts receivable dollars will either be paid or become uncollectible. Eventually, all the dollars do wind up either as collected or uncollectible, but XYZ wants to know the probability that a dollar of a 0-60 or a 61-120 receivable will eventually find its way into either paid bills or bad debts. It is convenient to partition the matrix of transition probabilities into four submatrices, as follows.

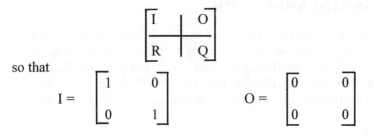

so that

$$I = \begin{bmatrix} 1 & 0 \\ 0 & 1 \end{bmatrix} \qquad O = \begin{bmatrix} 0 & 0 \\ 0 & 0 \end{bmatrix}$$

Now we are in a position to illustrate the procedure used to determine:

- Estimated collection and bad debt percentages by age category
- Estimated allowance for doubtful accounts

The procedure is as follows:

Step 1. Set up the matrix [I - Q].

$$[I - Q] = \begin{bmatrix} 1 & 0 \\ 0 & 1 \end{bmatrix} - \begin{bmatrix} .5 & .2 \\ .3 & .1 \end{bmatrix} = \begin{bmatrix} .5 & -.2 \\ -.3 & .9 \end{bmatrix}$$

Step 2. Find the inverse of this matrix, denoted by N.

$$N = [I - Q]^{-1} = \begin{bmatrix} 2.31 & .51 \\ .77 & 1.28 \end{bmatrix}$$

Note: The inverse of a matrix can be readily performed by spreadsheet programs such as *Lotus 1-2-3*, *Microsoft's Excel*, or *Quattro Pro*.

Step 3. Multiply this inverse by matrix R.

$$NR = \begin{bmatrix} 2.31 & .51 \\ .77 & 1.28 \end{bmatrix} \begin{bmatrix} .3 & 0 \\ .5 & .1 \end{bmatrix} = \begin{bmatrix} .95 & .05 \\ .87 & .13 \end{bmatrix}$$

NR gives us the probability that an account will eventually be collected or become a bad debt. Specifically, the top row in the answer is the 95 percent probability that $1 of XYZ's accounts receivable in the 0-60 category will be paid, and a 5 percent probability that it will eventually become a bad debt. Turning to the second row, the two entries represent the probability that $1 now in the 61-120 category will end up in the collected and bad debt categories. We can see that there is an 87 percent probability that $1 currently in the 61-120 will be collected and a 13 percent probability that it will become uncollectible.

If XYZ wants to estimate the future of its $10,000 accounts receivable ($7,000 in the 0-60 day category and $3,000 in the 61-120 day category), it must set up the following matrix multiplication:

$$[7,000 \ 3,000] \begin{bmatrix} .95 & .05 \\ .87 & .13 \end{bmatrix} = [9,260 \ 740]$$

Hence, of its $10,000 in accounts receivable, XYZ expects to collect $9,260 and to lose $740 to bad debts. Therefore, the estimated allowances for the collectible accounts is $740.

The variance of each component is equal to

$$A = be(cNR - (cNR)_{sq})$$

where $c_i = \dfrac{b_i}{\sum\limits_{i=1}^{} b_i}$ and e is the unit vector.

In our example, b = (7,000 3,000), c = (.7 .3). Therefore,

$$A = [7,000 \ 3,000] \begin{bmatrix} 1 \\ 1 \end{bmatrix} \left\{ [.7 \ .3] \begin{bmatrix} .95 & .05 \\ .87 & .13 \end{bmatrix} - [.7 \ .3] \begin{bmatrix} .95 & .05 \\ .87 & .13 \end{bmatrix}_{sq} \right\}$$

$$= 10,000 \ [\ [.926 \ .074] - [.857476 \ .005476] \ ]$$
$$= [685.24 \ 685.24]$$

which makes the standard deviation equal to $26.18 \sqrt{\$685.24}$. If we want to be 95 percent confident about our estimate of collections, we would set the interval estimate at $9,260 + 2(26.18), or $9,207.64 - $9,312.36, assuming t = 2 as a rule of thumb. We would also be able to set the allowance to cover the bad debts at $740 + 2(26.18), or $792.36.

SIMPLE AVERAGE

The most straightforward way to estimate collection percentages is to compute the average value realized from past data, i.e.,

$$P'_i = AVE \ (C_{t+i}/S_t)$$

$$= \frac{1}{N} \sum_{t=1}^{N} \frac{C_{t+2}}{S_t} \quad , i = 0,1,2...$$

where P'_t = an empirical estimate of collection percentages,
C_{t+i} = cash collection in month t+i from credit sales in month t,
S_t = credit sales in month t, and
N = the number of months of past data to compute the average.

LAGGED REGRESSION APPROACH

A more scientific approach to estimating cash collection percentages (or payment proportions) is to use multiple regression. We know that there is typically a time lag between the point of a credit sale and realization of cash. More specifically, the lagged effect of credit sales and cash inflows is distributed over a number of periods:

$$C_t = b_1 S_{t-1} + b_2 S_{t-2} + ...b_i S_{t-i}$$

where C_t = cash collection in month t,
S_t = credit sales made in period t,
$b_1, b_2, ...b_i$ = collection percentages (the same as P'_i), and
i = number of periods lagged.

By using the regression method already discussed, we can estimate these collection rates, using Excel or special packages such as *MicroTSP*, *SAS*, *Systat*, or *Minitab*. The cash collection percentages, $(b_1, b_2,...,b_i)$, may not add up to 100 percent because of the possibility of bad debts.

Once we estimate these percentages by using the regression method, we should be able to compute the bad debt percentage with no difficulty.

Table 13.2 shows the regression results using actual monthly data on credit sales and cash inflows for a real company. Equation I can be written as follows:

$$C_t = 60.6\%(S_{t-1}) + 24.3\%(S_{t-2}) + 8.8\%(S_{t-3})$$

The result indicates that the receivables generated by the credit sales are collected at the following rates: first month after sale, 60.6 percent; second month after sale, 24.3 percent; and third month after sale, 8.8 percent. The bad debt percentage is therefore 6.3 percent (100 - 93.7%).

Table 13.2—REGRESSION RESULTS FOR CASH COLLECTION (C_t)

Independent Variables	Equation I	Equation II
S_{t-1}	0.606[a]	0.596[a]
	(0.062)[b]	(0.097)
S_{t-2}	0.243[a]	0.142
	(0.085)	(0.120)
S_{t-3}	0.088	0.043
	(0.157)	(0.191)
S_{t-4}		0.136
		(0.800)
R^2	0.754	0.753
Durbin-Watson	2.52[c]	2.48[c]
Standard error of the estimate(S_e)	11.63	16.05
Number of monthly observations	21	20
Bad debt percentages	0.063	0.083

[a]Statistically significant at the 5% significance level.
[b]This figure in the parentheses is the standard error of the e estimate for the coefficient (S_b).
[c]No auto-correlation present at the 5% significance level.

Note, however, that these collection and bad debt percentages are probabilistic variables, variables whose values cannot be known with precision. However, the standard error of the regression coefficient and the 5-value permit us to assess the probability that the true percentage is within specified limits. The confidence interval takes the form:

$b \pm t \, S_b$

where S_b = standard error of the coefficient.

Example 13.1

Assuming t = 2 as rule of thumb at the 95 percent confidence level, the true collection percentage from the prior month's sales will be

60.6% ± 2(6.2%) = 60.6% ± 12.4%

In estimating cash collections and allowance for doubtful accounts, the following values are used for illustrative purposes:

S_{t-1} = $77.60,
S_{t-2} = $58.50,
S_{t-3} = $76.40, and

Forecast average monthly net credit sales = $75.20

(a) The forecast cash collection for period t would then be:

C_t = 60.6%(77.6) + 19.3%(58.5) + 8.8%(76.4) = $65.04

If the financial manager wants to be 95 percent confident about this forecast value, the interval would be set as follows:

$C_t \pm t \, S_e$

where S_e = standard error of the estimate.

Thus, the true value for cash collections in period t will be:

$65.04 ± 2(11.63) = $65.04 ± 23.26

(b) The estimated allowance for uncollectible accounts for period t will be:

6.3% ($75.2) = $4.74

By using these limits, financial planners can develop flexible (probabilistic) cash budgets where the lower limit can be interpreted as pessimistic and the upper limit as optimistic outcomes. They can also simulate a cash budget to try to determine both the expected change in cash collections for each period and the variation in this value.

In preparing a conventional cash inflow budget, the financial manager considers the sources of cash, including cash on account, sale of assets, incurrence of debt, and so on, with emphasis on cash collections from customers, since that is the greatest problem in this type of budget.

Example 13.2

The following data are given for Erich Stores:

	September Actual	October Actual	November Estimated	December Estimated
Cash sales	$7,000	$6,000	$ 8,000	$ 6,000
Credit sales	50,000	48,000	62,000	80,000
Total sales	$57,000	$54,000	$70,000	$86,000

Past experience indicates net collections normally occur in the following pattern:

- No collections are made in the month of sale.
- 80 percent of the sales of any month are collected in the following month.
- 19 percent of sales are collected in the second following month.
- 1 percent of sales are uncollectible.

We can project total cash receipts for November and December as follows:

	November	December
Cash sales	$ 8,000	$ 6,000
Cash collections		
September sales		
50,000 (19%)	9,500	
October sales		
48,000 (80%)	38,400	
48,000 (19%)		9,120
November sales		
62,000 (80%)		49,600
Total cash receipts	$55,900	$64,720

CASH FLOW FORECASTING SOFTWARE

Computer software allows for day-to-day cash forecasting and management, determining cash balances, planning and analyzing cash flows, finding cash shortages, investing cash surpluses, accounting for cash transactions, automating accounts receivable and payable, and dial-up banking. Computerization improves the availability, accuracy, timeliness, and monitoring of cash information at minimal cost. Daily cash information aids in planning how to use cash balances and allows for integration of different kinds of related information such as collections on customer accounts and cash balances and the effect of cash payments on cash balances.

Spreadsheet program software such as *Microsoft's Excel*, *Lotus 1-2-3*, and *Quattro Pro* can help you develop cash budgets and answer a variety of "what-if" questions. You can see, for example, the effect on cash flow from different scenarios (e.g., the purchase and sale of different product lines).

Two popular computer software packages specially designed for cash forecasting and management are briefly described here:

Up Your Cash Flow

This program automatically prepares spreadsheets for profit/loss forecasts, cash flow budgets, projected balance sheet, payroll analysis, term loan amortization schedule, sales/cost of sales by product, ratio analysis, and graphs. It is a menu-driven system that you can customize to your forecasting needs.

Granville Publications Software
10960 Wilshire Blvd., Suite 826
Los Angeles, CA 90024
(800) 873-7789

Cash Flow Analysis

This software projects cash inflow and outflow. You input data into eight categories: sales, cost of sales, general and administrative expense, long-term debt, other cash receipts, inventory build-up/reduction, capital expenditures (acquisition of long-term assets such as store furniture), and income tax. The program allows for changes in assumptions and scenarios and provides a complete array of reports.

Superior Software
16055 Ventura Blvd., Suite 725
Encino, CA 91436
(800) 421-3264
(818) 990-1135

CONCLUSION

Two methods of estimating patterns for expected collectibles and uncollectibles were presented. One advantage of the Markov model is that it
lets you determine the expected value and standard deviation of these percentages, making it possible to make probabilistic statements about these
figures. We have to be careful about these results, however, since the
model makes some strong assumptions. One serious assumption is that
the matrix of transition probabilities is constant over time. We do not
expect this to be perfectly true. The matrix may have to be updated, perhaps through the use of such techniques as exponential smoothing and
time series analysis.

The regression approach is relatively inexpensive to use because it
does not require a lot of data. All it requires is data on cash collections
and credit sales. Furthermore, credit sales values are all predetermined;
we use previous months' credit sales to forecast cash collections, so there
is no need to forecast credit sales. The model also allows you to make a
variety of statistical inferences about the cash collection percentages and
forecast values.

These models can be extended to setting credit and discount policies.
Corresponding to a given set of policies, there are

- An associated transition matrix in the Markov model
- Associated collection percentages in the regression model

By computing long-term collections and bad debts for each policy, an
optimal policy can be chosen that maximizes expected long-run profits.

CHAPTER 14
COST BEHAVIOR AND
COST PREDICTION

Not all costs behave in the same way. Certain costs, such as labor hours and machine hours, vary in proportion to changes in volume or activity. Other costs do not change even though volume changes. An understanding of cost behavior is helpful to budgeters, cost analysts, and managerial accountants as for:

1. Cost prediction

2. Break-even and contribution margin analysis

3. Appraisal of divisional performance

4. Flexible budgeting

5. Short-term decisions

6. Transfer pricing decisions

A LOOK AT COSTS BY BEHAVIOR

Depending on how they react or respond to changes in the level of activity, costs may be viewed as variable, fixed, or mixed (semi-variable). The classification is made within a specified range of activity, the relevant range. The relevant range is the volume zone within which the behavior of variable costs, fixed costs, and selling prices can be predicted with reasonable accuracy.

VARIABLE COSTS

Variable costs, those that vary with changes in volume or level of activity, include the costs of direct materials, direct labor, and sales commissions. Some examples are:

Variable Factory Overhead

Supplies	Receiving costs
Fuel and power	Overtime premium
Spoilage and defective work	

FIXED COSTS

Fixed costs such as advertising expense, salaries, and depreciation do not change regardless of the volume or level of activity. Some examples:

Fixed Factory Overhead

Property taxes	Rent on factory building
Depreciation	Indirect labor
Insurance	Patent amortization

MIXED (SEMI-VARIABLE) COSTS

Mixed costs have both a fixed and a variable element. Salespersons' compensation including salary and commission is an example. Some factory examples:

Mixed Factory Overhead

Supervision	Utilities	Compensation insurance
Inspection	Fringe benefits	Employer's payroll taxes
Service department costs	Maintenance and repairs	Rental of delivery truck

Factory overhead taken as a whole would be a perfect example of mixed costs. Figure 14.1 displays how each of these three types of costs varies with changes in volume.

ANALYSIS OF MIXED (SEMI-VARIABLE) COSTS

For forecasting, planning, control, and decision-making purposes, mixed costs need to be separated into their variable and fixed components. The analysis takes the following mathematical form, which is called a cost-volume formula (or cost function):

Y = a + bX

where Y = the mixed cost to be broken up,
       a = the fixed cost component,
       b = the variable rate per unit of X, and
       X = any given measure of activity such as direct labor hours,
           machine hours, or production volume.

Figure 14.1—COST BEHAVIOR PATTERNS

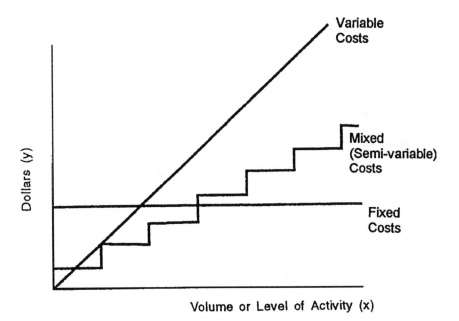

Separating the fixed and variable components of mixed costs is the same as estimating the parameter values a and b in the cost function. Among the methods that can be used for this purpose are the high-low method and regression analysis.

THE HIGH-LOW METHOD

The high-low method, as the name indicates, uses two extreme data points to determine the values of a (the fixed cost portion) and b (the variable rate) in the equation Y = a + bX. The extreme data points are the highest representative X-Y pair and the lowest representative X-Y pair. The activity level X, rather than the mixed cost item Y, governs their selection. To use the high-low method:

Step 1: Select the highest pair and the lowest pair.

Step 2: Compute the variable rate, b, using the formula:

$$\text{Variable rate} = \frac{\text{Difference in cost Y}}{\text{Difference in cost X}}$$

Step 3: Compute the fixed cost portion as:

Fixed cost portion = Total mixed cost - Variable cost

Example 14.1

Flexible Manufacturing Company decided to relate total factory overhead costs to direct labor hours (DLH) to develop a cost function in the form of Y = a + b X. Twelve monthly observations are collected (Table 14.1).

Table 14.1—DATA ON FACTORY OVERHEAD AND DIRECT LABOR HOURS

Month	Direct Labor Hours (X)	Factory Overhead (Y)
January	2510	82
February	2479	101
March	2080	88
April	2750	99
May	2330	93
June	2690	103
July	2480	77
August	2610	102
September	2910	122
October	2730	107
November	2760	101
December	2109	65

The high-low points selected from the monthly observations are:

	X	Y
High	122 hours	$2,920 (September pair)
Low	88	2,080 (March pair)
Difference	34 hours	$840

Thus,

$$\text{Variable rate b} = \frac{\text{Difference in Y}}{\text{Difference in X}} = \frac{\$840}{34 \text{ hours}} = \$24.71 \text{ per DLH}$$

The fixed cost portion is computed as:

	High	Low
Factory overhead (Y)	$2,920	$2,080
Variable expense		
($24.71 per DLH)	($3,014)	($2,174)
	($ 94)	($ 94)

The cost function for factory overhead is therefore:

-$94 fixed plus $24.71 per DLH.

The high-low method is simple to use. It has the disadvantage, however, of using extreme data points that may not be representative of normal conditions, so that the method may yield unreliable estimates of a and b in our formula. In this example, the negative value for a is questionable. In such a case, it would be wise to substitute two other points that are more representative of normal situations. Be sure to check the scatter diagram for this possibility.

SIMPLE REGRESSION

One popular method for estimating the cost function is regression analysis. As we discussed previously, simple regression involves one independent variable, e.g., DLH or machine hours alone, whereas multiple regression involves two or more variables. Unlike the high-low method, the regression method for estimating the variable and the fixed cost portions includes all the observed data and attempts to find a line of best fit.

Figure 14.2—SIMPLE REGRESSION (FOC VERSUS DLH)

Simple regression 1: $Y = b_0 + b_1 X_1$

	Regression Output:
Constant	1329.908
Standard error of Y estimate	150.7838
R-squared	0.693767
Number of observations	12
Degrees of freedom	10
X coefficient(s)	12.57958
Standard error of coefficient	2.642924
t-value	4.759720

$Y' = 1330 + 12.58 X_1$ with $R^2 = 69.38\%$

From the regression output (Figure 14.2), the cost function is

$$Y' = 1330 + 12.58 X$$

(factory overhead is $1,330 fixed plus $12.58 per DLH).

$R^2 = 69.38\%$, $S_e = 150.78$

Example 14.2

Assume 95 DLH are to be expended next year. Projected factory overhead for next year would be:

$$Y' = \$1,330 + 12.58 (95)$$
$$= \$1,330 + \$1,195 = \$2,525$$

If the cost forecaster wants to be 95 percent confident in a prediction, the confidence interval would be the estimated cost $(Y') \pm t\, S_e$. *Note:* As a rule of thumb, we use $t = 2$.

Example 14.3

From Example 14.2, $Y' = \$2,525$ and from Figure 14.2 we see $S_e = 150.78$, and $t = 2$.

Therefore, the range for the prediction, given direct labor hours of 95, would be:

$= \$2,525 \pm 2(150.78)$
$= \$2,525 \pm 301.56$, which means
$= \$2,826.56 - \$2,223.44$

MULTIPLE REGRESSION

Regression analysis allows cost analysts to consider more than one independent variable. If a simple regression does not provide a satisfactory cost function (as indicated typically by a low R-squared), the cost analyst should use multiple regression.

Example 14.4

We add data on machine hours to Table 14.1 to get Table 14.2.

Table 14.2—EXTENDED DATA FOR COST PREDICTION

Month	Factory Overhead Cost (Y)	Direct Labor Hours (X_1)	Machine Hours (X_2)
1	2510	82	88
2	2479	84	101
3	2080	74	88
4	2750	113	99
5	2330	77	93
6	2690	91	109
7	2480	95	77
8	2610	117	102
9	2910	116	122
10	2730	103	107
11	2760	120	101
12	2109	76	65

First, we present two simple regression results (one variable at a time):

Simple regression 1   Simple regression 2
$$Y = b_o + b_1 X_1$$ $$Y = b_o + b_2 X_2$$

Then, we present the following multiple regression result:

Multiple regression
$$Y = b_o + b_1 X_1 + b_2 X_2$$

Figure 14.3 shows simple and multiple regression results (SPSS output) for cost prediction.

Figure 14.3—SIMPLE AND MULTIPLE REGRESSION (SPSS OUTPUT)

Equation Number 1   Dependent Variable..   Y
Block Number 1.   Method: Enter
Variable(s) Entered on Step Number 1..   X2

Multiple R	.79890	Analysis of Variance			
R Square	.63825		DF	Sum of Squares	Mean Square
Adjusted R Square	.60207	Regression	1	473856.00635	473856.00635
Standard Error	163.88380	Residual	10	268578.99365	26857.89937
		F = 17.64308		Signif F = .0018	

VARIABLES IN THE EQUATION

Variable	B	SE B	Beta	T	Sig T	
X2	13.712698	3.264643	.798903	.200	.0018	$Y = b_0 + b_1 X_2$
(Constant)	1220.080952	316.956358			3.849	.0032

Equation Number 2   Dependent Variable..   Y
Block Number 1.   Method: Enter
Variable(s) Entered on Step Number 1..   X2
                                   2..   X1

Multiple R	.91977	Analysis of Variance			
R Square	.84598		DF	Sum of Squares	Mean Square
Adjusted R Square	.81176	Regression	2	628088.76563	314044.38282
Standard Error	112.71707	Residual	9	114346.23437	12705.13715
F = 24.71791		Signif F = .0002			

VARIABLES IN THE EQUATION

Variable	B	SE B	Beta	T	Sig T	
X2	7.814303	2.812060	.455262	2.779	.0214	$Y = b_0 + b_1 X_2 + b_2 X_2$
X1	8.479154	2.433626	.570814	3.484	.0069	
(Constant)	975.154527	229.052256			4.257	.0021

Simple regression 1 (overhead cost versus DLH) yielded:

Y' $= 1330 + 12.58$ X1
R^2 $= 69.38\%, S_e = 150.78$

Responding to the low R^2, trying the second regression (overhead cost versus MH) yielded:

Y' $= 1220 + 13.71$ X2
R^2 $= 63.82\%, S_e = 163.88$

MH did not fare any better. In fact, R^2 and S_e were worse.
   When we add machine-hours (MH) to the simple regression model, we get:

Y' $= 975 + 13.71$ X1 $+ 7.81$ X2
R^2 $= 84.59\%, S_e = 112.72$

The explanatory power (R^2) of the regression has increased dramatically to 84.59 percent, and the standard error of the regression has decreased to 112.72.

DUMMY VARIABLES

In many cost analyses, an independent variable may be discrete or categorical. For example, in estimating heating and fuel bills, the season will make a big difference. To control for this effect, a dummy variable can be included in the regression model. This variable will have a value equal to 1 during the winter months and 0 during all the other months.
   A dummy variable can also be used to account for jumps or shifts in fixed costs.
   A simple regression of overhead *versus* DLH gives (Figure 14.4):

$Y' = 1614 + 5.06\ X_1$ $R^2 = 22.42\%, S_e = 100.33$
       (2.98)

Figure 14.4—A SIMPLE REGRESSION OF OVERHEAD VERSUS DLH

Model: MODEL 1
Dependent variable: OVERHEAD

Analysis of Variance

Source	DF	Sum of Squares	Mean Square	F Value	Prob>F
Model	1	29094.33565	29094.33565	2.891	0.1199
Error	10	100652.33101	10054.23310		
C total	11	129746.66667			

Root MSE	100.32564	R-square	0.2242
Depreciation Mean	2123.6667	Adjusted R-square	0.1467
C.V.	4.72417		

		Parameter Estimates		$(Y = b_0 + b_1 X_1)$	
		Parameter	Standard	T for HO:	
Variable	DF	Estimate	Error	Parameter=0	Prob>|T|
INTERCEP	1	1614.844609	300.6752557	5.371	0.0003
LABOR	1	5.058711	2.97541537	1.700	0.1199

The explanatory power of the model is extremely low, and the coefficient of DLH is barely statistically significant (i.e., $t = 5.06/2.98 = 1.7 < 2$). The data suggest a possible decrease around the end of the sixth month. To test this hypothesis, we define a dummy variable, X2, as a shift or jump, where

$$X_2 = \begin{cases} 1 \text{ if } t = 1,2,...,6 \\ 0 \text{ if } t = 7,8,...,12 \end{cases}$$

Rerunning the regression with the shift variable leads to the following (Figure 14.5):

Table 14.5—RERUNNING THE REGRESSION

Model: MODEL 1
Dependent variable: OVERHEAD

Analysis of Variance

Source	DF	Sum of Squares	Mean Square	F Value	Prob>F
Model	2	104318.64415	52159.32208	18.461	0.0007
Error	9	25428.02251	2825.33583		
C total	11	129746.66667			

Table 14.5—RERUNNING THE REGRESSION, *con't.*

Root MSE	53.15389	R-square		0.8040
Depreciation Mean	2123.66667	Adjusted R-square		0.7605
C.V.	2.50293			

		Parameter Estimates		$(Y = b_0 + b_1X_1 + b_2X_2)$	
		Parameter	Standard	T for HO:	
Variable	DF	Estimate	Error	Parameter=0	Prob>|T|
INTERCEP	1	1258.127505	173.65577488	7.245	0.0001
LABOR	1	7.775297	1.66200606	4.678	0.0012
DUMMY	1	166.947667	32.35461912	5.160	0.0006

$$Y' = 1258 + 7.78\ X_1 + 166.95\ X_2 \qquad R^2 = 80.40\%, \qquad S_e = 53.15$$
$$(1.66) \qquad (32.35)$$

The explanatory power of the model is quite good, and both the DLH shift variables (t-values are 4.68 and 5.16) are highly significant.

COST PREDICTION

If we wish to predict costs for the first six months of the following year, the equation is:

$$
\begin{aligned}
Y' &= 1258 + 7.78\ X_1 + 166.95\ X_2 \\
&= 1258 + 7.78\ X_1 + 166.95\ (1) \\
&= 1424.95 + 7.78\ X_1
\end{aligned}
$$

If we wish to predict costs for the second six months of the following year, the model becomes:

$$
\begin{aligned}
Y' &= 1258 + 7.78\ X_1 + 166.95\ X_2 \\
&= 1258 + 7.78\ X_1 + 166.95\ (0) \\
&= 1258 + 7.78\ X_1
\end{aligned}
$$

THE CONTRIBUTION MARGIN INCOME STATEMENT

The traditional income statement for external reporting shows the functional classification of costs, that is, manufacturing vs. non-manufacturing (or operating) expenses. An alternative format of income statement, the *contribution margin income statement*, organizes costs by behavior rather than by function. It shows the relationship of variable and fixed costs associated with a given cost item, regardless of function.

The contribution approach to income determination provides data that are useful for managerial planning and decision making, for example:

1. For break-even and cost-volume-profit analysis,

2. In evaluating the performance of the division and its manager, and

3. For short-term and non-routine decisions

The contribution margin income statement is not acceptable, however, for income tax or external reporting purposes because it ignores fixed overhead as a product cost. It highlights the concept of *contribution margin*, the difference between sales and variable costs. The traditional format, on the other hand, emphasizes the concept of *gross margin*, the difference between sales and cost of goods sold.

These two concepts are independent of each other. Gross margin is available to cover non-manufacturing expenses, whereas contribution margin is available to cover fixed costs. Here is a comparison between the traditional format and the contribution format:

Traditional Format

	Sales		$15,000
Less:	Cost of goods sold		7,000
	Gross margin		$ 8,000
Less:	Operating expenses		
	Selling	2,100	
	Administrative	1,500	3,600
	Net income		$ 4,400

Contribution Format

	Sales		$15,000
Less:	Variable expenses		
	Manufacturing		$ 4,000
	Selling		1,600
	Administrative	500	6,100
	Contribution margin		$ 8,900
Less:	Fixed expenses		

Manufacturing	$3,000	
Selling	500	
Administrative	1,000	4,500
Net income		$ 4,400

CONCLUSION

Cost analysts and managerial accountants analyze cost behavior for break-even and cost-volume-profit analysis, for appraisal of managerial performance, for flexible budgeting, and to make short-term choice decisions. We have looked at three types of cost behavior—variable, fixed, and mixed. We illustrated two popular methods of separating the variable from the fixed components in mixed costs: the high-low method and regression analysis, with emphasis on the use of simple and multiple regression. To account for seasonal change or jumps or shifts in fixed costs, a dummy variable can be incorporated into the model.

Cost and managerial accountants prepare the income statement in a contribution format that organizes costs by behavior rather than by the functions of manufacturing, sales, and administration. The contribution income statement is widely used as an internal planning and decision-making tool.

CHAPTER 15
BANKRUPTCY
PREDICTION

Recently there has been an increasing number of bankruptcies. Will a company whose stock you own be among them? Who will go bankrupt? Will a major customer or supplier go bankrupt—or even your employer? What are the warning signs and what can be done to avoid corporate failure?

Bankruptcy is the final declaration that a company is unable to sustain current operation given the current debt obligations. The majority of firms require loans to function and therefore increase their liabilities during operations in order to expand, improve, or even just survive. The degree to which a firm has current debt in excess of assets is the most revealing factor in bankruptcy.

If you can predict with reasonable accuracy for a year or two ahead that the company you are interested in is developing financial distress, you might protect yourself better. For example, loan institutions face a major difficulty in calculating the degree of debt relative to assets—the likelihood of bankruptcy—yet that is precisely what these institutions must accomplish before issuing a loan.

NEED FOR PREDICTION

Businesspeople can reap significant rewards and benefits from a *predictive* model. It can be used, for example, in

1. *Merger analysis*, to help identify potential problems with a merger candidate.

2. *Turnaround management*, to develop emergency action plans and strategies to quickly correct a deteriorating situation.

3. *Insurance underwriting*, to evaluate the credit risk of the proposed insured and find solutions, such as risk sharing and self-insured retentions.

4. *Corporate governance*, for directors and audit committee analysis of going-concern capability, corporate risk, and merger and acquisition scenarios.

5. *Investment analysis*, to help an investor select stocks of potentially troubled companies, and for venture capitalists, investment bankers, and business valuation experts as they evaluate potential investments.

6. *Auditing analysis*, for external CPAs to evaluate whether a firm is a going concern and to formulate opinion qualification and financial statement disclosures.

7. *Legal analysis*, so that those investing or giving credit to your company may sue for losses incurred, and your company can defend itself.

8. *Loan credit analysis*, for bankers and other lenders, including vendors, to determine if they should extend a loan. If bankers can identify companies in danger of failure early enough, corrective action can be taken. The banker can: (a) decline to accept the company as a customer, (b) encourage the company to identify its problems and take steps to rectify them, (c) encourage the principals of the company to inject more capital into the business, and (d) encourage the company to seek other financing.

Analysts have tried and will continue to try to build early warning systems to detect the likelihood of bankruptcy. Investment bankers, financial analysts, security analysts, auditors, and others have used financial ratios as an indication of the financial strength of a company; however, financial ratio analysis is limited because the methodology is basically univariate. Each ratio is examined in isolation and the financial analyst must use professional judgment to determine whether a set of financial ratios is developing into a meaningful analysis.

In order to overcome the shortcomings of financial ratio analysis, it is necessary to combine mutually exclusive ratios into groups to develop a meaningful predictive model. *Regression analysis* and *multiple discriminant analysis* (MDA) are two statistical techniques that have been used to predict the financial strength of a company.

THREE MODELS

This chapter evaluates and, with the aid of a spreadsheet program, illustrates three predictive bankruptcy models: the Z-Score model, the Degree of Relative Liquidity model, and the Lambda Index.

The *Z-Score* model, developed by Edward Altman, uses multiple discriminant analysis to give a relative prediction of whether a firm will go bankrupt within five years. The *Degree of Relative Liquidity* model, on the other hand, evaluates a firm's ability to meet its short-term obligations. This model also uses discriminant analysis, combining several ratios to derive a percentage figure. The *Lambda Index* model also evaluates a firm's ability to generate or obtain cash on a short-term basis to meet current obligations and therefore predict solvency.

These models are described in detail below and applied to data extracted from *Moody's* and *Standard & Poor's* for two companies, Navistar International (formerly International Harvester), which continues to struggle in the heavy and medium truck industry, and Best Products, Inc., which declared bankruptcy in January 1991. Financial data were collected for the period 1979 through 1990 for Best and for the period 1979 through 1997 for Navistar.

Z-SCORE ANALYSIS

Using a blend of traditional financial ratios and multiple discriminant analysis, Altman[1] developed a bankruptcy prediction model that produces a Z-score as follows:

$$Z = 1.2*X_1 + 1.4*X_2 + 3.3*X_3 + 0.6*X_4 + 0.999*X_5$$

where
- X_1 = Working capital/total assets
- X_2 = Retained earnings/total assets
- X_3 = Earnings before interest and taxes (EBIT)/total assets
- X_4 = Market value of equity/book value of debt (or net worth for private firms)
- X_5 = Sales/total assets

Altman also established the following guideline for classifying firms:

[1]Edward I. Altman, *Corporate Financial Distress* (New York: John Wiley & Sons, 1983).

Z-score	Probability of Short-Term Illiquidity
1.8 or less	Very high
1.81 - 2.99	Not sure
3.0 or higher	Unlikely

The Z-score is about 90 percent accurate in forecasting business failure one year ahead and about 80 percent accurate in forecasting it two years ahead, though with the many important changes in reporting standards since the late 1960s, the original Z-score model is somewhat out of date. A second-generation model, *Zeta Analysis*, adjusts for these changes, especially the capitalization of financial leases. The resulting Zeta discriminant model is extremely accurate for up to five years. Since this analysis is proprietary, the exact weights for the model's seven variables are not available. The *Zeta* variables explaining corporate failure are.

X_1 = Return on assets: earnings before interest and taxes to total assets.

X_2 = Stability of earnings: measured by the "normalized measure of the standard error of estimate around a ten-year trend in X_1."

X_3 = Debt service: earnings before interest and taxes to total interest payments.

X_4 = Cumulative profitability: retained earnings to total assets.

X_5 = Liquidity: current assets to current liabilities.

X_6 = Capitalization: equity to total capital.

X_7 = Size measured by the firm's total assets.

APPLICATION

Navistar continues to struggle in the heavy and medium truck industry. Table 15.1 shows a 19-year financial history and the Z-scores of Navistar; the results are graphed in Figure 15.1.

Navistar performed at the edge of the ignorance zone ("unsure area") for 1979, but after 1980, the company started signaling failure. However, by selling stock and assets, the firm managed to survive. Since 1983, the company has shown improvement in its Z-scores, although it continually scored on the danger zone. Note that the 1994 Z-score of 1.19 is in the high probability range of <1.81. If the 1995 -1997 Z-scores increase over 1993 and 1994, it would indicate that Navistar is improving its financial position and becoming more viable.

Table 15.1—NAVISTAR INTERNATIONAL-NAV (NYSE): Z-SCORE PREDICTION OF FINANCIAL DISTRESS

	Balance Sheet					Income Statement			Stock Data	Calculations					Graph Values			
Year	Cur Asts (CA)	Total Asts (TA)	Cur Liab (CL)	Total Liab (TL)	Ret Erngs (RE)	Wrkng Captl (WC)	SALES	EBIT	Mkt Val/ Net WrthTA (MK-NW)	WC/ TA (X1)	RE/ TA (X2)	EBIT/ TA (X3)	MKT/-NW TA (X4)	SALES/ TA (X5)	Z Score	TOP GRAY	BTM GRAY	Year
1979	3266	5247	1873	3048	1505	1393	8426	719	1122	0.2655	0.2868	0.137	0.3681	1.6059	3	2.99	1.81	1979
1980	3427	5843	2433	3947	1024	994	6000	-402	1147	0.1701	0.1753	-0.0688	0.2906	1.0269	1.42	2.99	1.81	1980
1981	2672	5346	1808	3864	600	864	7018	-16	376	0.1616	0.1122	-0.003	0.0973	1.3128	1.71	2.99	1.81	1981
1982	1656	3699	1135	3665	-1078	521	4322	-1274	151	0.1408	-0.2914	-0.3444	0.0412	1.1684	-0.18	2.99	1.81	1982
1983	1388	3362	1367	3119	-1487	21	3600	-231	835	0.0062	-0.4423	-0.0687	0.2677	1.0708	0.39	2.99	1.81	1983
1984	1412	3249	1257	2947	-1537	155	4861	120	575	0.0477	-0.4731	0.0369	0.1951	1.4962	1.13	2.99	1.81	1984
1985	1101	2406	988	2364	-1894	113	3508	247	570	0.047	-0.7872	0.1027	0.2411	1.458	0.89	2.99	1.81	1985
1986	698	1925	797	1809	-1889	-99	3357	163	441	-0.0514	-0.9813	0.0847	0.2438	1.7439	0.73	2.99	1.81	1986
1987	785	1902	836	1259	-1743	-51	3530	219	1011	-0.0268	-0.9164	0.1151	0.803	1.8559	1.4	2.99	1.81	1987
1988	1280	4037	1126	1580	150	154	4082	451	1016	0.0381	0.0372	0.1117	0.643	1.011	1.86	2.99	1.81	1988
1989	986	3609	761	1257	175	225	4241	303	1269	0.0623	0.0485	0.084	1.0095	1.1751	2.2	2.99	1.81	1989
1990	2663	3795	1579	2980	81	1084	3854	111	563	0.2856	0.0213	0.0292	0.1889	1.0155	1.6	2.99	1.81	1990
1991	2286	3443	1145	2866	332	1141	3259	232	667	0.3314	0.0964	0.0674	0.2326	0.9466	1.84	2.99	1.81	1991
1992	2472	3627	1152	3289	93	1320	3875	-145	572	0.3639	0.0256	-0.04	0.1738	1.0684	1.51	2.99	1.81	1992
1993	2672	5060	1338	4285	-1588	1334	4696	-441	1765	0.2636	-0.3138	-0.0872	0.4119	0.9281	0.76	2.99	1.81	1993
1994	2870	5056	1810	4239	-1538	1060	5337	158	1469	0.2097	-0.3042	0.0313	0.3466	1.0556	1.19	2.99	1.81	1994
1995	3310	5566	1111	4696	-1478	2199	6342	262	966	0.3951	-0.2655	0.0471	0.2057	1.1394	1.52	2.99	1.81	1995
1996	2999	5326	820	4410	-1431	2179	5754	105	738	0.4091	-0.2687	0.0197	0.1673	1.0804	1.36	2.99	1.81	1996
1997	3203	5516	1267	4496	-1301	1936	6371	242	1374	0.351	-0.2359	0.0439	0.3055	1.155	1.57	2.99	1.81	1997

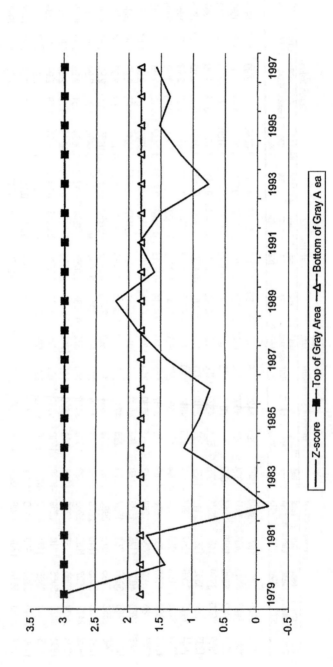

Figure 15.1—"Z"-SCORE GRAPH: NAVISTAR INTERNATIONAL

Best Products, Inc. had a Z-score in the 2.44 to 2.98 range from 1984 to 1988. The strong decline in 1989 may have correctly indicated the 1991 bankruptcy of Best (Table 15.2 and Figure 15.2).

DEGREE OF RELATIVE LIQUIDITY (DRL)

Though proposed as an alternative method for measuring the liquidity of a small firm, the DRL, developed by Skomp and Edwards[2], can have significant applications for larger companies. It has been compared to the two common liquidity ratios, the *current* and *acid-test* (or quick) ratios, that are often used to evaluate the liquidity of a firm. However, under certain circumstances, these two ratios sometimes give incomplete and misleading indications of a firm's ability to meet its short-term obligations. A logical approach to evaluating several liquidity measures simultaneously is to consider how appropriately each measure responds to changes in direction and degree of sensitivity. Examples of how these ratios may give misleading indications are:

- *Current:* May be distorted by an obsolete or slow-moving inventory and uncollectible accounts receivable.

- *Acid-test:* May be thrown off by uncollectible receivables and the exclusion of inventories.

The DRL calculates the percentage of a firm's cash requirements that could be secured from beginning working capital and from cash generated through the normal operating process. It emphasizes the availability of cash sources relative to cash needs, omitting such sources and uses of cash as:

- Sale of fixed assets
- Sale and extinguishment of capital stock
- Receipt and repayment of long-term borrowings
- Liquidations of marketable securities and bonds

The DRL is calculated by dividing the total cash potential by the expected cash expenditures:

---

[2]Stephen E. Skomp and Donald E. Edwards, "Measuring Small Business Liquidity: An Alternative to Current and Quick Ratios," *Journal of Small Business Management* (April 1978), Vol. 16:22.

Table 15.2—BEST PRODUCTS, INC.'S Z-SCORE

	Balance Sheet						Income Statement			Stock Data	Calculations						Graph Values			
Year	Cur Asts (CA)	Total Asts (TA)	Cur Liab (CL)	Total Liab (TL)	Ret Erngs (RE)	Net Worth (NW)	Wrkng Captl (WC)	SALES	EBIT	Mkt Val	WC/TA	RE/TA	EBIT/TA	MKT/TL	SALES/TA	Z Score (A)	TOP GRAY (B)	BTM GRAY (C)	Year (X)
1984	745228	1202138	468590	787135	186486	415003	276638	2081328	106952	319048	0.2301	0.1551	0.0890	0.4053	1.7314	2.76	2.99	1.81	1984
1985	723684	1178424	443752	759278	193568	419146	279932	2252656	66705	407604	0.2375	0.1643	0.0566	0.5368	1.9116	2.93	2.99	1.81	1985
1986	840686	1331975	529690	916579	189306	415396	310996	2234768	47271	253041	0.2335	0.1421	0.0355	0.2761	1.6778	2.44	2.99	1.81	1986
1987	816853	1265637	400403	878479	160465	387158	416450	2142118	25372	202988	0.3290	0.1268	0.0200	0.2311	1.6925	2.47	2.99	1.81	1987
1988	811314	1239960	426065	836956	190960	402904	385249	2066589	93226	672300	0.3107	0.1540	0.0752	0.8033	1.6668	2.98	2.99	1.81	1988
1989	877937	1735595	738837	1646302	39293	89293	139100	809457	96440	672300	0.0801	0.0226	0.0556	0.4084	0.4664	1.02	2.99	1.81	1989
1990	583773	1438208	412732	1366974	-14516	71234	171041	2094570	73512	672300	0.1189	-0.0101	0.0511	0.4918	1.4564	2.05	2.99	1.81	1990

Figure 15.2—ALTMAN'S Z-SCORE: BEST PRODUCTS, INC.

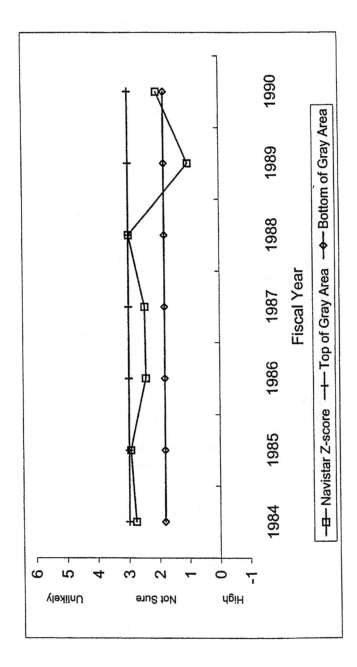

$$DRL = \frac{TCP}{E} \quad \text{or} \quad \frac{WC + (OT \times SVI)}{NSV - [(NI + NON) + WCC]}$$

where   TCP = Total cash potential
          E = Cash expenditures for normal operations
         WC = Beginning working capital (beginning current assets - beginning current liabilities)
         OT = Operating turnover, or

$$\frac{Sales}{Accounts\ receivable + Inventory \times Sales/cost\ of\ sales}$$

        SVI = Sales value of inventory (Inventory at cost x Sales/cost of sales)
        NSV = Net sales values
         NI = Net income
        NON = Non-cash expenditures (such as depreciation and amortization)
        WCC = Change in working capital

If the DRL ratio is greater than 1.00 (100%), the firm can meet its current obligations for the period and have net working capital available at the end of the period. If the DRL is less than 1.00, the firm should seek outside working capital financing soon.

The DRL may be derived by dividing TCP by E in the operating period. TCP is the sum of initial cash potential and the cash potential from normal operations. Initial cash potential is reflected in WC, assuming reported values can be realized in cash. The cash potential from operations can be determined by multiplying OT by SVI. OT reflects the number of times SVI (at retail) and accounts receivables (net of uncollectibles) are converted into cash in an operating period.

E is derived by subtracting cash flow from NSV. Cash flow from operations can be derived by NI plus NON plus WCC.

APPLICATION

The DRL is calculated for Navistar for 19 years (Table 15.3 and Figure 15.3). The results show a rather bleak liquidity position, with all figures under 1.00 except 1979. This indicates that Navistar has not been able to generate working capital internally through operations, but has had to continually seek outside working capital sources. However, the DRL appears to bottom out in 1988 and has shown some sign of stability since then.

Table 15.3—DRL: NAVISTAR INTERNATIONAL

| | Balance Sheet | | | | | | Income Statement | | | | Calculations | | | | | | Graph Values | | |
Year	Acts Rec (AR)	Inv (INV)	Cur Asts (CA)	Cur Liab (CL)	End W.C. (E-WC)	Beg W.C. (B-WC)	N.S.V. (NSV)	Cost of Sales (COS)	Net Inc (NI)	Non-Cash Exp (NON)	Op TO (OT=)	Sales Val Inv (SVI=)	Oper Cash Pot (OCP=)	Chng Wrkg Cap (WCC=)	Total Cash Pot (TCP=)	Expen-ditures (E=)	Degree of Rel Liq (DRL=)	BASE	Year
1979	806	2343	3266	1873	1393	1210	8392	6904	370	127	2.3	2848	6541	183	7751	7712	1.005	1.000	1979
1980	769	2332	3427	2480	947	1393	6312	5700	-397	130	1.9	2582	4864	-446	6257	7025	0.891	1.000	1980
1981	555	1634	2672	1846	826	947	6298	5750	-351	144	2.7	1790	4807	-121	5754	6626	0.868	1.000	1981
1982	306	759	1768	1135	633	826	4292	4150	-1738	149	3.9	785	3088	-193	3914	6074	0.644	1.000	1982
1983	255	619	1388	1366	22	633	3601	3325	-485	131	3.9	670	2609	-611	3242	4566	0.710	1.000	1983
1984	226	693	1412	1257	155	22	3382	2934	-55	100	3.3	799	2636	133	2658	3204	0.830	1.000	1984
1985	133	334	1101	988	113	155	3508	3084	-364	41	6.8	380	2598	-42	2753	3873	0.711	1.000	1985
1986	111	293	680	797	-117	113	3357	3009	2	40	7.7	327	2506	-230	2619	3545	0.739	1.000	1986
1987	114	266	785	836	-51	-117	3530	3054	33	41	8.4	307	2575	66	2458	3390	0.725	1.000	1987
1988	1854	316	3410	1126	2284	-51	4080	3574	244	49	1.8	361	665	2335	614	1452	0.423	1.000	1988
1989	1629	336	2965	1731	1234	2284	4023	3637	87	60	2.0	372	747	-1050	3031	4926	0.615	1.000	1989
1990	1627	343	2663	1579	1084	1234	3854	3376	-11	66	1.9	392	748	-150	1982	3949	0.502	1.000	1990
1991	1316	332	2286	1145	1141	1084	3259	2885	-165	73	1.9	375	723	57	1807	3294	0.549	1.000	1991
1992	1479	365	2472	1152	1320	1141	3685	3248	-212	77	1.9	414	806	179	1947	3641	0.535	1.000	1992
1993	1550	411	2682	1338	1344	1320	4510	3925	-501	75	2.2	472	1053	24	2373	4912	0.483	1.000	1993
1994	1517	429	2870	1710	1160	1344	5153	4500	82	72	2.6	491	1261	-184	2605	5183	0.503	1.000	1994
1995	1854	416	3310	933	2377	1160	6125	5288	164	81	2.6	482	1263	1217	2423	4663	0.520	1.000	1995
1996	1655	463	2999	820	2179	2377	5508	4827	65	105	2.5	528	1333	-198	3710	5536	0.670	1.000	1996
1997	1755	483	3203	1100	2103	2179	6147	5292	150	120	2.7	561	1489-	-76	3668	5953	0.616	1.000	1997

Figure 15.3—DRL GRAPH: NAVISTAR INTERNATIONAL

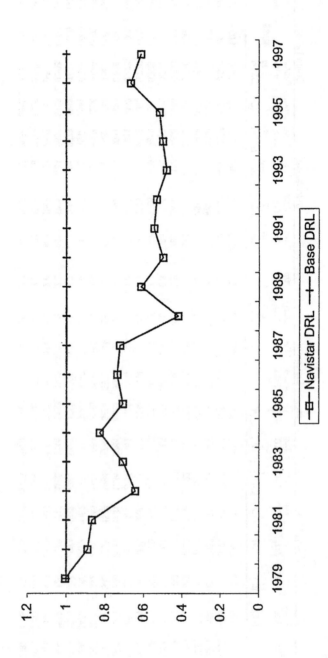

The DRL for Best Products, Inc. has remained above 1.00 since 1985, peaking at 1.194 in 1987 (Table 15.4 and Figure 15.4). However, after 1987 it began dropping and took a significant plunge in 1990, down to 1.039. Although the DRL was above 1.00, the significant drop may have indicated a worsening situation for Best and predicted their bankruptcy in January 1991.

From the evidence of these two companies, the DRL appears to have shown that the change in relative liquidity is more relevant than the absolute measure in predicting corporate bankruptcy.

LAMBDA INDEX

The Lambda index, developed by Gary Emery and 1990 Nobel Laureate Merton Miller,[3] is a ratio that focuses on two components of liquidity— short-term cash balances and available credit—to gauge the probability that a firm will become insolvent. The index takes into account the key aspect of uncertainty in cash-flow measurement by using a sample standard deviation. In consequence, it can be used like a z value from the standard normal distribution table.

For a given period, Lambda is the sum of a company's initial liquid reserve and net flow of funds divided by the uncertainty associated with the flows:

$$\frac{\text{Initial liquid reserve} \quad + \quad \text{Total anticipated net cash flow during the analysis horizon}}{\text{Uncertainty about net cash flow during the analysis horizon.}}$$

Unused lines of credit, short-term investments, and cash balances make up the initial liquid reserve. Net cash flow is the balance of cash receipts less cash outlays. Uncertainty is based on the standard deviation of net cash flow. A cash forecast should be used to calculate the Lambda index.

The worksheet should contain 12 line items in the following order: short-term line of credit, beginning liquid assets, adjustments, initial liquid reserve, total sources of funds, total uses of funds, ending liquid assets, ending liquid reserve, standard deviation, the Lambda index, and, finally, additional cash required to maintain a Lambda of three.

The *short-term line of credit* may not change during the course of the forecast (i.e., one year), which simplifies calculations. *Liquid assets* by

---

[3]As cited by Kelly R. Conaster, "Can You Pay the Bills," *Lotus*, January, 1991.

Table 15.4—DRL: BEST PRODUCTS, INC.

Year	Balance Sheet						Income Statement					Sales Val Inv	Calculations				Graph Values		Year
	Acts Rec (AR)	Inv (INV)	Cur Asts (CA)	Cur Liab (CL)	End W.C. (E-WC)	Beg W.C. (B-WC)	N.S.V. (NSV)	Cost of Sales (COS)	Net Inc (NI)	Non-Cash Exp (NON)	Op TO (OT=)	(SVI=)	Oper Cash Pot (OCP=)	Chng Wrkg Cap Pot (WCC=)	Total Cash Pot (TCP=)	Expen-ditures (E=)	Degree of Rel Liq (DRL=)	BASE	Year
1985	46746	658880	723684	443752	279932	276638	2252656	1692568	13609	65764	2.4	876910	2138650	3294	2415288	2169989	1.113	1.000	1985
1986	45050	757051	840686	529690	310996	279932	2234768	1685198	2223	67341	2.1	1003937	2138793	31064	2418725	2134140	1.133	1.000	1986
1987	29670	649162	816853	400403	416450	310996	2142118	1592984	-25593	66647	2.4	872941	2071704	105454	2382700	1995610	1.194	1.000	1987
1988	28571	670236	811314	426065	385249	416450	2066589	1499641	30527	38544	2.2	923623	2004580	-31201	2421030	2028719	1.193	1.000	1988
1989	32614	579651	877937	738837	139100	385249	809457	575467	39297	13216	1.0	815342	778324	-246149	1163573	1003093	1.160	1.000	1989
1990	32213	509617	583773	412732	171041	139100	2094570	1529598	-53809	56008	2.9	697849	2002150	31941	2141250	2060430	1.039	1.000	1990

Figure 15.4—DRL GRAPH: BEST PRODUCTS, INC.

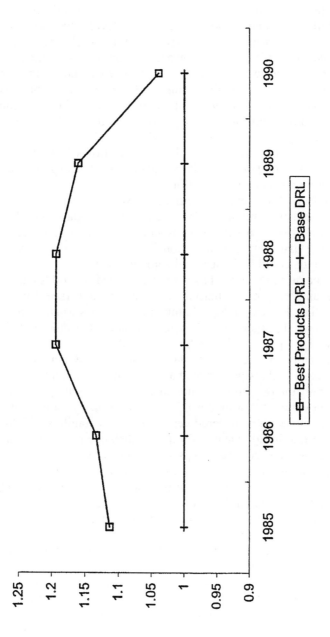

definition include marketable securities and cash available at the start of the forecast summary. The *adjustments* line item allows one to see the result of decreasing or increasing the cash level. The *initial liquid reserve* is the total short-term line of credit with any adjustments. *Total sources* and *total uses of funds* are forecasts by company management, resulting in a positive or negative net cash flow. The Lambda value should rise if short-term credit does not change and the firm has a positive net cash flow. *Ending liquid assets* is the sum of three values: beginning liquid assets, adjustments, and net cash flow. *Ending liquid reserve* is the sum of two values: short-term line of credit and ending liquid assets. The *standard deviation* is drawn from the net cash flows from period to period. Finally, the *Lambda index* is calculated by dividing the ending liquid reserve by the standard deviation.

The last line item is *additional cash needed* to hold a Lambda of three. A negative number here indicates a Lambda value of greater than three and, hence, a safer firm financially. A very high negative value, assuming that management is confident of its forecasts, may signal that those funds could be better used somewhere else.

Once an index value has been determined, the odds can be found by referencing a standard normal distribution table (see Table A.1 in the Appendix). For example, a Lambda of 2.33 has a table value of .9901, which says that there is a 99 percent chance that there will be no problems and a 1 percent chance that there will.

A Lambda value of 3 translates to one chance in a thousand that necessary cash outlays will exceed available cash on hand. A Lambda value of 3.9 puts the probability at one in 20,000. Generally, then, a firm with a Lambda value of 9 or higher is financially healthy. Firms with a Lambda of 15 or more are considered very safe. A low Lambda of 1.64 is equivalent to a one in 20 chance of required disbursements exceeding cash on hand. A work sheet that keeps a running tally of Lambda shows how changes in the financial picture affect future cash balances.

There are a number of positive aspects to using the Lambda index. The index focuses on the key factors of liquidity, available unused credit, and cash flows, which by contrast are ignored by standard cash forecasts. Further, by including the standard deviation of cash flows, Lambda penalizes irregular cash flows. Higher changes in cash flows would result in a lower Lambda.

A drawback to Lambda, however, is the fact that it is significantly tied to revenue forecasts, which, depending on the time horizon and the industry, can be suspect. A strong Lambda does not carry much weight if a firm is not confident about its forecast.

APPLICATION

Table 15.6 and Figure 15.5 show that Navistar's Lambda index was very low in 1979, dropping to a low point of 2.16 in 1982, though it moved up to 5.98 in 1989.

Though the Navistar Lambda value increased from 1986 through 1989, it dropped again in 1990 though not to its previous lows. Using a Lambda value of 9 as the benchmark for a healthy firm, Navistar was in trouble for some time. Since 1989, however, the Lambda appears to have been improving constantly over time.

In the 1980s Best Product's Lambda index was far lower than Navistar's, with a low of 2.39 in 1986 and a high of 4.52 in 1989. Its Lambda index dropped even further in 1990, hitting 0.80. It is not surprising that in January 1991, Best filed for bankruptcy protection (Table 15.7 and Figure 15.6).

Table 15.5 summarizes guidelines for classifying firms under the three models.

Table 15.5—CLASSIFYING GUIDELINES UNDER THE THREE MODELS

Model	Guidelines
Z-Score Model	
Z-Score	Probability of Short-Term Illiquidity
1.8 or less	Very high
1.81 - 2.99	Not sure
3.0 or higher	Unlikely
Degree of Relative Liquidity (DRL) Model	
DRL Score	Probability of Short-Term Illiquidity
Less than 1.00	Very high
Higher than 1.00	Unlikely
Lambda Index	
Lambda score	Probability of Short-Term Illiquidity
1.64	1 in 20
3.90	1 in 20,000
9.00 or higher	Unlikely

Table 15.6—NAVISTAR LAMBDA INDEX

Year	1979	1980	1981	1982	1983	1984	1985	1986	1987	1988	1989	1990	1991	1992	1993	1994	1995	1996	1997
Short-term line of credit	100000	100000	100000	100000	100000	100000	100000	100000	100000	100000	100000	100000	100000	100000	100000	100000	100000	100000	100000
Beginning liquid assets	27256	25205	137103	393879	259452	391619	412970	323220	217745	383900	562400	674000	588000	604000	638000	734000	870000	798000	800000
Adjustments																			
Initial liquid reserve	127256	125205	237103	493879	359452	491619	512970	423220	317745	483900	662400	774000	688000	704000	738000	834000	970000	898000	900000
Total sources of funds	-2051	111898	256776	-134427	132167	21351	-89750	-105475	166155	178500	111600	-86000	16000	34000	96000	136000	-72000	2000	-122000
Total uses of funds																			
Net cash flow	-2051	111898	256776	-134427	132167	21351	-89750	-105475	166155	178500	111600	-86000	16000	34000	96000	136000	-72000	2000	122000
Ending liquid assets, short-term debt, and adjustments (net)	5205	137103	393879	259452	391619	412970	323220	217745	383900	562400	674000	588000	604000	638000	734000	870000	798000	800000	922000
Ending liquid reserve	125205	237103	493879	359452	491619	512970	423220	317745	483900	662400	774000	688000	704000	738000	834000	970000	898000	900000	1022000
Standard deviation	NA	80574	129721	166384	147856	133909	135398	135604	135181	129435	130297	125041	120167	116583	114801	115195	112221	110558	
Calculated Lambda index	NA	2.94	3.81	2.16	3.32	3.83	3.13	2.34	3.57	4.90	5.98	5.28	5.63	6.14	7.15	8.45	7.80	8.02	9.24
Additional cash required (remaining) to maintain Lambda of 3.0	NA	4619	-104716	139701	-48050	-111243	-17027	89666	-77087	-256856	-385696	-297108	-328877	-377498	-484250	-625596	-552415	-563336	-690326
Very Safe	15.00	15.00	15.00	15.00	15.00	15.00	15.00	15.00	15.00	15.00	15.00	15.00	15.00	15.00	15.00	15.00	15.00	15.00	15.00
Healthy	9.00	9.00	9.00	9.00	9.00	9.00	9.00	9.00	9.00	9.00	9.00	9.00	9.00	9.00	9.00	9.00	9.00	9.00	9.00
Slight: 1 in 20000	3.90	3.90	3.90	3.90	3.90	3.90	3.90	3.90	3.90	3.90	3.90	3.90	3.90	3.90	3.90	3.90	3.90	3.90	3.90
Low: 1 in 20	1.64	1.64	1.64	1.64	1.64	1.64	1.64	1.64	1.64	1.64	1.64	1.64	1.64	1.64	1.64	1.64	1.64	1.64	1.64

Figure 15.5—LAMBDA INDEX GRAPH: NAVISTAR INTERNATIONAL

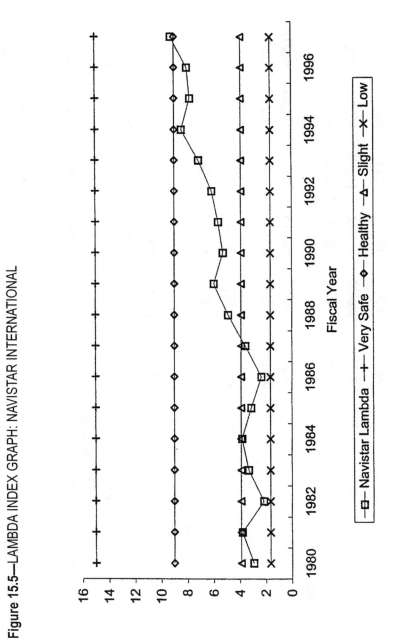

Table 15.7—LAMBDA INDEX: BEST PRODUCTS, INC.

Year	1985	1986	1987	1988	1989	1990
Short-term line of credit	100000	100000	100000	100000	100000	100000
Beginning liquid assets	62933	4915	15126	103197	110243	253278
Adjustments						
Initial liquid reserve	162933	104915	115126	203197	210243	353278
Total sources of funds	-58018	10211	88071	7046	143035	-244843
Total uses of funds						
Net cash flow	-58018	10211	88071	7046	143035	-244843
Ending liquid assets, short-term debt, and adjustments (net)	4915	15126	103197	110243	253278	8435
Ending liquid reserve	104915	115126	203197	210243	353278	108435
Standard deviation	NA	48245	73097	59769	78245	135047
Calculated Lambda index	NA	2.39	2.78	3.52	4.52	0.80
Additional cash required (remaining) to maintain Lambda of 3.0	NA	29610	16095	-30936	-118542	296706
Very Safe		15.00	15.00	15.00	15.00	15.00
Healthy		9.00	9.00	9.00	9.00	9.00
Slight: 1 in 20000		3.90	3.90	3.90	3.90	3.90

Figure 15.6—LAMBDA INDEX: BEST PRODUCTS, INC.

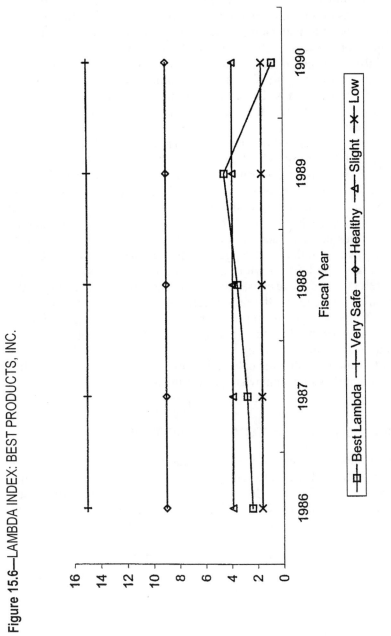

A WORD OF CAUTION

The Z-score may be used by different people for varying uses. It offers an excellent measure of the probability of a firm's insolvency, but, like any tool, it must be used with care and skill. The Z-score should be evaluated over a number of years; it should not be the sole basis of evaluation.

It is also important to be careful when the Z-score is used to compare the stability of different firms. In order to eliminate external environmental factors, the firms must be in the same market, offering the same or very similar products, and the measure must be taken across the same period of years.

The DRL is a more comprehensive measure of liquidity than the current ratio or the acid-test ratio. However, like them, the DRL is a relative measure, to be used only in relation to either the firm's own historical DRL or to those of other businesses. Since the DRL does not incorporate timing of and variances in cash flows (assuming them to be uniform and continuous), comparing the DRL of two dissimilar firms is hazardous. The DRL *does* correctly identify an improved or deteriorated liquidity position; however, it does not suggest explicit causes for any change. On the other hand, the DRL provides a basis from which to pursue analysis and interpretation of those causes of change, because the derivation of the DRL requires input for all the factors relevant to liquidity position.

As with the DRL, in using the Lambda index to gauge a firm's liquidity, it is necessary to consider a firm's historical background—and always to use common sense in evaluating any calculated value. A weak point of this model is that the calculation uses forecasted figures, making the final Lambda value somewhat suspect in some cases.

NEURAL BANKRUPTCY PREDICTION

Neural networks use some of the tools already in place to improve bankruptcy prediction. If the ratios chosen for the Z model are used but the neural network is allowed to form its own functions, the predictive abilities of the Z formula can be much improved upon. This is of significant value to managers, creditors, and investors since misclassification, particularly of a firm that is going bankrupt, has huge monetary implications.

The *Neural Bankruptcy Prediction Program* developed in 1995 by Dorsey, Edmister, and Johnson[4] is a good example of the model. This is a DOS-based software that can be downloaded from the University of

[4]Dorsey, R.E., Edmister, R.O. and Johnson, J.D. *Bankruptcy Prediction Using Artificial Neural Systems*, University of Missouri Business School's Internet web page.

Missouri Business School's Internet web page (www.bus.olemiss.edu/johnson/compress/compute.htm).

As an illustration, 1994 financial reports for a number of companies were obtained from the America Online Financial Reports database. Then, the 18 ratios required by the Neural Network Bankruptcy Prediction Program were calculated (Table 15.8):

Table 15.8—DATA SET RATIO DEFINITIONS

Ratio	Definition
CASH/TA	Cash/Total assets
CASH/TS	Cash/Net sales
CF/TD	Cash flow operations income/Total liabilities
CA/CL	Total current assets/Total current liabilities
CA/TA	Total current assets/Total assets
CA/TS	Total current assets/Net sales
EBIT/TA	(Interest expense + Income before tax)/Total assets
LOG (INT+15)	LOG(Interest expense + Income before tax)/Total assets + 15)
LOG (TA)	LOG(Total assets)
MVE/TK	Shareholder's equity/(Total assets - Total current liabilities)
NI/TA	Net income/Total assets
QA/CL	(Total current assets - Inventories)/Total current liabilities
QA/TA	(Total current assets - Inventories)/Total assets
QA/TS	(Total current assets - Inventories)/Net sales
RE/TA	Retained earnings/Total assets
TD/TA	Total liabilities/Total assets
WK/TA	(Total assets/Net sales)/(Working capital/Total assets)
WK/TS	1/(Net sales/Working capital)

Table 15.9 shows the result of 1994 data analysis for a selected group of firms.

Insolvency was predicted for those companies with values over 0.4 (threshold value). Three of ten solvent companies received values over 0.4, indicating bankruptcy. Although those companies did not go bankrupt in 1995, they can still be considered as high risk. It is impressive that all of the insolvent corporations are recognized.

The Neural Network Bankruptcy Prediction Program is a reliable tool for screening financially distressed large companies. Despite the small sample size, 100 percent accuracy in predicting insolvency was remarkable. The program is a relatively simple and easy process; it holds promise even to those who are not proficient in mathematics.

Table 15.9—BANKRUPTCY ANALYSIS FOR SELECTED FIRMS

Year	Company	Bankrupt (1-yes/ 0-no)	Value	Insolvency Predicted (1-yes/0-no)	Error
1994	Apparel Ventures Inc.	0	0.38085095	0	
1994	Apple Computer Inc.	0	0.00267937	0	
1994	Biscayne Apparel Inc.	0	0.43153563	1	
1994	Epitope Inc.	0	0.18238553	0	
1994	Montgomery Ward Holding Co.	0	0.06268501	0	30%
1994	Schwerman Trucking Co.	0	0.57828138	1	
1994	Signal Apparel Co.	0	0.37081639	0	
1994	Southern Pacific Transportation	0	-0.3514775	0	
1994	Time Warner Inc.	0	0.57828138	1	
1994	Warner Insurance Services	0	-0.1020344	0	
1994	Baldwin Builders	1	0.57828138	1	
1994	Bradlees Inc.	1	1.00828347	1	
1994	Burlington Motor Holdings	1	1.00828347	1	
1994	Clothestime Inc.	1	0.43153563	1	
1994	Dow Corning	1	0.65517535	1	0%
1994	Edison Brothers Stores	1	0.61124180	1	
1994	Freymiller Trucking Co.	1	1.00828347	1	
1994	Lamonts Apparel Inc.	1	1.28955072	1	
1994	Plaid Clothing Group Inc.	1	1.28955072	1	
1994	Smith Corona Co.	1	0.43153563	1	

CONCLUSION

The three major models discussed in this chapter appear to have worked well for both Navistar International and Best Products in the sense that they all pointed to early signs of financial distress. The Z-score model seems to be a more positive predictor for bankruptcy than the other two since it covers a wider range of financial ratios—especially, retained earnings divided by total assets. Retained earnings (of course backed by cash balance) are the factor that will save a company in financial trouble especially in economic hard times.

All developers of prediction models warn that their techniques should be considered as just another tool and are not intended to replace experienced and informed personal evaluation. Perhaps the best use of any of these models is as a filter to identify companies requiring further review, or to establish a trend for a company over a number of years. If, for example, over a number of years the trend for a company is downward, that company has problems that, if caught in time, could be corrected to allow the company to survive.

CHAPTER 16
FORECASTING
FOREIGN EXCHANGE
RATES

This chapter addresses the problem of forecasting foreign exchange rates. It then establishes a framework for the international exchange markets and explores the relationship between exchange rates, interest rates, and inflation rates. After discussing the types of forecasting techniques used to predict foreign exchange rates, the chapter concludes by setting up a framework within which forecasts can be evaluated.

WHY FORECAST EXCHANGE RATES?

In today's global environment, companies trading across national boundaries are often exposed to transaction risk, the risk that comes from fluctuation in the exchange rate between the time a contract is signed and the time payment is received. Yet some companies choose to ignore forecasting exchange rates; others rely on their banks. Very few companies dedicate resources to forecasting foreign exchange rates themselves.

Many companies argue that because forecasts of international exchange rates are often inaccurate, they are invalid. Therefore, there is no need to forecast. These companies fail to understand, however, that because forecasting is not an exact science but rather an art form, the quality of forecasts generally tends to improve with experience.

Historically, exchange rates have been fixed, with very few short-term fluctuations. Today, when most exchange rates are floating, a rate can easily vary as much as 5 percent within a week. The recent crisis in the European monetary market illustrates the need for accurate exchange rate information. There are four primary reasons why it is imperative to forecast the foreign exchange rates.

HEDGING DECISIONS

Multinational companies (MNCs) are constantly faced with the decision of whether or not to hedge payables and receivables in foreign currency. An exchange rate forecast can help them determine whether to hedge. As an example, if forecasts suggest that the Swiss franc will appreciate in value relative to the dollar, a company expecting payment from a Swiss partner may decide not to hedge. However, if the forecasts showed the Swiss franc depreciating relative to the dollar, the U.S. partner should hedge.

SHORT-TERM FINANCING DECISIONS

An MNC has several sources of capital market and several currencies in which it can borrow. Ideally, it would borrow a currency with a low interest rate that would depreciate over the financial period. For example, if a U.S. firm borrowed in German marks that depreciated in value during the loan period, at the end of the period, the company would have to use fewer dollars to buy the same amount of marks.

INTERNATIONAL CAPITAL BUDGETING DECISIONS

Accurate cash flow figures are imperative in order to make good capital budgeting decisions. In the case of international projects, it is necessary not only to establish accurate cash flows but also to convert them into the MNC's home currency. This requires the use of foreign exchange forecasts first to convert the cash flows and then to evaluate the decision.

SUBSIDIARY EARNING ASSESSMENTS

When an MNC reports its earning, international subsidiary earnings are often translated into the MNC's home currency. For example, when IBM makes an earnings projection, it needs to translate its projected earnings in Germany from Deutsche marks to dollars. A depreciation in marks would decrease a subsidiary's earnings, and vice versa. Thus, it is necessary to generate an accurate forecast of marks to create a legitimate earnings assessment.

SOME BASIC TERMS AND RELATIONSHIPS

At this point, it is necessary to address some of the basic terminology used in foreign exchange as well as address the fundamental laws of international monetary economics. It is also necessary to establish a basic international monetary framework before forecasting.

SPOT RATE

Spot rate is the rate that exists in today's market. Table 16.1 illustrates a typical listing of foreign exchange rates found in the *Wall Street Journal.* The British pound is quoted at 1.5685, the spot rate. It means you can go to the bank today and exchange $1.5685 for £1.00. In reality, if, for example, you need £10,000 to pay off an import transaction on a given day, you would ask your bank to purchase £10,000. Rather than handing you the money, the bank would instruct its English subsidiary to pay £10,000 to your English supplier and it would debit your account $15,685.

Table 16.1—SAMPLE FOREIGN EXCHANGE RATES

The New York foreign exchange selling rates below apply to trading among banks in amounts of $1 million and more, as quoted at 3 p.m. Eastern time by Bankers Trust Co., Telerate and other sources. Retail transactions provide fewer units of foreign currency per dollar.

Country	U.S.$ equiv.		Currency per U.S.$	
	Wed.	Tues.	Wed.	Tues.
Argentina (Peso)	1.01	1.01	.99	.99
Australia (Dollar)	.6952	.6932	1.4384	1.4426
Austria (Schilling)	.09050	.09134	11.05	10.95
Bahrain (Dinar)	2.6522	2.6522	.3771	.3771
Belgium (Franc)	.03092	.03122	32.34	32.03
Brazil (Cruzeiro)	.0000978	.0000987	10226.10	10128.01
Britain (Pound)	1.5685	1.6005	.6376	.6248
30-Day Forward	1.5637	1.5958	.6395	.6266
90-Day Forward	1.5551	1.5868	.6430	.6302
180-Day Forward	1.5440	1.5752	.6477	.6348
Canada (Dollar)	.7862	.7859	1.2720	1.2725
30-Day Forward	.7830	.7827	1.2772	1.2776
90-Day Forward	.7783	.7782	1.2848	1.2850
180-Day Forward	.7718	.7722	1.2957	1.2950
Chile (Peso)	.032704	.002704	369.87	369.87
China (Renminbi)	.181028	.181028	5.5240	5.5240
Colombia (Peso)	.001636	.001636	611.15	611.15
Czechoslovakia (Koruna)				
Commercial Rate	.0358938	.0357270	27.8600	27.9900
Denmark (Krone)	.1641	.1659	6.0935	6.0291
Ecuador (Sucre)				
Floating Rate	.000551	.000551	1814.03	1814.03
Finland (Markka)	.19790	.19998	5.0529	5.0004

FORWARD RATE

Besides the spot rate, Table16.1 also quotes the forward rate. The 90-day forward rate for the pound is 1.5551. In forward market, you buy and sell currency for future delivery, usually one, three or six months in advance. If you know you will soon need to buy or sell currency, you can hedge against a loss by selling in the forward market. Let's say that in three months you must pay £10,000 to your English supplier. You can purchase £10,000 today for delivery in 90 days by paying $15,551 (10,000 x 1.5551). No matter what the exchange rate of pound or U.S. dollar is in 90 days, you are assured delivery at the quoted price.

The cost of purchasing pounds in the forward market ($15,551) is less than the price in the spot market ($15,685). This implies that the pound is selling at a forward discount relative to the dollar, so you can buy more pounds in the forward market. It could also mean that the U.S. dollar is selling at a forward premium.

INTEREST RATE PARITY THEORY

The interest rate parity theory says that the interest rate differential must equal the difference between the spot and the forward rate. The validity of this theory can be easily tested by a simple example. Assume that the interest rate in the U.S. is 10 percent. An identical investment in Switzerland yields 5 percent. The exchange rate is .7097 dollar per Swiss franc. An investor can invest $100,000 in the U.S. and earn interest of $5,000 (100,000 x 10/2) over six months. The same investor can use that $100,000 today to buy 140,905 francs and invest it in a Swiss bank, where it will earn 3,525 francs.

When the investor decides to transfer his currency to the U.S., what will be the exchange rate? If the investor has sold francs in the 180-day forward market, the exchange rate should be .7270 and earnings would translate to $5,000. If the exchange rate were lower, e.g., .7100, the amount would be $2,543 and no one would be interested in investing in Switzerland. All Swiss investors would want to invest in U.S., so they would buy dollars and the drive exchange rate down to .7270, where excess profits would disappear.

THE FISHER PRICE EFFECT

The Fisher price effect states that a difference in interest rates must equal the expected difference in inflation rates. The interest rate is made up several different components:

Interest rate $= K_r + K_i + K_{drp}$

where K_r = the real interest rate,
       K_i = the inflation premium, and
       K_{drp} = the default risk premium.

Fisher argued that the real interest rate remains the same for all countries. Thus differences in the exchange rate are a direct result of differences in the inflation rate. (It is assumed that the investments are identical and therefore the default risk would be the same.) If real interest rates were different, there would be an excellent opportunity for currency arbitrage and eventually the market would make the exchange rates such that the real interest rate was identical.

PURCHASING POWER PARITY

The law of purchasing power parity states that the expected difference in inflation rate equals the difference between the forward and the spot rate. This can be easily proven. According to the interest rate parity theory, the difference in interest rate equals the difference between the forward and spot rate. According to the Fisher price effect, the difference in interest rate also equals the difference in inflation rate. Therefore, the difference in the inflation rate should equal the difference between the forward and the spot rates.

These three theories form the cornerstone of international finance. The theories are very important in that they are used to develop some fundamental forecasting models. They have been kept relatively simple, although real life is not this simple. These models are often modified to account for real world and market imperfections.

FORECASTING TECHNIQUES

The international financial markets are very complex. Therefore, a variety of forecasting techniques are used to forecast the foreign exchange rate. One method of forecasting may be more suited to one particular exchange rate scenario.

The four major ways of forecasting foreign exchange rates are fundamental forecasting, market-based forecasting, technical forecasting, and a mixture of the three.

FUNDAMENTAL FORECASTING

Fundamental forecasting is based on the fundamental relationships between economic variables and exchange rates. Given current values for economic variables along with their historical impact on the value of a currency, MNCs can develop exchange rate projections.

In previous sections, we established a basic relationship between exchange rates, inflation rates, and interest rates. This relationship can be used to develop a simple linear forecasting model for Deutsche mark.

$$DM = a + b \, (INF) + c \, (INT)$$

where   DM   = quarterly percentage change in the German mark,
            INF   = quarterly percentage change in inflation differential
                      (U.S. inflation rate − German inflation rate), and
            INT   = quarterly percentage change in interest rate differential
                      (U.S. interest rate − German interest rate).

This model is relatively simple, with only two explanatory variables. Though other variables are often added, the essential methodology remains the same.

The following example illustrates how exchange rates can be forecast using the fundamental approach. Table 16.2 shows the basic input data for ten quarters. Table 16.3 summarizes the regression output produced by *Microsoft Excel*.

Table 16.2—BASIC INPUT DATA

Period	US CPI	US Inf	G CPI	G INF	US INT	G INT	DM/$	INF Diff	INT Diff
Apr-95	123.7	1.56%	104.0	0.87%	9.64%	6.97%	1.8783	0.69%	2.67%
Jul-95	124.7	0.81%	104.5	0.48%	9.51%	6.87%	1.8675	0.33%	2.64%
Oct-95	125.9	0.96%	105.2	0.67%	9.92%	7.40%	1.8375	0.29%	2.52%
Jan-96	128.1	1.75%	105.9	0.67%	10.82%	8.50%	1.6800	1.08%	2.32%
Apr-96	129.4	1.01%	106.4	0.47%	11.42%	8.87%	1.6820	0.54%	2.55%
Jul-96	131.6	1.70%	107.3	0.85%	11.25%	8.93%	1.5920	0.85%	2.32%
Oct-96	133.8	1.67%	108.4	1.03%	10.83%	9.00%	1.5180	0.65%	1.83%
Jan-97	134.9	0.82%	108.7	0.28%	10.06%	9.70%	1.4835	0.55%	0.36%
Apr-97	135.7	0.59%	108.7	0.00%	10.16%	8.40%	1.7350	0.59%	1.76%
Jul-97	136.6	0.66%	109.7	0.92%	9.84%	8.60%	1.7445	-0.26%	1.24%
Oct-97	137.8	0.88%	111.8	1.91%	9.62%	8.40%	1.6750	-1.04%	1.22%
Jan-98	138.8	0.73%	112.7	0.81%	9.36%	8.00%		-0.08%	1.36%

Table 16.2—BASIC INPUT DATA, *con't.*

Period		Quaterly % Change	
	INF Diff.	INT Diff	DM/$
Jul-95	-0.523	-0.01124	-0.00575
Oct-95	-0.107	-0.04545	-0.01606
Jan-96	2.6998	-0.07937	-0.08571
Apr-96	-0.498	0.099138	0.00119
Jul-96	0.5742	-0.0972	-0.05351
Oct-96	-0.243	-0.02112	-0.04648
Jan-97	-0.157	-0.80328	-0.02273
Apr-97	0.0874	3.888889	0.169532
Jul-97	-1.433	-0.29545	0.005476
Oct-97	3.0346	-0.01613	-0.03984
Jan-98	-0.923	0.114754	

Table 16.3—*MICROSOFT EXCEL* REGRESSION OUTPUT

Analysis of Variance	df	Sum of Squares	Mean Square	F	Significance F
Regression	2	0.039325	0.01966	41.317	0.00013
Residual	7	0.003331	0.00048		
Total	9	0.042656			

	Coefficients	Standard Error	t-Statistic	P-value	Lower 95%	Upper 95%
Intercept	-0.0149	0.0072502	-2.057589	0.06975	-0.0321	0.00223
INF Diff.	-0.0171	0.0050964	-3.352584	0.00849	-0.0291	-0.005
INT Diff.	0.04679	0.0055715	8.39862	1.5E-05	0.0336	0.05997

Regression Statistics	
Multiple R	0.9602
R Square	0.9219
Adjusted R-Square	0.8996
Standard Error	0.0218
Observations	10

The forecasting model that can be used to predict the DM/$ exchange rate for the next quarter is:

$$DM = -0.0149 - 0.0171 \, (INF) + 0.0468 \, (INT)$$
$$R^2 = 92.19\%$$

Ex post predictions are summarized in Table 16.4 and plotted against
actual values in Figure 16.1.

Table 16.4—PREDICTED EXCHANGE RATE VALUES FOR DM/$

Observation	Predicted Y	Residuals	Stdzd Residuals	Percentile	DM/$
1	-0.00651	0.000756	0.034667	5	-0.0857
2	-0.01521	-0.00085	-0.039159	15	-0.0535
3	-0.06476	-0.02095	-0.960496	25	-0.0465
4	-0.00176	0.002953	0.135359	35	-0.0398
5	-0.02895	-0.02456	-1.125773	45	-0.0227
6	-0.02065	-0.02584	-1.184324	55	-0.0161
7	-0.04983	0.027104	1.242462	65	-0.0057
8	0.165562	0.00397	0.181967	75	0.0012
9	-0.00426	0.009735	0.446276	85	0.0055
10	-0.06752	0.027684	1.269022	95	0.1695

Figure 16.1—PLOT OF PREDICTED AND ACTUAL Y VALUES

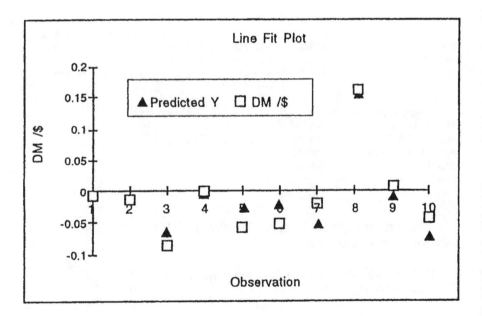

Assuming that INT   = -0.9234 and INF = 0.1148 for the next quarter,
  DM   = -0.0149 - 0.0171 (-0.9234) + 0.0468 (0.1148) =
      0.00623
  DM/$ = (1 + 0.00623) x (1.6750) = 1.6854

According to the forecast, the exchange rate in the first quarter of 1998 should have been 1.6854. The actual rate was 1.6392. The error in the forecast was .0462 (1.6854 - 1.6392) and the mean percentage error (MPE) for the forecast was 2.78 percent.

This simple fundamental forecasting model for foreign exchange rates is especially useful if the exchange rates are floating freely and there is minimum government or central bank intervention in the currency market. Note that this model relies on relationships between macroeconomic variables.

However, there are certain problems with the model. First, it will not be very effective with fixed exchange rates. The technique also relies on forecast to forecast; that is, one must project the future interest rate and the future inflation rate in order to compute the differentials that will be used to compute the exchange rate. (*Note*: These estimates are frequently published in trade publications and bank reports.) Second, the technique often ignores other variables that influence the foreign exchange rate.

MARKET-BASED FORECASTING

Market-based forecasting, which develops forecasts from market indicators, is perhaps the easiest forecasting model, very simple, but also very effective. The model relies on the spot and the forward rate to forecast price. It assumes that the spot rate reflects the foreign exchange rate in the near future.

Let us suppose that the Italian lira is expected to depreciate against the U.S. dollar, which would encourage speculators to sell lira and later buy them back at the lower future price. This process if continued would drive down the prices of lira until excess (arbitrage) profits were eliminated.

The model also suggests that the forward exchange rate equals the future spot price. Suppose the 90-day forward rate is .987. Market forecasters believe that the exchange rate in 90 days will be .965. This provides an arbitrage opportunity. Traders will keep selling the currency in the forward market until the opportunity for excess profit is eliminated.

This model, however, assumes that capital markets and currency markets are highly efficient and that there is perfect information in the market place. Under these circumstances, this model can provide accurate forecasts. Indeed, many of the world currency markets, such as those for the U.S. dollar, German mark, and Japanese yen, *are* highly efficient; this model is well suited for them. However, market imperfections or lack of perfect information reduces the model's effectiveness. In some cases, it cannot be used.

TECHNICAL FORECASTING

Technical forecasting uses historical exchange rates to predict future values. It is sometimes a process of pure judgment, without statistical analysis. Often, however, statistical analysis is applied to detect historical trends. There are also time series models that examine moving averages.

Most technical models, then, rely on the past to predict the future. They try to identify a historical pattern that seems to repeat. Models range from a simple moving average to a complex autoregressive integrated moving average (ARIMA). Most models try to break down the historical series to identify and remove the random element. Then they try to forecast the overall trend with cyclical and seasonal variations.

A moving average is useful to remove minor random fluctuations. A trend analysis is useful to forecast a long-term linear or exponential trend. Winter's seasonal smoothing and Census XII decomposition are useful to forecast long term cycles with additive seasonal variations. ARIMA is useful to predict cycles with multiplicative seasonality. Many forecasting and statistical packages such as *Forecast Pro, Sibyl/Runner, Minitab,* and *SAS* can handle these computations.

Table 16.5 is an example of technical forecasting using the previous six years of monthly data of the German mark (DM/$) exchange rate to forecast the DM/$ for the first 9 months in 1998; the data are plotted in Figure 16.2.

Table 16.5—GERMANY CURRENCY 7-YEAR MONTHLY CLOSING

Month	1992	1993	1994	1995	1996	1997	1998
January	2.3892	1.8298	1.6785	1.8648	1.6805	1.4835	1.6190
February	2.2185	1.8268	1.6884	1.8296	1.6930	1.5195	1.6395
March	2.3175	1.8028	1.8219	1.8927	1.6947	1.7000	1.6445
April	2.1865	1.7985	1.6773	1.8783	1.6822	1.7350	1.6590
May	2.3127	1.8215	1.7015	1.9858	1.6913	1.7255	1.6080
June	2.1986	1.8240	1.8211	1.9535	1.6645	1.8120	1.5255
July	2.0940	1.8590	1.8810	1.8675	1.5920	1.7445	1.4778
August	2.0520	1.8145	1.8748	1.9608	1.5680	1.7425	1.4055
September	2.0207	1.8460	1.8798	1.8730	1.5650	1.6612	1.4105
October	2.0630	1.7255	1.7684	1.8353	1.5180	1.6750	

Table 16.5—GERMANY CURRENCY 7-YEAR MONTHLY CLOSING, *con't.*

Month	1992	1993	1994	1995	1996	1997	1998
November	2.9880	1.6375	1.7354	1.7895	1.5030	1.6327	
December	1.9188	1.5713	1.7803	1.6915	1.4955	1.5175	

Source: The raw data was derived from *Business International*, December 1998.

Figure 16.2—PLOT OF 6-YEAR DM/$ RATE

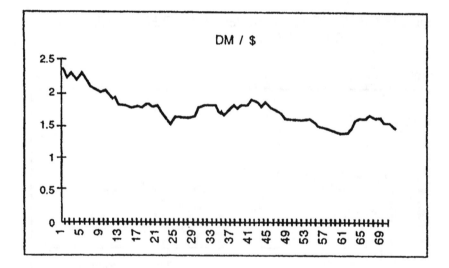

The data pattern seems to show a mild cycle with additive seasonality. Winter's seasonal smoothing is the ideal method under these situations. The data were run in Forecast Pro for Windows, a PC software package. The forecast is summarized in Table 16.6 and plotted against actual values in Figure16.3.

Table 16.6—SUMMARY OF DM/$ EXCHANGE RATE FORECAST

Forecast	Actual	Error	% Error
1.6080	1.6190	-0.0110	-0.68%
1.6507	1.6395	0.0112	0.68%
1.7248	1.6445	0.0803	4.77%
1.6593	1.6590	0.0003	0.02%
1.6079	1.6080	-0.0001	-0.01%
1.5879	1.5255	0.0624	4.01%
1.4863	1.4778	0.0085	0.57%
1.4526	1.4055	0.0471	3.30%
1.3834	1.4105	<u>-0.0271</u>	<u>-1.94%</u>
	Average:	0.0191	1.19%

Figure 16.3—PLOT OF ACTUAL VERSUS SMOOTHED VALUES FOR A 6-YEAR DM/$ RATE

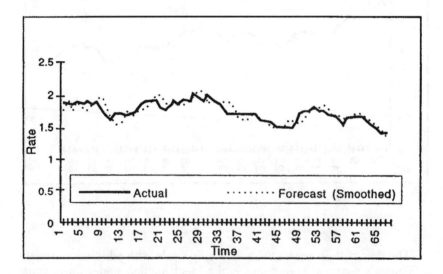

Table 16.6 also summarizes the predictive performance of the model. The mean percentage error (MPE) was somewhat low (1.19%), which generally indicates a good forecast.

MIXED FORECASTING

Mixed forecasting is a combination of the three methods previously discussed. In some cases, mixed forecast is nothing but a weighted average of a variety of forecasting techniques. The techniques can be weighted arbitrarily or by assigning a higher weight to the more reliable technique. Mixed forecasting can often lead to a better result than a single forecast.

EVALUATING FORECASTS

Forecasting foreign exchange is an ongoing process. Due to the dynamic nature of international markets, forecasts may not be accurate. However, the quality of forecast does improve with a forecaster's experience. Therefore, it is necessary to set up a framework within which a forecast can be evaluated.

The simplest framework would be to measure errors in forecasting, which was discussed in detail in Chapter 4. Several measures such as MAD, MSE, and MPE can be calculated and tracked. If more than one forecasting technique, i.e., a mixed forecast, is used, a company may be able to decide which technique is superior in order to adjust the weighting scale.

A good framework makes it easy for a company to predict errors in forecasting. For example, if a forecaster is consistently forecasting the foreign exchange rate for the German mark above its actual rate, this would suggest the need for an adjustment for this bias. Furthermore, the tracking signal and turning point error need to be systematically monitored.

CONCLUSION

Failure to accurately forecast currency can have a disastrous impact on earnings. Yet currency forecasting is neglected in many MNCs. They often argue that forecasting is useless since it does not provide an accurate estimate. They do not even have a hedging strategy.

It is important to realize that forecasting is often undertaken not only so that the corporation has a general idea about the overall trend of the future but also to avoid being caught off guard. Even if currency forecasts are not 100 percent accurate, they do provide some advance warning of future trends.

The quality of forecasts tends to improve over time as the forecaster gains experience. Although evidence shows that forecasts using qualitative techniques are not as accurate as those using quantitative techniques, judgment and intuition do have value in forecasting. An experienced forecaster uses both qualitative and quantitative techniques to create a reasonable forecast.

CHAPTER 17
INTEREST RATE
FORECASTING

While a number of efforts have been devoted to evaluating the accuracy of forecasts of sales and earnings per share, little attention has been given to the reliability of interest forecasts. With interest rates and earnings more closely linked than ever before, interest rates must be forecast accurately.

Many corporate financial decisions, such as the timing of a bond refunding, depend on anticipated changes in interest rate. Especially for financial institutions, changes in interest rates can be one of the variables most important to the success of the enterprise since both lending and investing decisions are heavily influenced by anticipated movements in interest rates.

Clearly, the accuracy of interest rate forecasts is important from the perspective of the producer and the consumer of such forecasts. Whether refinancing a mortgage or completing a multimillion-dollar acquisition, the future direction of interest rates is key. It is important to develop a tracking and forecasting system that considers not only economic factors but also the psychological and political forces affecting interest rates.

INTEREST RATE FUNDAMENTALS

Today's supply of and demand for credit determines today's short-term interest rate. Expectations about the future supply of and demand for credit determine the long-term interest rate. Both short- and long-term interest rates are impacted by similar factors.

What are the specific factors that determine interest rates? The business cycle is one. The cycle tends to dictate credit demands by both government and businesses. Economic growth is driven by credit and liquidity in our economy. As the demand for funds strengthens during an expansion, there is upward pressure on interest rates. The reverse occurs during a business contraction.

Although the demand side is stressed in this explanation of the cyclical effect on interest rates, the supply side of credit and liquidity should not be ignored. For example, foreign credit supplies are certainly an important factor these days. The larger the trade deficit, the larger will be the influx of foreign capital into the U.S.—which, all things being equal, helps lower interest rates.

Any gap between demand and supply can be accentuated by monetary policy. The Federal Reserve is supposed to "lean against the wind." M-1 (growth of the monetary aggregates), the Fed's net addition to liquidity, will tend to raise interest rates near cyclical peaks and diminish them at cyclical troughs.

In addition, inflation affects short- and long-term interest rates. One key factor is compensation for anticipated inflation, which would otherwise erode the purchasing power of principal and interest and hence ruin the supply of savings.

The stage is set for interest rate forecasting. Interest rates are the dependent variable within a multiple regression framework in which the state of the business cycle, monetary policy, and inflation anticipations are explanatory variables.

The difficulty is that the correct measurement of the explanatory factors is hard to find. For example, how do you represent the business cycle? It can be characterized by a multitude of business conditions and their statistical representations. The Fed's monetary policy is another example. Finding the right proxies is burdensome.

Furthermore, the interest rate, the dependent variable, is also hard to define, since there are short-term, intermediate-term, and long-term rates. Table 17.1 presents a guide to selecting the dependent variable and conceivable independent variables. By no means an exhaustive list, the table is only a suggested guide based on a review of past efforts at forecasting interest rates.

Table 17.2 provides a list of variables that emerged from empirical testing by interest rate experts.

Table 17.1—VARIABLES COMMONLY USED IN INTEREST RATE FORECASTING

DEPENDENT VARIABLES

1. *Short-Term Rates*
   U.S. Treasury bill rates (notably three-month)
   Federal funds rate
   Prime rate
2. *Long-Term Rates*
   New AA utility bond yields
   10-year U.S. Treasury bond yields
   20-year U.S. Treasury bond yields
   30-year U.S. Treasury bond yields
   Commercial mortgage rates
   Residential mortgage rates

INDEPENDENT VARIABLES

1. *Real Economic Activity*
   Real GDP
   Change in real GDP
   Change in non-agricultural payroll employment
   Confidence index
   Leading economic indicators
2. *Capacity Utilization*
   Rate of growth in productivity
   Vendor performance
   New capacity utilization estimates
   Manufacturers capacity utilization
   Operating rates to preferred rates
   Utilization rate . . . manufacturing
   Capacity utilization . . . primary materials
   Capacity utilization . . . advanced processing
   Buying policy
   Business equipment/consumer goods
   Help wanted/unemployment
   Number of initial jobless claims
   Change in unfilled orders
   Output/capacity
3. *Credit Demands by Government and Businesses*
   Income velocity (GDP/M-1)
   Federal budget deficit/GDP
   Change in mortgage debt

Table 17.1—VARIABLES COMMONLY USED IN INTEREST RATE FORECASTING, *con't.*

    Change in bank loans to business
    Change in installment debt
4. *Inflation Rate*
    Change in Consumer Price Index (CPI)
    Change in Producer Price Index (PPI)
5. *Monetary Aggregates*
    Change in money supply (M-1)
    Change in money supply (M-2)
    Real money base money supply in constant dollars (M-1)
6. *Liquidity*
    Money supply (M-1)/GDP
    Money supply (M-2)/GDP
7. *Banking*
    Member bank borrowing
    Loans/deposits...commercial banks
    Loans/investments...commercial banks
8. *Households*
    Change in household net worth (flow of funds)
9. *Corporations*
    Internal cash flow/business capital spending
10. *Foreign Credit Supplies and Foreign Influences*
    Size of the current account (i.e., foreign trade) deficit/GDP Foreign interest rates
11. *Expectational Variables*
    Moving average of prior years of actual inflation
    Moving average of the change in the 3-month T-bill yield
    Polynomial distributed lag of the percentage change in the CPI

Table 17.2—KEY VARIABLES IN INTEREST RATE FORECASTING FOUND IN THE LITERATURE

Dependent Variable	Independent (Explanatory) Variables
1. Roger Williams[1]	
Federal fund rate	Vendor performance Change in money supply M-1 or M-2 Rate of change in the CPI
New AA utility bond yields	Vendor performance Rate of change in the CPI lagged one period

Table 17.2—KEY VARIABLES IN INTEREST RATE FORECASTING FOUND IN THE LITERATURE, *con't.*

Dependent Variable	Independent (Explanatory) Variables
	Ratio of bank loans to investments lagged one period
2. The Prudential[2]	
10-year Treasury bond yields	Government deficits/GDP Foreign trade/GDP Rate of growth in productivity Moving average of the five prior years of actual inflation Lagged change in GDP Foreign interest rates Variance and momentum indexes
3. Schott[3]	
20-year Treasury bond yields	Log (unemployment rate) Percentage change in M-1 Polynomial distributed lag of the percentage Change in the CPI Volatility = moving average of the change in the 3-month T-bill
4. Horan[4]	
New AA utility bond yield	Income volatility (GDP/M-1) Moving average of CPI change Commercial paper rate RHO (autoregressive error term)

[1]Roger Williams, "Forecasting Interest Rates and Inflation," *Business Economics*, 57-60. January 1979, pp. 57-60.

[2]The Prudential, "Understanding Long-Term Interest Rates," *Economic Review*. July 1991, pp. 1-8.

[3]Francis H. Schott, "Forecasting Interest Rates: Methods and Application," *Journal of Business Forecasting*, Fall 1986, pp. 11-19.

[4]Lawrence J. Horan, "Forecasting Long-Term Interest Rates—A New Method," *Business Economics*, September 1978, pp. 5-8.

STATISTICAL METHODOLOGY AND A SAMPLE MODEL

Despite many difficulties, business economists often attempt statistical forecasts of interest rates structured along the lines of the sample equation shown in Table 17.3. Multiple regression analysis appears to be the dominant approach to building the model for interest rate forecasting.

In Table 17.3, we show the 20-year U.S. Treasury bond yield as a function of the unemployment rate, the growth in money supply, a weighted average of past inflation, and volatility in the three-month Treasury bill.

Table 17.3—MODEL AND VALUES OF PARAMETERS

MODEL
20-Year T-Bond Yield = b_0 + b_1 ˇ log (Unemployment Rate) + b_2 x % Change in M-1 + b_3 x Change in CPI, Annualized + b_4 x Volatility

VALUE OF PARAMETERS

Independent Variable	Coefficient	t-value*
1. Constant	11.137	4.36
2. Log (unemployment rate)	-3.297	-3.65
3. Percentage change in M-1	-0.026	-2.16
4. Polynomial distributed lag of the percentage change in the CPI annualized; lag of 4 quarters, 2nd degree polynomial	-0.24	-2.73
5. Volatility; 4-year moving average of the absolute value of the change in the 3-month T-bill	1.726	2.05

n = 47
S_e = 0.4709
R^2 = 0.975
Durbin-Watson =1.64**

*Statistically significant at the 5 percent significance level.
**No auto-correlation (serial correlation) at the 1 percent level.

Source: Francis H. Schott, "Forecasting Interest Rates: Methods and Application," *Journal of Business Forecasting*, Fall 1986, p18.

CHECKLIST FOR SCREENING OUT EXPLANATORY FACTORS

In order to pick the best regression equation for interest forecasting, follow the criteria presented in Chapter 5 (Multiple Regression). Some are repeated here.

1. Many independent variables listed in Table 17.2 tend to be highly correlated with each other (*multicollinearity*). This helps to eliminate a number of overlapping series.

2. Variables cannot be retained unless the positive or negative signs of regression coefficients are consistent with theoretical expectations.

4. Traditional yardsticks such as R^2, t-test, F-test, and Durbin-Watson test must be used to select preliminary equations.

5. The predictive performance of the preliminary models needs to be tested based on ex ante and ex post forecasts.
   (a) It is usually measured by such metrics as MPE, RSME, MSE, MAD, and/or the Theil U Coefficient.
   (b) Compare the forecasts with some naive (but much less costly) approach, such as assuming that rates in the future will be the same as today.
   (c) Compare quantitative approaches such as econometric forecasting with judgmental forecasts. Judgment can be the overriding factor in interest rate forecasting.
   (d) *Turning point error* needs to be evaluated separately. A turning point error takes place when either an increase in interest levels was projected but rates declined or vice versa. It often is argued that the ability of forecasters to anticipate reversals of interest rate trends is more important than the precise accuracy of the forecast. Substantial gains or losses may arise from a move from generally upward rate trends to downward rate trends (or vice versa), but gains or losses from incorrectly predicting the extent of a continued increase or decrease in rates may be much more limited.

A WORD OF CAUTION

Judgments and expert opinions can help determine the future direction of interest rates. The right marriage between a quantitative evaluation and expert judgments is a must. No reasonable business planners will rely solely on statistical methods such as multiple regression. Other quantitative methods need to be attempted. Differences among forecasting methods and assumptions and the choice of proxies for the explanatory variables can yield vastly different results from analyst to analyst. Consensus forecasts such as those of the National Association of Business Economists (NABE), which receives wide coverage in the financial press, and econometric forecasts made by consulting firms like The Wharton Econometric Associates, Chase Econometrics, and DRI/McGraw-Hill should be consulted as well.

The cost of errors in interest rate forecasting can be as severe as exchange rate forecasting mistakes. Francis Schott at Equitable Life suggests that businesses use specific strategies and policies to reduce their exposure to interest rate forecasting mistakes (e.g., asset/liability maturity matching and hedging with futures).

CONCLUSION

Interest rate forecasting is as treacherous as other economic forecasting. This chapter touched briefly upon fundamentals: business cycles, the outlook for the demand and supply of credits, monetary policy, and the inflation rate. It also presented a sample model that reflects the fundamental theory. The forecasting ability of the model should be judged in terms of its ability to anticipate major changes in the direction (turning point) of rates.

CHAPTER 18
TECHNOLOGICAL
FORECASTING

Technological forecasting is a discipline concerned with identifying new products based on innovative technologies that will produce growth markets. It attempts to predict changes in technology and to estimate the time frame in which new technologies are likely to be economically feasible. By its very nature, it is one of the most difficult kinds of forecasts to make because of the innumerable variables, unknowns and possible outcomes. However, being able to forecast technology with a reasonable degree of accuracy is becoming increasing important to the success of business managers in gaining a competitive edge—or even remaining viable in the long run, as evidenced by the tremendous pace of change occurring today.

It is probably very safe to say that we have experienced greater technological change in the last 50 years than in all the years before from the beginning of recorded history. The implication is that technological growth will continue at an ever accelerating rate.

In order to remain competitive, and possibly even gain a competitive advantage, in these times of change, management must engage in technological forecasting. Nothing can be more damaging to a company than to allow competitors to get a jump on it in new products or techniques. Technological developments may be a requirement not only for competitiveness but also for self-preservation.

Planning for most areas affecting the operations of an enterprise will be predicated on assumptions about future technology. Planning for capital investment in new machinery or equipment, for new facilities, and for the research and development activities of the enterprise are some examples.

ACCURACY OF TECHNOLOGICAL FORECASTING

The need for technological forecasting is clear, but the ability to produce accurate forecasts is lacking. There are so many intangibles involved in the development of technological breakthroughs that the forecaster is severely limited. It is doubtful that anyone could have predicted the many technical spin-offs from the space program, for example. Nor, for that matter, can we surmise the full results of the unforeseen development of a method of immunization against cancer or AIDS.

Once a breakthrough occurs, however, prediction of its development is more feasible. A historical analysis of the progress of the technology of any given development is most likely to show an exponential improvement rate. Progress can be represented by a curve like that shown in Figure 18.1.

Figure 18.1—PROJECTION OF BIT DENSITY IN COMPUTER MEMORY

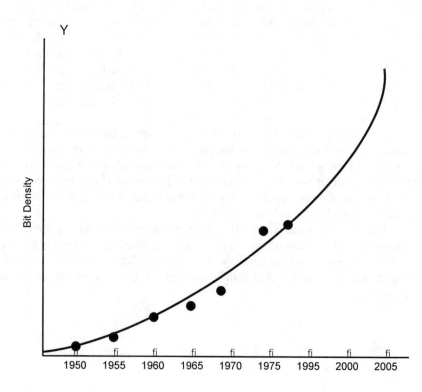

This curve has certain underlying assumptions. Early progress is very small for a period of time. At some point very rapid progress begins, probably as a result of a specific breakthrough. This may be the result of a discovery making a useful item possible, as splitting the atom made atomic energy feasible. The discovery could result from a production technology making economical production possible. Following the period of rapid growth, a leveling off is seen. This could represent a period of saturation, where only by another breakthrough could any further significant progress take place. It is also conceivable that another curve of the same shape could start where this curve left off. For example, television could be represented by two sequential curves, the first showing progress for black and white, the second for color television.

THE S-CURVE AS A GUIDE

The S-curve reveals the life cycle of a particular product or process. It graphs the relationship between the effort put into improving a product or process and the results from making the investment. It shows how one technology eventually outperforms another previously higher-performance technology when there is a discontinuity. It can be used as a guide because at the point of maturity (increased efforts and investment resulting in smaller productivity improvements) firms need to look for higher-performing technologies, which frequently involve radical changes. It is strategically important to organizations because otherwise they may be leapfrogged by competitors who adopt a radically different technology to achieve a competitive advantage. The notion of S-curves suggests that organizations need to manage a portfolio of technologies in order to compete in the long term.

METHODOLOGY OF TECHNOLOGICAL FORECASTING

Despite what has been said about the problems of accurate technological forecasting, a company should nevertheless make this kind of forecast. In the short term, forecasts based of historical trends and statistical probability analysis should be acceptable. This does not mean, however, that history repeats itself, or that because certain progress took place in the past there will be continued similar progress.

It is possible to determine the pertinent elements of the environment and to be cognizant of their impact. Technological forecasting must recognize the strong influence of environmental factors. This type of forecast is only part of a total attempt to relate the enterprise to its environment. It is not possible to produce a technological forecast without this recognition. The relationship of technology to society appears to be of particular significance.

Methods that have been devised to forecast technology are:

1. Delphi method

2. Simple trend extrapolation and lead-lag relationships

3. Input-output models

4. Production models

5. Diffusion models

THE DELPHI METHOD

According to surveys and expert opinions on technological forecasting, intuition seems to play a very important role in exploratory technological forecasting. For instance, suppose that a company wants to forecast the maximum speed of PCs in the year 2010. One way to obtain such a forecast would simply be to ask an expert or a group of experts to make an educated guess about what they think the speed will be at that time.

Though this approach is relatively straightforward and inexpensive, it suffers from a number of difficulties. First, answers are likely to vary depending on the expert. Second, even when the experts are distinguished, the forecasts can contain major errors. For example, Stableford and Langford[1] predicted in 1985 that there would be a near disaster of small nuclear war."

The Delphi method can be used to deal with some of the inherent problems involved in simply asking a group of experts for a consensus guess. To forecast the maximum speed of PCs in the year 2010, users of the Delphi method would ask a number of experts to formulate independent estimates. The median and interquartile range of the estimates would then be communicated to each of the experts, and they would be asked to reconsider their previous answers and revise them if they wanted to.

---

[1]B. Stableford and David Langford, *The Third Millennium: A History of the World: AD 2000-3000* (Alfred Knopf, 1985).

Those people whose answers lay outside the interquartile range would be asked to state why they disagree with the other members of the group. Their replies would be circulated among the group, and the members would be asked once again to make a forecast. The interactive process would continue until there was a reasonable convergence of the individual forecasts.

This method is not without its flaws. For example, in 1973, DuPont, Scott Paper, Lever Brothers, and Monsanto funded Project Aware, a comprehensive Delphi study conducted by the Institute of the Future. The study was a unique attempt to predict long-range changes in the social, economic, and technological environment that the companies would face in the next decade. The experts who participated in the study reached a consensus that there was a 90 percent probability that National Health Insurance would be enacted by 1985.

Kaiser Aluminum fared no better with a consensus-generating technique. In 1966 it conducted a Delphi study called Future. The study had experts estimate the probability that each of 60 events would occur in the next 20 years (by 1986). Most of the forecasts were stated vaguely and hence were difficult to evaluate. But the experts foresaw the greatest likelihood (80 percent) that (1) worldwide production of fresh water from the oceans would be economic, and (2) there would be widespread use of lasers and ultra-light metal substitutes. No one predicted the event that most affected the future of the industry: the inexorable decline of domestic steel production. It was not that the experts got the probabilities wrong; they just did not consider the right issues. Instead of issues of the future, they focused on issues of their own time.

The results of the Delphi method obviously can be no better than the foresight of the individual experts. This foresight, as noted, can be very imperfect. Moreover, by relying so heavily on consensus, the Delphi method assumes that collective judgment is better than individual judgment. This is a dangerous assumption, as evidenced by the many important technological advances that have been made by individuals and groups that acted contrary to prevailing majority—and elite—opinion.

SIMPLE TREND EXTRAPOLATION AND LEAD-LAG RELATIONSHIPS

Another technique that plays an important role in exploratory technological forecasting is *simple trend extrapolation*. To forecast the maximum speed of PCs in 2010, one would obtain a time series of the maximum speed of the PC at various points in history and project the historical trend into the future. In fact, Naisbitt[2] used this approach to project future trends in our society, such as a shift from an industrial to an information society and globalization of the economy.

The problem with these types of naive extrapolation is that, unless the fundamental factors determining the technological parameter in question operate much as they have in the past, previous trends will not necessarily be a good guide to the future. For example, a host of factors, including the allocation of R & D resources, data processing needs, and the competitive pressure of the industry, may see to it that the maximum speed of PCs increases at quite a different rate than it has in the immediate past. Or take the case of productivity increase: There is considerable evidence that productivity has not increased at a constant rate in the United States. The moral, well known to economists, is that a naive projection of historical trends is a dangerous business, particularly over the long term.

Besides trend extrapolation, technological forecasters have adopted another old favorite of economic forecasters: *lead-lag relationships*. To forecast the maximum speed of PCs in 2010, the forecaster would plot the maximum speed of PCs against the maximum speed of mainframes. Finding that PC speeds have lagged mainframe speeds, he or she might be able to use this relationship to make the desired forecast. Again, the problem is that the historical relationship may not prevail into the future.

There are plenty of examples of technological forecasting that used a combination of simple extrapolation and lead-lag relationships. Marvin Minsky, a pioneer in the field of artificial intelligence, sees computerized robots and smarter machines as a growing trend. Jack Kilby predicts that integrated circuit research will result in many new products and applications of technology. Jerome Feldman sees neutral networks, connectionist systems, and parallel-distributed processing systems becoming practical in the next decade. The huge growth of genetic engineering and biotechnology is already underway. By the year 2000, $100 billion worth of biotech drugs, plants, chemicals, and other products are expected to be sold worldwide.[3]

---

[2]John Naisbitt, *Megatrends: Ten New Directions Transforming Our Lives* (NY: Warner Books, 1982); John Naisbitt, *Megatrends 2000: Ten New Directions for the 1990's* (NY: William Morrow & Co., 1990).
[3]Business Week, *Reinventing America*, and various weekly issues.

INPUT-OUTPUT MODELS

There has been some experimentation with the projection of input-output structures into the future.[4] To make such projections one must forecast both the input requirements of future techniques and their rate of diffusion, since the input-output coefficients will be a weighted average of existing and future techniques, the weights depending on the rate of diffusion.

One way that economists have tried to forecast input-output coefficients in a particular industry is to assume that new technologies have a weight proportional to investment in new capacity. By observing changes in the industry's average input-output structure and its expenditures on new plant and equipment, one can estimate what the input-output coefficients for the new layer of capital must have been. To make short-term projections, one can then assume that the coefficients for the new layer will remain constant and increase the weight given to these coefficients in proportion to expected investment. This method is crude at best. All that its users claim is that it gives ballpark estimates.

Another way of projecting input-output structures is by using expert opinion. This method, however, suffers from the same difficulties as Delphi method, along with other problems. For one thing, the industrial classification employed in the input-output model is broader than the product categories the technologists making the forecasts are used to dealing with. For another, it is difficult to include qualitative changes, like new products, within the input-output framework. At present, the use of input-output analysis in connection with technological forecasting is still in its infancy. All that can be said is that it represents a promising area for future research.

PRODUCTION MODELS

Some economists suggest the use of production models based on R & D expenditures for technological forecasting. In recent years, many researchers have attempted to formulate econometric models of production in which R & D plays a role. Though these models are oversimplified and incomplete in many respects, they provide reasonably persuasive evidence that R & D has a significant effect on the rate of productivity increase in the industries and time periods studied. The models use regression and econometric techniques.

---

[4]A. Carter, "Technological Forecasting and Input-Output Analysis," *Technological Forecasting and Social Change.*

These models can be used to forecast the effects on productivity or output of a certain investment in R & D at various points in time, and future requirements for labor and other inputs. Of course, they cannot be used to forecast the precise nature of the technology that will result from an investment in R & D, but they can provide some idea of the input-output relationships that this technology will permit—and for many purposes these relationships are what really count. For example, if we can be reasonably sure that a given investment in R & D will result in a reduction in cost or in the use of crucial inputs (for example, alternative energy sources such as hydropower, solar energy, alcohol fuels, photovoltaic cells, and geothermal energy), this may be all that is really relevant for making certain decisions. The precise nature of the new technology may not matter much.

Some government agencies have become interested in these models in recent years. Their models suggest that the marginal rate of return from certain types of civilian R & D is very high, and that we may be underinvesting in it. It is difficult, of course, to tell how much influence these models had on the recent decisions by the American government to experiment with various devices to encourage additional civilian R & D, but we can rest assured that they are one of the influences. However, lest anyone get the impression that these models are sufficiently dependable to play a dominant role in influencing such decisions, let us add that they are extremely crude and subject to considerable error. Much more work still needs to be done.

DIFFUSION MODELS

In the past 30 years, a number of studies have been made of the diffusion of innovations. The results suggest that it is possible, on the basis of simple econometric models, to explain fairly well the differences among industrial innovations in their rate of diffusion. Mansfield[5] presented a simple model based on variables like the profitability of the innovation, the size of the investment required to adopt the innovation, and the organization of the industry of potential users—to explain differences in the rate at which innovations spread. This model explained very well the rates of diffusion of a dozen major innovations in the United States. Subsequent work has shown that it is also useful in explaining the rates of diffusion of other innovations, and in other countries.

---

[5]E. Mansfield, *The Economics of Technological Change* (New York: Norton, 1968).

For many purposes, it is extremely important to know how rapidly a new technique will displace an old one. Obviously, this is of crucial importance to the firm marketing the new technique, but it may be of great importance to others as well. For example, government agencies, labor unions, and competing firms are sometimes concerned with the extent to which labor will be displaced and how particular areas will be affected. For many purposes, the important consideration is not when an entirely new process or product will be invented in the future but how rapidly new processes and products that have already been invented will diffuse. Certainly, in view of the long time lags in many sectors of the economy, this often is all that matters in the short run—and the intermediate run as well.

For forecasting growth markets, however, research arising out of the diffusion of innovations has some problems. One stems from the fact that market growth is not automatic, or even likely. Forecasts based on such theories have a built-in tendency to be overly optimistic. They presuppose strong market growth and do not address adequately the possibility of failure. There is no law or inherent tendency for products to exhibit growth, as some formulations would have people believe. In fact, nearly every study that has looked at the issue has concluded that most products never make it past stage one.

This is not to suggest that the work in these areas is flawed but rather to point out that since the theories rely so heavily on after-the-fact explanations, they are of little help in predicting which technologies will go on to spawn huge growth markets and which will repeat previous failures.[6]

Diffusion models nevertheless have found a variety of uses in technological forecasting. One leading electronics firm has been experimenting with the use of this model to forecast the market penetration of its new products. Of course, the fact that this model has been used does not mean that it is other than a simple first approximation. It is continually being refined and tested on a wider and wider variety of technological and product areas, though we are still far from having a satisfactory understanding of the diffusion process.

AN EVALUATION

The present state of the art in technological forecasting can be characterized as follows:

---

[6]OECD Publication and Information Center, *New Technologies in the 1990s: A Socio-Economic Strategy* (OECD: 1988).

1. Most of the techniques commonly used for exploratory forecasting seem crude and inaccurate. Among other things, there have been no studies measuring the track record of various kinds of technological forecasting techniques. It would be useful to have some idea of how well these techniques have performed under various circumstances, and which techniques seem to do better under which circumstances. Without such information, it is hard for anyone to decide which exploratory forecasting activities are worth carrying out.

2. Despite the crudeness of most existing techniques, technological forecasting remains a necessary part of the decision-making process for firms and government agencies. The potential gains seem to outweigh the costs. However, given the lack of reliable data regarding the likely gains from various kinds of technological forecasting, it is not easy to compare techniques.

3. There is a great need for a better understanding of the process of technological change. Until the fundamental processes are somewhat better understood, it seems unlikely that exploratory forecasting techniques will improve much. The area perhaps best understood at present is the diffusion process, and this is the area where forecasting currently seems most effective. More emphasis must be placed on the accumulation of the basic knowledge that is required if this field is to become more a science and less an art.

4. If normative technological forecasting is to become widespread, it is important that better methods be developed to estimate development cost, time, probability of success, and the value of the outcome if achieved. At present, such estimates tend to be so biased and error-ridden that it is difficult to depend on their results. In view of the inaccuracy of these estimates, companies that use normative technological forecasting techniques must carry out "what-if" analyses to see the effect of errors. Further, they must see how big errors in these estimates have been in the recent past—since there seems to be some tendency to underestimate their size.

5. The work of technological forecasters needs to be integrated properly with the decisions of strategic planners. Frequently, the work of the technological forecasters is largely ignored. If this work is worth doing at all, it should be coupled with long range planning and decision-making.

6. It is important to recognize that one cannot estimate the probability that a particular technology will come into being on the basis

of technological considerations alone. Economic, social, political, and business anomalies are often equally important. Managers cannot decide how a firm's technological resources should be allocated and used on the basis of technological considerations alone.

CHAPER 19
FORECASTING IN THE
21ST CENTURY

Any discipline or managerial function can be expected to change over time, and forecasting is no exception. Alterations in the methodology and uses of forecasting can be expected to increase. These changes are likely to take the form of more sophisticated forecasting techniques, wide availability of expert-system-based forecasting software, and the increased use of forecasting by management.

MORE SOPHISTICATED TECHNIQUES AND USER-FRIENDLY SOFTWARE

The passage of time should witness advances in the quality of forecasting technology. Among the forces contributing to the elevation of the art are new developments in the social sciences, mathematics, research techniques, and information technology. Progress to date has been considerable, as witnessed by the many analysts who use innovations in simulation, brand-share models, and survey techniques.

A survey of the literature suggests that sensitivity ("what-if") analysis—a refined feature of model building—is being widely adopted. Sensitivity analysis involves manipulating a mathematical model and observing the effect on the dependent variable. If the effect is small, analysts need not concern themselves with attempting to develop more precise estimates of the magnitude of that variable. If the effect is substantial, attempts to improve precision may be in order. Increasing use of sensitivity analysis is only one indicator of advances in methodology. Virtually every phase of the forecasting process can be expected to become more sophisticated soon.

INCREASED USE OF FORECASTING

Managers of the future are likely to use forecasting to a larger extent than is the case now. Part of the impetus for this development will evolve from the increasing educational levels of executives. Larger numbers of managers have MBA degrees. The modern manager is more likely to have the training required to understand the methodology and even to construct forecast models. These better-educated managers are therefore likely to give more importance to forecasting as a planning and control tool than did their predecessors.

The increased pace of change is a second force that contributes to increased employment of forecasting. More and more products are displaying shorter life cycles. Industry sales change abruptly, producing rapid and significant fluctuations in company sales. These changes make it necessary for managers to have methods to signal what is expected to take place in the future. No longer can managers sit back and assume that sales will grow more or less automatically at a pace of 5 percent annually. They must continually monitor sales levels and be prepared to respond to change.

Cost pressures on management are likely to be continued. These take the form of increments in wages, power rates, interest rates, and costs of raw materials, supplies, parts, and equipment. These cost advances put pressure on management to produce effective plans and controls. These plans and controls are dependent on the sales forecast.

Business valuations that are essential for such key strategic activities as mergers and acquisitions require more precise prediction of future earnings, cash flows, and sales.

Increases in the intensity of competition can be expected to generate increments in forecasting use. Rivalry from both foreign and domestic firms is increasing, especially in industries like packaged foods, automobiles, and computers. As competition steps up, managers are forced to use effective forecasting processes to compete with rivals who are enhancing their own forecasting abilities.

Advancing inability to predict the future behavior of the consumer through simplistic methods that were effective in the past tends to induce further use and sophistication in sales forecasting. Increases in consumer education and discretionary income tend to render consumers less brand-loyal and more inclined to change their behavior, including purchase and use of previously unknown products. Consumers are becoming more fickle and their behavior more difficult to predict, despite considerable advances in the quality of consumer behavior research and theory.

The increasing sophistication of forecasting methods and modeling software should help produce greater usage of forecasting. Better tools and computer software are likely to yield wider use. As the methodology becomes more accurate and precise, managers can be expected to rely on forecasting more than they did in the past.

CONCLUSION

Some generalizations help in placing the forecasting process in proper perspective. One is that forecasting is an ongoing process; another is that it is essential. Forecasting is *not* an activity that takes place at periodic intervals, such as once a year, and ceases entirely between these intervals. Both short- and long-term forecasts are continually being made, evaluated, and revised. As new products are considered or are adopted, their sales potential is assessed.

Changes in the environment and internal structure of the firm are likely to be continual. Factors such as price alterations by competitors, strikes by labor unions, and changes in a firm's advertising strategy occur from time to time. Many of these phenomena are of sufficient significance to warrant alterations in existing sales forecasts. Forecasting is not a one-time, static activity. It is a continuing process that should merit constant attention.

Forecasting is essential. It is difficult, in some cases impossible, for a firm to develop and implement effective plans in the absence of well-conceived sales forecasts that provide managers with the means for planning, organizing, and controlling all of the resources at their disposal. In the absence of forecasts, these activities would have to be based on mere guesswork. The dynamic and uncertain nature of the business world dictates that sales forecasts be the springboard for virtually all major decisions made by management.

GLOSSARY

A

ACCURACY: The criterion for evaluating the performance of alternative forecasting methods and models. It refers to the correctness of the forecast as measured against actual events. Accuracy can be measured using such statistics as mean squared error (MSE) and mean absolute percentage error (MAPE).

ARIMA: An abbreviation for autoregressive integrated moving average. This name describes a broad class of time series models. In an ARIMA model, the past series (autoregressive terms) and past error values from forecasting (the moving average terms) are combined.

AUTO-CORRELATION: The extent to which a time series variable, lagged one or more time periods, is correlated with itself. (1) One of the assumptions required is a regression in order to make it reliable, also called serial correlation. When there is auto-correlation (i.e., the error terms are not independent), the standard errors of the regression coefficients are seriously underestimated. The problem of auto-correlation usually is detected by the Durbin-Watson statistic (*see also* Durbin-Watson statistic). (2) The pattern of auto-correlation coefficients is used to identify whether seasonality is present in a given time series (and the length of that seasonality), to identify appropriate time series models for specific situations, and to determine the presence of stationarity in the data.

AUTOREGRESSIVE (AR): A form of regression where the dependent variable is related to past values of itself at varying time lags. Thus an autoregressive model would express the forecast as a function of previous values of that time series.

AUTOREGRESSIVE / MOVING AVERAGE SCHEME: This type of time series forecasting model can be autoregressive (AR) in form, moving average (MA) in form, or a combination of the two (ARIMA).

B

BANKRUPTCY PREDICTION: Prediction of the financial distress of corporations, municipalities, universities, and other institutions.

BOX-JENKINS METHODOLOGY: The general methodology suggested by Box and Jenkins for applying autoregressive / moving average (ARIMA) models to time series forecasting problems. A time series model is proposed, statistically tested, modified, and re-tested until satisfactory.

BOX-PIERCE Q STATISTIC: A test on the auto-correlations of the residuals of the ARIMA model.

BUSINESS VALUATION: The process of determining the value of a business or an asset.

C

CASH BUDGET: A budget for cash planning and control presenting expected cash inflow and outflow for a designated time period. The cash budget helps management keep its cash balances in reasonable relationship to its needs. It helps the company avoid maintaining idle cash or suffering possible cash shortages.

CASH FLOW FORECASTING: Forecasts of cash flow, including cash collections from customers, investment income, and cash disbursements.

CAUSAL FORECASTING MODEL: A model that relates the variable to be forecast to a number of other variables that can be observed.

CENSUS X-II DECOMPOSITION: A refinement of the classical decomposition method, developed by the U.S. Bureau of Census.

CLASSICAL DECOMPOSITION METHOD: The approach to forecasting that seeks to decompose the underlying pattern of a time series into cyclical, seasonal, trend, and random sub-patterns. These sub-patterns are then analyzed individually, extrapolated into the future, and recombined to obtain forecasts from the original series.

COEFFICIENT OF DETERMINATION: A statistical measure of how good the estimated regression equation is, designated as R^2 (read as R-squared). It is a measure of "goodness of fit" in the regression. Therefore, the higher the R-squared, the more confidence we can have in our equation.

CONSTANT VARIANCE: *See* Homoscedasticity.

CORRELATION: The degree of relationship between business and economic variables such as cost and volume. Correlation analysis evaluates cause/effect relationships. It looks consistently at how the value of one variable changes when the value of the other is changed. Predictions can be made based on the relationships uncovered. An example is the effect of advertising on sales. A degree of correlation is measured statistically by the coefficient of determination (R-squared).

CORRELATION COEFFICIENT (R): A measure of the degree of correlation between two variables. The range of values for R is between -1 and +1. A negative value of R indicates an inverse relationship; a zero value of R indicates that the two variables are independent of each other; the closer R is to +1, the stronger the relationship between the two variables.

COST OF PREDICTION ERRORS: The cost of failure to predict a certain variable (such as sales, earnings, or cash flow) accurately.

COST PREDICTION: Forecast of costs for managerial decision-making purposes. The terms "cost estimation" and "cost prediction" are used interchangeably. To predict future costs, a cost function often is specified and estimated statistically. The cost function may be either linear or nonlinear. The estimated cost function must pass some statistical tests, such as having a high R^2 and a high t-value, to provide sound cost prediction.

D

DEGREE OF FREEDOM (DF): The number of data items that are independent of one another. Given a sample of data and the computation of some statistic (e.g., the mean), DF is defined as (number of observations included in the formula) minus (number of parameters estimated using the data). For example, the mean statistic for N sample data points has n DF, but the variance formula has (n-1) DF because one parameter (the mean X) has to be estimated before the variance formula can be used.

DEGREE OF RELATIVE LIQUIDITY (DRL): The percentage of a firm's cash expenditures that can be secured from (1) beginning fund and (2) cash generated from normal operations.

DELPHI METHOD: A qualitative forecasting method that seeks to use the judgment of experts systematically in arriving at a forecast of what future events will be or when they may occur. It draws upon a group of experts who have access to each other's opinions in an environment where no majority opinion is disclosed.

DEPENDENT VARIABLE: A variable whose value depends on the values of other variables and constants. For example, in the relationship $Y = f(X)$, Y is the dependent variable influenced by independent variables such as earnings per share, debt/equity ratio, and beta (*see also* Independent Variable).

DESEASONALIZED DATA: Removal of the seasonal pattern in a data series. Deseasonalizing facilitates the comparison of month-to-month changes.

DUMMY VARIABLE: Often referred to as a binary variable whose value is either 0 or 1, a dummy variable is used to quantify qualitative or categorical events. For example, a peace or war option could be represented by a dummy variable.

DURBIN-WATSON STATISTIC: A summary measure of the amount of auto-correlation in the error terms of the regression. By comparing the computed value of the Durbin-Watson test with the appropriate values from the table of values of the D-W statistic (Appendix Table A.4), its significance can be determined (*see also* Auto-correlation).

E

EARNINGS FORECAST: Projection of earnings or earnings per share (EPS) by management and independent security analysts. Examples of forecast sources include (1) Lynch, Jones, and Ryan's Institutional Brokers Estimate System (IBES), (2) Standard & Poor's *The Earnings Forecaster*, and (3) Zacks Investment Research's Icarus Service.

ECONOMETRIC FORECASTING: A method that uses a set of equations intended to be used simultaneously to capture how endogenous and exogenous variables are interrelated. The value of econometric forecasting is connected intimately to the value of the assumptions underlying the model equations.

ERROR TERM: Deviation of the actual value of an observation from the true regression line (*see also* Residual).

EX ANTE FORECAST: A forecast that uses only the data available when the actual forecast is prepared.

EX POST FORECAST: A forecast that uses some information estimated beyond the period for which the actual forecast is made.

EXPONENTIAL SMOOTHING: A technique that uses a weighted moving average of past data as the basis for a forecast. The procedure gives heaviest weight to more recent information and smaller weights to observations in the more distant past. The method is effective when there is random demand and no seasonal fluctuations in the data. The method is popular for short-run forecasting.

EXPONENTIAL SMOOTHING ADJUSTED FOR TREND: Also called Holt's two-parameter method, it adds a trend adjustment to the single smoothed value.

EXPONENTIAL SMOOTHING, SEASONAL: Also called Winter's three-parameter method, it is an extension by Winters of Holt's two-parameter exponential smoothing by including an additional equation that is used to adjust the smoothed forecast to reflect seasonality.

F

F-TEST: In statistics the ratio of two mean squares (variances) often can be used to test the significance of some item of interest. For example, in regression, the ratio of (mean square due to the regression) to (mean square due to error) can be used to test the overall significance of the regression model. By looking up F-tables, the degree of significance of the computed F-value can be determined.

FINANCIAL PROJECTION: An essential element of planning that is the basis for budgeting activities and estimating future financing needs of a firm. Financial projections (forecasts) begin with forecasting sales and their related expenses.

FORECAST: 1. A projection or an estimate of future sales revenue, earnings, or costs (*see also* Sales Forecasting). 2. A projection of future financial position and operating results of an organization (*see also* Financial Projection).

G

GOODNESS OF FIT: The degree to which a model fits the observed data. In a regression analysis, goodness of fit is measured by the coefficient of determination (R-squared).

GROSS DOMESTIC PRODUCT (GDP): A measure of the value of all goods and services produced by the economy within national boundaries; a nation's broadest gauge of economic health.

H

HOLT'S TWO-PARAMETER EXPONENTIAL SMOOTHING: *See* Exponential Smoothing Adjusted for Trend.

HOMOSCEDASTICITY: One of the assumptions required in a regression in order to make valid statistical inferences about population relationships; also known as constant variance. Homoscedasticity requires that the standard deviation and variance of the error terms is constant for all Xs, and that the error terms are drawn from the same population, indicating a uniform scatter or dispersion of data points about the regression line. If the assumption does not hold, the accuracy of the b coefficient is open to question.

I

INDEPENDENT VARIABLE: A variable that may take on any value in a relationship: in a relationship $Y = f(X)$, X is the independent variable. Independent variables that influence sales are, e.g., advertising and price (*see also* Dependent Variable).

INPUT-OUTPUT ANALYSIS: Models concerned with the flows of goods among industries in an economy or among branches of a large organization. An input-output matrix table is the source of this method. The table is very useful in evaluating the effects of a change in demand in one industry on other industries (e.g., the effect of a change in oil prices on demand for cars, then steel sales, then iron ore and limestone sales).

INTEREST RATE FORECASTING: Projection of short-term or long-term interest rates. The future direction of interest rates must be projected, for instance, when re-funding a bond or completing an acquisition.

J

JUDGMENTAL (QUALITATIVE) FORECAST: A method that brings together in an organized way personal judgments about the process being analyzed.

L

LEAST-SQUARES METHOD: A statistical technique for fitting a straight line through a set of points in such a way that the sum of the squared distances from the data points to the line is minimized.

LIFE CYCLE: The movement of a firm or its product through stages of development, growth, expansion, maturity, saturation, and decline. Not all products go through such a life cycle, for example, paper clips, nails, knives, drinking glasses, and wooden pencils. Most new products seem to, however; current examples include high-tech items such as computers, VCRs, and black-and-white TVs (*see also* Product Life Cycle).

LIFE-CYCLE ANALYSIS: A forecast of new product growth based on S-curves. Central to the analysis are the phases of product acceptance by various groups such as innovators, early adapters, early majority, late majority, and laggards.

LINEAR REGRESSION: A regression in the form of $Y = a + bX$ that deals with a straight line relationship between variables. *See also* Nonlinear Regression and Regression Analysis.

LOGISTIC CURVE: This curve has the typical S-shape often associated with the product life cycle. It frequently is used in connection with long-term curve fitting as a technological method.

M

MARKOV ANALYSIS: A method of analyzing the current behavior of a variable to predict the future behavior of that portion of the accounts receivable that will eventually become uncollectible.

MEAN ABSOLUTE DEVIATION (MAD): The mean or average of the sum of all the forecast errors with regard to sign.

MEAN ABSOLUTE PERCENTAGE ERROR (MAPE): The mean or average of the sum of all the percentage errors for a given data set taken without regard to sign. (That is, their absolute values are summed and the average computed.) It is a common measure of accuracy in quantitative methods of forecasting.

MEAN SQUARE ERROR (MSE): A measure of accuracy computed by squaring the individual error for each item in a data set and then finding the average or mean value of the sum of the squares. MSE gives greater weight to large errors than to small errors.

MOVING AVERAGE (MA): (1) For a time series, an average that is updated as new information is received. With the moving average, the analyst uses the most recent observations to calculate an average that is used as the forecast for next period. (2) In Box-Jenkins modeling, the MA in ARIMA, meaning that the value of the time series at time t is influenced by a current error term and (possibly) weighted error terms in the past.

MULTI-COLLINEARITY: The condition that exists when the independent variables are highly correlated. In the presence of multi-collinearity, the estimated regression coefficients may be unreliable. The presence of multi-collinearity can be tested by investigating the correlation between independent variables.

MULTIPLE DISCRIMINANT ANALYSIS (MDA): A statistical classificatory technique similar to regression analysis that can be used to evaluate financial ratios.

MULTIPLE REGRESSION ANALYSIS: A statistical procedure that attempts to assess the relationship between the dependent variable and two or more independent variables. For example, sales of Coca-Cola are a function of various factors such as advertising, taste, its price, and the prices of competitive products. For forecasting purposes, a multiple regression equation falls into the category of a causal forecasting model (*see also* Regression Analysis).

N

NAIVE FORECAST: Forecasts obtained with a minimal amount of effort and data manipulation and based solely on the most recent information available. One such naive method would be to use the most recent datum available as the future forecast.

NONLINEAR REGRESSION: A regression that deals with curvilinear relationships such as exponential and quadratic functions (*see also* Linear Regression and Regression Analysis).

O

OPTIMAL PARAMETER OR WEIGHT VALUES: Those values that give the best performance for a given model applied to a specific set of data. The optimal parameters are then used in forecasting.

P

PRODUCT LIFE CYCLE: The concept, particularly useful in forecasting and analyzing historical data of new products, that presumes that demand for a product follows an S-shaped curve, growing slowly in the early stages, achieving rapid and sustained growth in the middle stages, and slowing again in the mature stage.

PROGRAM EVALUATION AND REVIEW TECHNIQUE (PERT): Useful management tool for planning, coordinating and controlling large complex projects.

PROJECTED (BUDGETED) BALANCE SHEET: A schedule for expected assets, liabilities, and stockholders' equity as of the end of the budgeting year. A budgeted balance sheet: (1) discloses unfavorable financial conditions that management may want to avoid; (2) serves as a final check on the mathematical accuracy of all other budgets; and (3) highlights future resources and obligations.

PROJECTED (BUDGETED) INCOME STATEMENT: A summary of projections of component revenues and expenses for the budget period. It indicates expected net income for the period.

Q

QUANTITATIVE FORECASTING: A technique that can be applied when information about the past is available—if that information can be expressed in numbers and if the pattern included in past information can be assumed to continue into the future.

R

R-SQUARED: *See* Coefficient of Determination.

R-BAR SQUARED ($\bar{R}^2$): R^2 adjusted for the degrees of freedom. (*See* R-Squared.)

REGRESSION ANALYSIS: A statistical procedure for estimating mathematically the average relationship between the dependent variable (e.g., sales) and one or more independent variables (e.g., price and advertising).

REGRESSION COEFFICIENTS: When a dependent variable, Y, is regressed against a set of independent measures, X1 through Xk, the analyst may wish to estimate the values of the unknown coefficients by least-squares procedures. For example, in a linear regression equation $Y = a + bX$, a and b are regression coefficients. Specifically, a is called the y-intercept or constant, while b is called a slope. The properties of these regression coefficients can be used to understand the importance of each independent variable (as it relates to Y) and the interrelatedness among the independent variables (as they relate to Y).

REGRESSION EQUATION (MODEL): A forecasting model that relates the dependent variable (sales, for example) to one or more independent variables (advertising and income, for example).

RESIDUAL: A synonym for error. It is calculated by subtracting the forecast value from the actual value to give the error value for each forecast period.

ROOT MEAN SQUARED ERROR (RMSE): The square root of the mean squared error (MSE).

S

S-CURVE: The form most often used to represent the product life cycle. Several different mathematical forms, such as the logistic curve, can be used to fit an S-curve to actual observed data.

SALES FORECASTING: Projection or prediction of future sales. It is the foundation for the quantification of the entire business plan and a master budget, and for capacity planning, budgeting, production and inventory planning, manpower planning, and purchasing planning.

SEASONAL INDEX: A number that indicates the seasonality for a given time period. For example, a seasonal index for observed values in July would indicate how the July value is affected by the seasonal pattern in the data. Seasonal indexes are used to obtain deseasonalized data.

SERIAL CORRELATION: *See* Auto-correlation.

SIMPLE REGRESSION: A regression analysis that involves one independent variable, for example, the demand for automobiles as a function of price only (*see also* Multiple Regression; Regression Analysis).

SLOPE: The steepness and direction of the line. More specifically, slope is the change in Y for every unit change in X.

STANDARD ERROR OF THE ESTIMATE: The standard deviation of the regression. The statistic can be used to gain some idea of the accuracy of predictions.

STANDARD ERROR OF THE REGRESSION COEFFICIENT: A measure of the amount of sampling error in a regression coefficient.

T

t-STATISTIC: *See* t-value.

t-TABLE: A table that provides t-values for various degrees of freedom and sample sizes. The t-table is based on the student t-probability distribution (*see also* t-value).

t-TEST: In regression analysis, a test of the statistical significance of a regression coefficient made by (1) computing the t-value of the regression coefficient as follows: t-value = coefficient / standard error of the coefficient; and then (2) comparing the value with the t-table value. High t-values enhance confidence in the coefficient as a predictor. Low values (as a rule of thumb, under 2.0) indicate low reliability of the coefficient as a predictor (*see also* t-Value).

t-VALUE: A measure of the statistical significance of an independent variable b in explaining the dependent variable Y. It is determined by dividing the estimated regression coefficient b by its standard error.

TEMPLATE: A worksheet or computer program that includes the formulas for a particular application but not the data. It is a blank worksheet on which data are saved as needed for future forecasting and budgeting applications.

THEIL U STATISTIC: A measure of the predictive ability of a model based on a comparison of the predicted change with the observed change. The smaller the value of U, the more accurate the forecasts. If U is greater than or equal to 1, the predictive ability of the model is lower than a naive no-change extrapolation.

TIME SERIES MODEL: A function that relates the value of a time series to previous values of that time series, its errors, or other related time series (*see* ARIMA).

TRACKING SIGNALS: A method of monitoring how well a forecast is predicting actual values. The running sum of forecast error is divided by the mean absolute deviation (MAD). When the signal goes beyond a set range, corrective action may be required.

TREND ANALYSIS: A special form of simple regression in which time is the independent variable (*see also* Trend Equation).

TREND EQUATION: A special case of simple regression, where the X variable is a time variable. This equation is used to determine a trend in the variable Y that can be used for forecasting.

TREND LINE: A line fitted to sets of data points that describe the relationship between time and the dependent variable.

TURNING POINT ERROR: Also known as "error in the direction of prediction." It represents the failure to forecast reversals of trends. For example, it may be argued that the ability to anticipate reversals of interest rate trends is more important than the precise accuracy of the forecast.

W

WEIGHT: The relative importance given to an individual item included in forecasting, such as alpha in exponential smoothing. In the method of moving averages, all past values included in the moving average are given equal weight.

WINTERS' THREE-PARAMETER METHOD: *See* Exponential Smoothing, Seasonal.

Z

Z-SCORE: A score produced by Altman's bankruptcy prediction model, known to be about 90 percent accurate in forecasting business failure one year in the future and about 80 percent accurate in forecasting it two years in the future.

APPENDIX

Table A.1—STANDARD NORMAL DISTRIBUTION TABLE

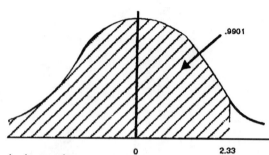

Areas under the normal curve

Z	0	1	2	3	4	5	6	7	8	9
.0	.5000	.5040	.5080	.5120	.5160	.5199	.5239	.5279	.5319	.5359
.1	.5398	.5438	.5478	.5517	.5557	.5596	.5636	.5675	.5714	.5753
.2	.5793	.5832	.5871	.5910	.5948	.5987	.6026	.6064	.6103	.6141
.3	.6179	.6217	.6255	.6293	.6331	.6368	.6406	.6443	.6480	.6517
.4	.6554	.6591	.6628	.6664	.6700	.6736	.6772	.6808	.6844	.6879
.5	.6915	.6950	.6985	.7019	.7054	.7088	.7123	.7157	.7190	.7224
.6	.7257	.7291	.7324	.7357	.7389	.7422	.7454	.7486	.7517	.7549
.7	.7580	.7611	.7642	.7673	.7703	.7734	.7764	.7794	.7823	.7852
.8	.7881	.7910	.7939	.7967	.7995	.8023	.8051	.8078	.8106	.8133
.9	.8159	.8186	.8212	.8238	.8264	.8289	.8315	.8340	.8365	.8389
1.0	.8413	.8438	.8461	.8485	.8508	.8531	.8554	.8577	.8599	.8621
1.1	.8643	.8665	.8686	.8708	.8729	.8749	.8770	.8790	.8810	.8830
1.2	.8849	.8869	.8888	.8907	.8925	.8944	.8962	.8980	.8997	.9015
1.3	.9032	.9049	.9066	.9082	.9099	.9115	.9131	.9147	.9162	.9177
1.4	.9192	.9207	.9222	.9236	.9251	.9265	.9278	.9292	.9306	.9319
1.5	.9332	.9345	.9357	.9370	.9382	.9394	.9406	.9418	.9430	.9441
1.6	.9452	.9463	.9474	.9484	.9495	.9505	.9515	.9525	.9535	.9545
1.7	.9554	.9564	.9573	.9582	.9591	.9599	.9608	.9616	.9625	.9633
1.8	.9641	.9648	.9656	.9664	.9671	.9678	.9686	.9693	.9700	.9706
1.9	.9713	.9719	.9726	.9732	.9738	.9744	.9750	.9756	.9762	.9767
2.0	.9772	.9778	.9783	.9788	.9793	.9798	.9803	.9808	.9812	.9817
2.1	.9821	.9826	.9830	.9834	.9838	.9842	.9846	.9850	.9854	.9857
2.2	.9861	.9864	.9868	.9871	.9874	.9878	.9881	.9884	.9887	.9890
2.3	.9893	.9896	.9898	.9901	.9904	.9906	.9909	.9911	.9913	.9916
2.4	.9918	.9920	.9922	.9925	.9927	.9929	.9931	.9932	.9934	.9936
2.5	.9938	.9940	.9941	.9943	.9945	.9946	.9948	.9949	.9951	.9952
2.6	.9953	.9955	.9956	.9957	.9959	.9960	.9961	.9962	.9963	.9964
2.7	.9965	.9966	.9967	.9968	.9969	.9970	.9971	.9972	.9973	.9974
2.8	.9974	.9975	.9976	.9977	.9977	.9978	.9979	.9979	.9980	.9981
2.9	.9981	.9982	.9982	.9983	.9984	.9984	.9985	.9985	.9986	.9986
3.	.9987	.9990	.9993	.9995	.9997	.9998	.9998	.9999	.9999	1.0000

Table A.2—t-DISTRIBUTION TABLE

Values of t

d.f.	$t_{0.100}$	$t_{0.050}$	$t_{0.025}$	$t_{0.010}$	$t_{0.005}$	d.f.
1	3.078	6.314	12.706	31.821	63.657	1
2	1.886	2.920	4.303	6.965	9.925	2
3	1.638	2.353	3.182	4.541	5.841	3
4	1.533	2.132	2.776	3.747	4.604	4
5	1.476	2.015	2.571	3.365	4.032	5
6	1.440	1.943	2.447	3.143	3.707	6
7	1.415	1.895	2.365	2.998	3.499	7
8	1.397	1.860	2.306	2.896	3.355	8
9	1.383	1.833	2.262	2.821	3.250	9
10	1.372	1.812	2.228	2.764	3.169	10
11	1.363	1.796	2.201	2.718	3.106	11
12	1.356	1.782	2.179	2.681	3.055	12
13	1.350	1.771	2.160	2.650	3.012	13
14	1.345	1.761	2.145	2.624	2.977	14
15	1.341	1.753	2.131	2.602	2.947	15
16	1.337	1.746	2.120	2.583	2.921	16
17	1.333	1.740	2.110	2.567	2.898	17
18	1.330	1.734	2.101	2.552	2.878	18
19	1.328	1.729	2.093	2.539	2.861	19
20	1.325	1.725	2.086	2.528	2.845	20
21	1.323	1.721	2.080	2.518	2.831	21
22	1.321	1.717	2.074	2.508	2.819	22
23	1.319	1.714	2.069	2.500	2.807	23
24	1.318	1.711	2.064	2.492	2.797	24
25	1.316	1.708	2.060	2.485	2.787	25
26	1.315	1.706	2.056	2.479	2.779	26
27	1.314	1.703	2.052	2.473	2.771	27
28	1.313	1.701	2.048	2.467	2.763	28
29	1.311	1.699	2.045	2.462	2.756	29
Inf.	1.282	1.645	1.960	2.326	2.576	Inf.

The t-value describes the sampling distribution of a deviation from a population value divided by the standard error.

Degrees of freedom (d.f.) are in the first column. The probabilities indicated as subvalues of t in the heading refer to the sum of a one-tailed area under the curve, that lies outside the point t.

For example, in the distribution of the means of samples of size n = 10, d.f. = n – 2 = 8; then 0.0025 of the area under the curve falls in one tail outside the interval t ± 2.306.

Table A.3—VALUES OF F FOR F WITH 0.05 OF THE AREA IN THE RIGHT TAIL

Example: For a test at a significance level of 0.05 where there are 15 degrees of freedom for the numerator and 6 degrees of freedom for the denominator, the appropriate F value is found by looking under the 15 degrees of freedom column and proceeding down to the 6 degrees of freedom row; there one finds the appropriate F value to be 3.94.

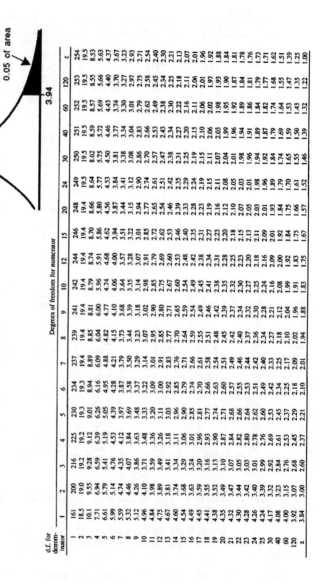

d.f. for denom-inator	Degrees of freedom for numerator																		
	1	2	3	4	5	6	7	8	9	10	12	15	20	24	30	40	60	120	z
1	161	200	216	225	230	234	237	239	241	242	244	246	248	249	250	251	252	253	254
2	18.5	19.0	19.2	19.2	19.3	19.3	19.4	19.4	19.4	19.4	19.4	19.4	19.4	19.5	19.5	19.5	19.5	19.5	19.5
3	10.1	9.55	9.28	9.12	9.01	8.94	8.89	8.85	8.81	8.79	8.74	8.70	8.66	8.64	8.62	8.59	8.57	8.55	8.53
4	7.71	6.94	6.59	6.39	6.26	6.16	6.09	6.04	6.00	5.96	5.91	5.86	5.80	5.77	5.75	5.72	5.69	5.66	5.63
5	6.61	5.79	5.41	5.19	5.05	4.95	4.88	4.82	4.77	4.74	4.68	4.62	4.56	4.53	4.50	4.46	4.43	4.40	4.37
6	5.99	5.14	4.76	4.53	4.39	4.28	4.21	4.15	4.10	4.06	4.00	3.94	3.87	3.84	3.81	3.77	3.74	3.70	3.67
7	5.59	4.74	4.35	4.12	3.97	3.87	3.79	3.73	3.68	3.64	3.57	3.51	3.44	3.41	3.38	3.34	3.30	3.27	3.23
8	5.32	4.46	4.07	3.84	3.69	3.58	3.50	3.44	3.39	3.35	3.28	3.22	3.15	3.12	3.08	3.04	3.01	2.97	2.93
9	5.12	4.26	3.86	3.63	3.48	3.37	3.29	3.23	3.18	3.14	3.07	3.01	2.94	2.90	2.86	2.83	2.79	2.75	2.71
10	4.96	4.10	3.71	3.48	3.33	3.22	3.14	3.07	3.02	2.98	2.91	2.85	2.77	2.74	2.70	2.66	2.62	2.58	2.54
11	4.84	3.98	3.59	3.36	3.20	3.09	3.01	2.95	2.90	2.85	2.79	2.72	2.65	2.61	2.57	2.53	2.49	2.45	2.40
12	4.75	3.89	3.49	3.26	3.11	3.00	2.91	2.85	2.80	2.75	2.69	2.62	2.54	2.51	2.47	2.43	2.38	2.34	2.30
13	4.67	3.81	3.41	3.18	3.03	2.92	2.83	2.77	2.71	2.67	2.60	2.53	2.46	2.42	2.38	2.34	2.30	2.25	2.21
14	4.60	3.74	3.34	3.11	2.96	2.85	2.76	2.70	2.65	2.60	2.53	2.46	2.39	2.35	2.31	2.27	2.22	2.18	2.13
15	4.54	3.68	3.29	3.06	2.90	2.79	2.71	2.64	2.59	2.54	2.48	2.40	2.33	2.29	2.25	2.20	2.16	2.11	2.07
16	4.49	3.63	3.24	3.01	2.85	2.74	2.66	2.59	2.54	2.49	2.42	2.35	2.28	2.24	2.19	2.15	2.11	2.06	2.01
17	4.45	3.59	3.20	2.96	2.81	2.70	2.61	2.55	2.49	2.45	2.38	2.31	2.23	2.19	2.15	2.10	2.06	2.01	1.96
18	4.41	3.55	3.16	2.93	2.77	2.66	2.58	2.51	2.46	2.41	2.34	2.27	2.19	2.15	2.11	2.06	2.02	1.97	1.92
19	4.38	3.52	3.13	2.90	2.74	2.63	2.54	2.48	2.42	2.38	2.31	2.23	2.16	2.11	2.07	2.03	1.98	1.93	1.88
20	4.35	3.49	3.10	2.87	2.71	2.60	2.51	2.45	2.39	2.35	2.28	2.20	2.12	2.08	2.04	1.99	1.95	1.90	1.84
21	4.32	3.47	3.07	2.84	2.68	2.57	2.49	2.42	2.37	2.32	2.25	2.18	2.10	2.05	2.01	1.96	1.92	1.87	1.81
22	4.30	3.44	3.05	2.82	2.66	2.55	2.46	2.40	2.34	2.30	2.23	2.15	2.07	2.03	1.98	1.94	1.89	1.84	1.78
23	4.28	3.42	3.03	2.80	2.64	2.53	2.44	2.37	2.32	2.27	2.20	2.13	2.05	2.01	1.96	1.91	1.86	1.81	1.76
24	4.26	3.40	3.01	2.78	2.62	2.51	2.42	2.36	2.30	2.25	2.18	2.11	2.03	1.98	1.94	1.89	1.84	1.79	1.73
25	4.24	3.39	2.99	2.76	2.60	2.49	2.40	2.34	2.28	2.24	2.16	2.09	2.01	1.96	1.92	1.87	1.82	1.77	1.71
30	4.17	3.32	2.92	2.69	2.53	2.42	2.33	2.27	2.21	2.16	2.09	2.01	1.93	1.89	1.84	1.79	1.74	1.68	1.62
40	4.08	3.23	2.84	2.61	2.45	2.34	2.25	2.18	2.12	2.08	2.00	1.92	1.84	1.79	1.74	1.69	1.64	1.58	1.51
60	4.00	3.15	2.76	2.53	2.37	2.25	2.17	2.10	2.04	1.99	1.92	1.84	1.75	1.70	1.65	1.59	1.53	1.47	1.39
120	3.92	3.07	2.68	2.45	2.29	2.18	2.09	2.02	1.96	1.91	1.83	1.75	1.66	1.61	1.55	1.50	1.43	1.35	1.25
z	3.84	3.00	2.60	2.37	2.21	2.10	2.01	1.94	1.88	1.83	1.75	1.67	1.57	1.52	1.46	1.39	1.32	1.22	1.00

Table A.3—VALUES OF F FOR F WITH 0.05 OF THE AREA IN THE RIGHT TAIL, *con't*.

Example: For a test at a significance level of 0.01 where there are 7 degrees of freedom for the numerator and 5 degrees of freedom for the denominator, the appropriate F value is found by looking under the 7 degrees of freedom column and proceeding down to the 5 degrees of freedom row; there one finds the appropriate F value to be 10.5.

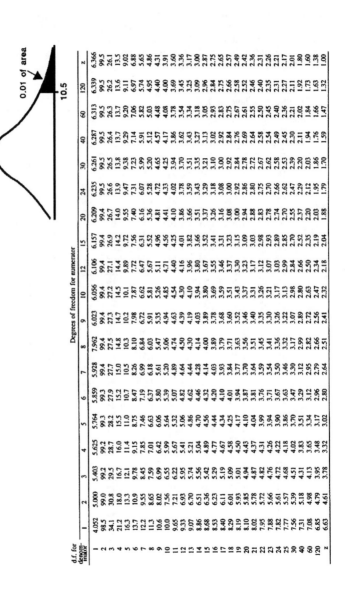

0.01 of area

10.5

d.f. for denominator	Degrees of freedom for numerator																		
	1	2	3	4	5	6	7	8	9	10	12	15	20	24	30	40	60	120	z
1	4,052	5,000	5,403	5,625	5,764	5,859	5,928	7,962	6,023	6,056	6,106	6,157	6,209	6,235	6,261	6,287	6,313	6,339	6,366
2	98.5	99.0	99.2	99.2	99.3	99.3	99.4	99.4	99.4	99.4	99.4	99.4	99.4	99.5	99.5	99.5	99.5	99.5	99.5
3	34.1	30.8	29.5	28.7	28.2	27.9	27.7	27.5	27.3	27.2	27.1	26.9	26.7	26.6	26.5	26.4	26.3	26.2	26.1
4	21.2	18.0	16.7	16.0	15.5	15.2	15.0	14.8	14.7	14.5	14.4	14.2	14.0	13.9	13.8	13.7	13.7	13.6	13.5
5	16.3	13.3	12.1	11.4	11.0	10.7	10.5	10.3	10.2	10.1	9.89	9.72	9.55	9.47	9.38	9.29	9.20	9.11	9.02
6	13.7	10.9	9.78	9.15	8.75	8.47	8.26	8.10	7.98	7.87	7.72	7.56	7.40	7.31	7.23	7.14	7.06	6.97	6.88
7	12.2	9.55	8.45	7.85	7.46	7.19	6.99	6.84	6.72	6.62	6.47	6.31	6.16	6.07	5.99	5.91	5.82	5.74	5.65
8	11.3	8.65	7.59	7.01	6.63	6.37	6.18	6.03	5.91	5.81	5.67	5.52	5.36	5.28	5.20	5.12	5.03	4.95	4.86
9	10.6	8.02	6.99	6.42	6.06	5.80	5.61	5.47	5.35	5.26	5.11	4.96	4.81	4.72	4.65	4.57	4.48	4.40	4.31
10	10.0	7.56	6.55	5.99	5.64	5.39	5.20	5.06	4.94	4.85	4.71	4.56	4.41	4.33	4.25	4.17	4.08	4.00	3.91
11	9.65	7.21	6.22	5.67	5.32	5.07	4.89	4.74	4.63	4.54	4.40	4.25	4.10	4.02	3.94	3.86	3.78	3.69	3.60
12	9.33	6.93	5.95	5.41	5.06	4.82	4.64	4.50	4.39	4.30	4.16	4.01	3.86	3.78	3.70	3.62	3.54	3.45	3.36
13	9.07	6.70	5.74	5.21	4.86	4.62	4.44	4.30	4.19	4.10	3.96	3.82	3.66	3.59	3.51	3.43	3.34	3.25	3.17
14	8.86	6.51	5.56	5.04	4.70	4.46	4.28	4.14	4.03	3.94	3.80	3.66	3.51	3.43	3.35	3.27	3.18	3.09	3.00
15	8.68	6.36	5.42	4.89	4.56	4.32	4.14	4.00	3.89	3.80	3.67	3.52	3.37	3.29	3.21	3.13	3.05	2.96	2.87
16	8.53	6.23	5.29	4.77	4.44	4.20	4.03	3.89	3.78	3.69	3.55	3.41	3.26	3.18	3.10	3.02	2.93	2.84	2.75
17	8.40	6.11	5.19	4.67	4.34	4.10	3.93	3.79	3.68	3.59	3.46	3.31	3.16	3.08	3.00	2.92	2.83	2.75	2.65
18	8.29	6.01	5.09	4.58	4.25	4.01	3.84	3.71	3.60	3.51	3.37	3.23	3.08	3.00	2.92	2.84	2.76	2.66	2.57
19	8.19	5.93	5.01	4.50	4.17	3.94	3.77	3.63	3.52	3.43	3.30	3.15	3.00	2.92	2.84	2.76	2.67	2.58	2.49
20	8.10	5.85	4.94	4.43	4.10	3.87	3.70	3.56	3.46	3.37	3.23	3.09	2.94	2.86	2.78	2.69	2.61	2.52	2.42
21	8.02	5.78	4.87	4.37	4.04	3.81	3.64	3.51	3.40	3.31	3.17	3.03	2.88	2.80	2.72	2.64	2.55	2.46	2.36
22	7.95	5.72	4.82	4.31	3.99	3.76	3.59	3.45	3.35	3.26	3.12	2.98	2.83	2.75	2.67	2.58	2.50	2.40	2.31
23	7.88	5.66	4.76	4.26	3.94	3.71	3.54	3.41	3.30	3.21	3.07	2.93	2.78	2.70	2.62	2.54	2.45	2.35	2.26
24	7.82	5.61	4.72	4.22	3.90	3.67	3.50	3.36	3.26	3.17	3.03	2.89	2.74	2.66	2.58	2.49	2.40	2.31	2.21
25	7.77	5.57	4.68	4.18	3.86	3.63	3.46	3.32	3.22	3.13	2.99	2.85	2.70	2.62	2.53	2.45	2.36	2.27	2.17
30	7.56	5.39	4.51	4.02	3.70	3.47	3.30	3.17	3.07	2.98	2.84	2.70	2.55	2.47	2.39	2.30	2.21	2.11	2.01
40	7.31	5.18	4.31	3.83	3.51	3.29	3.12	2.99	2.89	2.80	2.66	2.52	2.37	2.29	2.20	2.11	2.02	1.92	1.80
60	7.08	4.98	4.13	3.65	3.34	3.12	2.95	2.82	2.72	2.63	2.50	2.35	2.20	2.12	2.03	1.94	1.84	1.73	1.60
120	6.85	4.79	3.95	3.48	3.17	2.96	2.79	2.66	2.56	2.47	2.34	2.19	2.03	1.95	1.86	1.76	1.66	1.63	1.38
z	6.63	4.61	3.78	3.32	3.02	2.80	2.64	2.51	2.41	2.32	2.18	2.04	1.88	1.79	1.70	1.59	1.47	1.32	1.00

Table A.4—VALUES OF THE DURBIN-WATSON d FOR SPECIFIED SAMPLE SIZES (T) AND EXPLANATORY VARIABLES (K' = K - 1)

This table gives the significance points for dL and dU for tests on the auto-correlation of residuals (when no explanatory variable is a lagged endrogenous variable) using the Durbin-Watson test statistics at the 0.05 significance level. The number of explanatory variables, K', excludes the constant term. The next page of the table gives corresponding values for the 0.01 significance level.

Significance level = 0.05

Number of residuals	K = 1		K = 2		K = 3		K = 4		K = 5	
T	d_L	d_U	d_L	d_U	d_L	d_U	d_L	d_U	d_L	d_U
15	1.08	1.36	0.95	1.54	0.82	1.75	0.69	1.97	0.56	2.21
16	1.10	1.37	0.98	1.54	0.86	1.73	0.74	1.93	0.62	2.15
17	1.13	1.38	1.02	1.54	0.90	1.71	0.78	1.90	0.67	2.10
18	1.16	1.39	1.05	1.53	0.93	1.69	0.82	1.87	0.71	2.06
19	1.18	1.40	1.08	1.53	0.97	1.68	0.86	1.85	0.75	2.02
20	1.20	1.41	1.10	1.54	1.00	1.68	0.90	1.83	0.79	1.99
21	1.22	1.42	1.13	1.54	1.03	1.67	0.93	1.81	0.83	1.96
22	1.24	1.43	1.15	1.54	1.05	1.66	0.96	1.80	0.86	1.94
23	1.26	1.44	1.17	1.54	1.08	1.66	0.99	1.79	0.90	1.92
24	1.27	1.45	1.19	1.55	1.10	1.66	1.01	1.78	0.93	1.90
25	1.29	1.45	1.21	1.55	1.12	1.66	1.04	1.77	0.95	1.89
26	1.30	1.46	1.22	1.55	1.14	1.65	1.05	1.76	0.98	1.88
27	1.32	1.47	1.24	1.56	1.16	1.65	1.08	1.76	1.01	1.86
28	1.33	1.48	1.26	1.56	1.18	1.65	1.10	1.75	1.03	1.85
29	1.34	1.48	1.27	1.56	1.20	1.65	1.12	1.74	1.05	1.84
30	1.35	1.49	1.28	1.57	1.21	1.65	1.14	1.74	1.07	1.83
31	1.36	1.50	1.30	1.57	1.23	1.65	1.16	1.74	1.09	1.83
32	1.37	1.50	1.31	1.57	1.24	1.65	1.18	1.73	1.11	1.82
33	1.38	1.51	1.32	1.58	1.26	1.65	1.19	1.73	1.13	1.81
34	1.39	1.51	1.33	1.58	1.27	1.65	1.21	1.73	1.15	1.81
35	1.40	1.52	1.34	1.58	1.28	1.65	1.22	1.73	1.16	1.80
36	1.41	1.52	1.35	1.59	1.29	1.65	1.24	1.73	1.18	1.80
37	1.42	1.53	1.36	1.59	1.31	1.66	1.25	1.72	1.19	1.80
38	1.43	1.54	1.37	1.59	1.32	1.66	1.26	1.72	1.21	1.79
39	1.43	1.54	1.38	1.60	1.33	1.66	1.27	1.72	1.22	1.79
40	1.44	1.54	1.39	1.60	1.34	1.66	1.29	1.72	1.23	1.79
45	1.48	1.57	1.43	1.62	1.38	1.67	1.34	1.72	1.29	1.78
50	1.50	1.59	1.46	1.63	1.42	1.67	1.38	1.72	1.34	1.77
55	1.53	1.60	1.49	1.64	1.45	1.68	1.41	1.72	1.38	1.77
60	1.55	1.62	1.51	1.65	1.48	1.69	1.44	1.73	1.41	1.77
65	1.57	1.63	1.54	1.66	1.50	1.70	1.47	1.73	1.44	1.77
70	1.58	1.64	1.55	1.67	1.52	1.70	1.49	1.74	1.46	1.77
75	1.60	1.65	1.57	1.68	1.54	1.71	1.51	1.74	1.49	1.77
80	1.61	1.66	1.59	1.69	1.56	1.72	1.53	1.74	1.51	1.77
85	1.62	1.67	1.60	1.70	1.57	1.72	1.55	1.75	1.52	1.77
90	1.63	1.68	1.61	1.70	1.59	1.73	1.57	1.75	1.54	1.78
95	1.64	1.69	1.62	1.71	1.60	1.73	1.58	1.75	1.56	1.78
100	1.65	1.69	1.63	1.72	1.61	1.74	1.59	1.76	1.57	1.78

Table A.4—VALUES OF THE DURBIN-WATSON d FOR SPECIFIED SAMPLE SIZES (T) AND EXPLANATORY VARIABLES (K' = K - 1), *con't*

Significance level = 0.05

Number of residuals T	K = 1 d_L	K = 1 d_U	K = 2 d_L	K = 2 d_U	K = 3 d_L	K = 3 d_U	K = 4 d_L	K = 4 d_U	K = 5 d_L	K = 5 d_U
15	1.08	1.36	0.95	1.54	0.82	1.75	0.69	1.97	0.56	2.21
16	1.10	1.37	0.98	1.54	0.86	1.73	0.74	1.93	0.62	2.15
17	1.13	1.38	1.02	1.54	0.90	1.71	0.78	1.90	0.67	2.10
18	1.16	1.39	1.05	1.53	0.93	1.69	0.82	1.87	0.71	2.06
19	1.18	1.40	1.08	1.53	0.97	1.68	0.86	1.85	0.75	2.02
20	1.20	1.41	1.10	1.54	1.00	1.68	0.90	1.83	0.79	1.99
21	1.22	1.42	1.13	1.54	1.03	1.67	0.93	1.81	0.83	1.96
22	1.24	1.43	1.15	1.54	1.05	1.66	0.96	1.80	0.86	1.94
23	1.26	1.44	1.17	1.54	1.08	1.66	0.99	1.79	0.90	1.92
24	1.27	1.45	1.19	1.55	1.10	1.66	1.01	1.78	0.93	1.90
25	1.29	1.45	1.21	1.55	1.12	1.66	1.04	1.77	0.95	1.89
26	1.30	1.46	1.22	1.55	1.14	1.65	1.05	1.76	0.98	1.88
27	1.32	1.47	1.24	1.56	1.16	1.65	1.08	1.76	1.01	1.86
28	1.33	1.48	1.26	1.56	1.18	1.65	1.10	1.75	1.03	1.85
29	1.34	1.48	1.27	1.56	1.20	1.65	1.12	1.74	1.05	1.84
30	1.35	1.49	1.28	1.57	1.21	1.65	1.14	1.74	1.07	1.83
31	1.36	1.50	1.30	1.57	1.23	1.65	1.16	1.74	1.09	1.83
32	1.37	1.50	1.31	1.57	1.24	1.65	1.18	1.73	1.11	1.82
33	1.38	1.51	1.32	1.58	1.26	1.65	1.19	1.73	1.13	1.81
34	1.39	1.51	1.33	1.58	1.27	1.65	1.21	1.73	1.15	1.81
35	1.40	1.52	1.34	1.58	1.28	1.65	1.22	1.73	1.16	1.80
36	1.41	1.52	1.35	1.59	1.29	1.65	1.24	1.73	1.18	1.80
37	1.42	1.53	1.36	1.59	1.31	1.66	1.25	1.72	1.19	1.80
38	1.43	1.54	1.37	1.59	1.32	1.66	1.26	1.72	1.21	1.79
39	1.43	1.54	1.38	1.60	1.33	1.66	1.27	1.72	1.22	1.79
40	1.44	1.54	1.39	1.60	1.34	1.66	1.29	1.72	1.23	1.79
45	1.48	1.57	1.43	1.62	1.38	1.67	1.34	1.72	1.29	1.78
50	1.50	1.59	1.46	1.63	1.42	1.67	1.38	1.72	1.34	1.77
55	1.53	1.60	1.49	1.64	1.45	1.68	1.41	1.72	1.38	1.77
60	1.55	1.62	1.51	1.65	1.48	1.69	1.44	1.73	1.41	1.77
65	1.57	1.63	1.54	1.66	1.50	1.70	1.47	1.73	1.44	1.77
70	1.58	1.64	1.55	1.67	1.52	1.70	1.49	1.74	1.46	1.77
75	1.60	1.65	1.57	1.68	1.54	1.71	1.51	1.74	1.49	1.77
80	1.61	1.66	1.59	1.69	1.56	1.72	1.53	1.74	1.51	1.77
85	1.62	1.67	1.60	1.70	1.57	1.72	1.55	1.75	1.52	1.77
90	1.63	1.68	1.61	1.70	1.59	1.73	1.57	1.75	1.54	1.78
95	1.64	1.69	1.62	1.71	1.60	1.73	1.58	1.75	1.56	1.78
100	1.65	1.69	1.63	1.72	1.61	1.74	1.59	1.76	1.57	1.78

Note: K = number of explanatory variables excluding the constant term.

Table A.5—AREA IN THE RIGHT TAIL OF A CHI-SQUARED (χ^2) DISTRIBUTION

Example: In a chi-square distribution with 11 degrees of freedom, find the appropriate chi-square value of 0.20 of the area under the curve (the shaded area in the right tail), look under the 0.20 column in the table and proceed down to the 11 degrees of freedom row; the appropriate chi-square value there is 14.631.

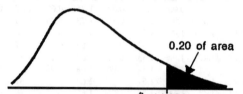

0.20 of area

Value of χ^2 14.631

Degrees of freedom	Area in right tail				
	0.99	0.975	0.95	0.90	0.800
1	0.00016	0.00098	0.00398	0.0158	0.0642
2	0.0201	0.0506	0.103	0.211	0.446
3	0.115	0.216	0.352	0.584	1.005
4	0.297	0.484	0.711	1.064	1.649
5	0.554	0.831	1.145	1.610	2.343
6	0.872	1.237	1.635	2.204	3.070
7	1.239	1.690	2.167	2.833	3.822
8	1.646	2.180	2.733	3.490	4.594
9	2.088	2.700	3.325	4.168	5.380
10	2.558	3.247	3.940	4.865	6.179
11	3.053	3.816	4.575	5.578	6.989
12	3.571	4.404	5.226	6.304	7.807
13	4.107	5.009	5.892	7.042	8.634
14	4.660	5.629	6.571	7.790	9.467
15	5.229	6.262	7.261	8.547	10.307
16	5.812	6.908	7.962	9.312	11.152
17	6.408	7.564	8.672	10.085	12.002
18	7.015	8.231	9.390	10.865	12.857
19	7.633	8.907	10.117	11.651	13.716
20	8.260	9.591	10.851	12.443	14.578
21	8.897	10.283	11.591	13.240	15.445
22	9.542	10.982	12.338	14.041	16.314
23	10.196	11.689	13.091	14.848	17.187
24	10.856	12.401	13.848	15.658	18.062
25	11.524	13.120	14.611	16.473	18.940
26	12.198	13.844	15.379	17.292	19.820
27	12.879	14.573	16.151	18.114	20.703
28	13.565	15.308	16.928	18.939	21.588
29	14.256	16.047	17.708	19.768	22.475
30	14.953	16.791	18.493	20.599	23.364

INDEX